The Insidious Momentum of American Mass Incarceration

The Insidious Momentum of American Mass Incarceration

Franklin E. Zimring

OXFORD
UNIVERSITY PRESS

Oxford University Press is a department of the University of Oxford. It furthers the University's objective of excellence in research, scholarship, and education by publishing worldwide. Oxford is a registered trade mark of Oxford University Press in the UK and certain other countries.

Published in the United States of America by Oxford University Press
198 Madison Avenue, New York, NY 10016, United States of America.

© Oxford University Press 2020

All rights reserved. No part of this publication may be reproduced, stored in a retrieval system, or transmitted, in any form or by any means, without the prior permission in writing of Oxford University Press, or as expressly permitted by law, by license, or under terms agreed with the appropriate reproduction rights organization. Inquiries concerning reproduction outside the scope of the above should be sent to the Rights Department, Oxford University Press, at the address above.

You must not circulate this work in any other form
and you must impose this same condition on any acquirer.

Library of Congress Cataloging-in-Publication Data
Names: Zimring, Franklin E., author.
Title: The insidious momentum of American mass incarceration / Franklin E. Zimring.
Description: New York, NY : Oxford University Press, 2020. |
Includes bibliographical references and index.
Identifiers: LCCN 2020008086 (print) | LCCN 2020008087 (ebook) |
ISBN 9780197513170 (hardback) | ISBN 9780197513200 | ISBN 9780197513187 |
ISBN 9780197513194 (epub)
Subjects: LCSH: Imprisonment—United States—History—20th century. |
Imprisonment—United States—History—21st century. | Imprisonment—United
States—Forecasting.
Classification: LCC HV9471 .Z56 2020 (print) | LCC HV9471 (ebook) |
DDC 365/.973—dc23
LC record available at https://lccn.loc.gov/2020008086
LC ebook record available at https://lccn.loc.gov/2020008087

For Jim Jacobs

Teacher and Friend

Contents

Preface ix

Acknowledgments xiii

Part I: The Road to 2020

1. An American Surprise 3
2. Crime, Law Enforcement, and Sentencing in an Era of Prison Expansion 22
3. Why the Prison-Boom Generation? 44
4. How American Institutions Encourage and Sustain High Rates of Imprisonment 61
5. What Happens Next? 82

Part II: Strategies of Sentencing Reform

6. Two Categorical Alternatives to Prisons 103
7. Restructuring the Governance of Imprisonment 121
8. Prosecutorial Power and Adversarial Focus 141

Afterword: Explaining the Limited Estimates of Decarceration 154

Part III: Policy Problems for a Million-Cell Future

9. Strategy and Tactics for Building Institutions   159
10. The Epidemic of Penal Disabilities   180

References   199

Index   209

Preface

Why this book?

The literature reacting to the explosive growth of imprisonment in the United States got off to a slow start but has now produced a bumper crop of documentation and advocacy. Only five books on prison policy were issued in the 1990s, compared to 32 volumes on the topic since 2010. A National Academy of Sciences panel report was published on the growth of penal confinement in 2014 (National Academy 2014), and several other serious scholarly efforts to document and understand the prison boom are part of the recent literature.[1] Why yet another volume?

The overuse of secure confinement in American criminal justice has in recent years become a priority concern for those seeking to minimize the harms of criminal justice at every level of government. The problem has been given an evocative label—mass incarceration—and the costs of this overuse of prisons and jails on those locked up, their families, and the communities they come from have been carefully documented. Even in an era of wide gaps between ideological camps in partisan politics, there is substantial

---

[1] See, e.g., Garland 2001b; Pattillo, Western, and Weiman 2004; Jacobson 2005; Gottschalk 2006; Western 2007; Useem and Piehl 2008; Alexander 2011; Raphael and Stoll 2013; Mears and Cochran 2015; Enns 2016; Hinton 2017; Kohler-Hausmann 2017; Pfaff 2017; Forman 2018; Barkow 2019; and Bazelon 2019; complete bibliographic information in references.

consensus that overpunishment is an American disease. The political Left emphasizes the devastating impact of epidemic imprisonment on minority males. The political Right has recently come to view campaigns like the war on drugs and its epic levels of incarceration as just another failed government program. As a matter of current sentiment, mass incarceration seems to be a practice that is ripe for reform.

But the path from public sentiment to effective and substantial reform is paved with uncertainty and ignorance. How much incarceration is too much and why? What are the circumstances that make secure confinement necessary and for whom? What are the appropriate sanctions that can be substituted for prisons and jails and in what cases?

Behind these questions of appropriate penal policy there are also questions of how and why governments in the United States produced the levels of confinement we now regard as mass incarceration. Is mass incarceration a distinguishing characteristic of American government and society over the long term or a more recent phenomenon? Are the large differences between different states and regions in rates of incarceration of critical importance, or is the major difference between the United States and other nations? Are there differences in rates of crime or types of offender that play a major role in explaining the extraordinary rates of imprisonment in the United States?

While the literature on mass incarceration is unanimous in condemning the current epidemic of penal confinement in American prisons and jails, there is no consensus on the causes of the one-generation growth in levels of confinement and no persuasive analysis of what is likely to happen in the coming decades in the United States.

This book is an effort to make a comprehensive statement about the causes of a one-generation, nationwide, fivefold expansion in prison population and the most probable future trends in penal confinement for the generation after the peak rate of imprisonment was reached in 2007. How much of the epic growth of confinement will remain in place in the United States of 2050, and why? How does the prospect of mass incarceration as a chronic condition influence the range of reforms in law and policy that need to become priorities for penal reform?

My effort in these pages is to explain the scale of penal expansion as a nationwide phenomenon that persisted much longer than the particular problems that were its policy justifications and now is sustained as the new normal in a low-crime era.

Understanding when and how and why the United States became the homeland of mass incarceration is a necessary part of determining how the emphasis on confinement can be reduced and will also provide indications of how much room for reduction in levels of confinement might be achievable. The first part of this book will profile the growth of imprisonment in the generation after 1970 in the United States and will then examine why imprisonment dominated sanction policy for serious or repetitive offenders.

This analysis emphasizes the important roles that both the federal system and the distribution of power and fiscal responsibility among the levels of government in American states played in expanding prison usage.

Chapter 1 will show both the singular status of the United States in imprisonment and the relatively short explosion of growth in 1970–2005 that was the primary cause of mass incarceration. My analysis of this first chapter justifies treating the 35 years after 1972 as both a nationwide phenomenon and as a single policy push rather than separate eras of street crime emphasis and war on drugs throughout the generation of increase. This decision in Chapter 1 sets the analysis in the next nine chapters apart from all prior studies.

Chapter 2 will look at changes in crime rates and criminal sentences that caused the singular growth in imprisonment. Chapter 3 explores the changes in policy and practice that happened during the era after 1970 when the prison population soared. Chapter 4 examines the institutions in American government and society that encourage high imprisonment.

Chapter 5 will focus on whether and to what extent cyclical forces can be expected to moderate patterns of mass incarceration without destabilizing the institutional patterns that evolved over the period after 1970. Might the volume of persons sent to prison regress to anywhere near the preboom mean level without major changes in institutions, incentives, or laws? If not, what is the likely scale of incarceration we can expect in the United States of 2050? Without major structural change, very high levels of prison confinement will be chronic in the middle of the twenty-first century.

The second part of the book examines changes in types of legal response to crime and in the governance of punishment that might reduce levels of confinement more quickly. Chapter 6 addresses two shifts from prison eligibility to other legal responses for whole categories of behavior. Chapter 7 discusses structural changes in the institutions in state government that influence criminal sentencing policy for offenses that continue to carry potential for imprisonment. Chapter 8 focuses on the powers and preferences of local prosecutors in the United States.

The final part of this book broadens the focus from policies that increase or decrease rates of imprisonment to analyze as well policies toward prison and jail construction (Chapter 9) and the epidemic of legal, social, and regulatory disabilities that increase the pain of criminal convictions (Chapter 10). The larger the population of persons convicted of felonies, the greater the magnitude of protracted stigma and disadvantage. And if there are substantial limits on the capacity to reduce the scale of imprisonment in the short- and middle-term American future, the fivefold expansion of felony convictions will also persist. Minimizing the avoidable collateral damage from experience with criminal conviction is both a moral and a policy necessity.

* * * * *

There are two peculiar aspects of this volume that deserve preliminary mention—the book's odd title and its pessimistic expectations for the American midrange future. The odd element in the book's title is its central emphasis on the "momentum" of mass incarceration. What does momentum mean in this context, and why is it important?

The most powerful enemy of efforts to reduce excess incarceration is not a crisis in crime or in the administration of criminal justice. It is instead the strong tendency in state and local criminal justice to conduct business as usual. The organizational and political circumstances that produce continual high levels of imprisonment are not essential elements of American social values or deeply felt public demands for harsh punishment. Crime rates are not high in 2020, and neither are public passions. It is the mundane features of state and local government—local elections of prosecutors, state support for prison budgets, the habit of prosecutors to regard prison sentences as indications of their adversarial effectiveness that have created a new normal—that suggest levels of imprisonment are likely to stay at least three times as high in 2050 as in the four decades in the middle of the twentieth century.

But just because the causes of persisting high levels of incarceration are mundane does not mean they will be easy to undo. The United States has 51 different criminal justice systems, each with its own penal code, and thousands of county governments with independent centers of prosecutorial power and law enforcement policy. Business as usual is a powerful influence on such decentralized institutions, and the business as usual in American criminal justice is mass incarceration.

Can we reverse the momentum of mass incarceration? In one sense the answer to that question is obvious and affirmative. This book demonstrates that substantial declines in imprisonment are far from impossible. But there is no strong sense of social crisis or political priority that has yet developed in the opening decades of the twenty-first century. We could reverse the momentum of mass incarceration in the United States, but we probably will not do so.

Acknowledgments

A SMALL ARMY of human resources contributed to my education on the topics covered in this volume and to the specific content in these pages. Norval Morris and Gordon Hawkins inspired my interest in prisons, and Gordon coauthored my first book on the topic. The statistical research and analysis necessary to the project involved data collection by Johann Koehler, James Stone, Ginger Jackson-Gleich, Stephen Rushin, and Patrick Booth and technical assistance from Jeffrey Fagan and Justin McCrary. Anthony Doob was an indispensable resource on Canadian government and prosecution and linked me to the empirical work critical to the analysis in Chapter 8. Kevin Reitz served as both inspiration and critic for the analysis of penal federalism and also for sentencing commissions. Critical readers of early chapters are always essential to my work, but doubly so in pursuing a project of this breadth. James Jacobs was particularly generous with his time and expertise as each chapter emerged in draft form, and Kevin Reitz, Mona Lynch, Keramet Reiter, Jonathan Simon, and James Cook provided helpful assistance as the manuscript took shape. The *Minnesota Law Review* sponsored a symposium on the book manuscript in November 2019 that provoked helpful critical analysis from Rachel Barkow, Richard Frase, Kevin Reitz, John Pfaff, Alfred Blumstein, Mark Bergstrom, Jessica Eaglin, and Robert Weisberg. Sarah Trautman was the editor of the effort.

One reason I write so much is that there is probably no other academic legal setting as supportive of the production of books as the University of California, Berkeley. Erwin Chemerinsky provided enthusiastic support for this project from its inception. Toni Mendicino is an expert at organizing and assembling manuscripts for publication, and I am one of her grateful beneficiaries.

Part I

THE ROAD TO 2020

1

An American Surprise

THE CURRENT CIRCUMSTANCES of American imprisonment are unprecedented both in American history and in comparison with any other developed nation.

Figure 1.1 shows the scale of US imprisonment as of 2010 in comparison with several other fully developed nations. This is a close-to-current snapshot of the United States in comparative context.

There are several dimensions of the international contrast in rates of imprisonment that deserve consideration. The first is the simple arithmetic of American prominence—the rate per 100,000 in prison in the United States is between 3.2 and 12 times as large as any of the European and developed Commonwealth nations profiled in the figure. It is possible, of course, when visualizing Figure 1.1 to try to identify which country is in second place, but in a real sense *none* of the other nations are in close enough proximity to the United States' 500 per 100,000 to be in second place. The United States is separated from all the other nations by about 350 per 100,000, which is more than twice the imprisonment rate of any of the other nations in the developed world.

One other implication of the visual suggestion that none of the other nations in Figure 1.1 are in second place to the United States' 500 per 100,000 is that all of the other national imprisonment rates profiled in the figure look rather close to each other when compared to the outlier status of US imprisonment rates. But if we were to remove the bar representing American imprisonment, the visual impression of the relationship of the other national imprisonment levels changes rather substantially. Without the US 500 bar, the distance between England and Wales at 153 per 100,000

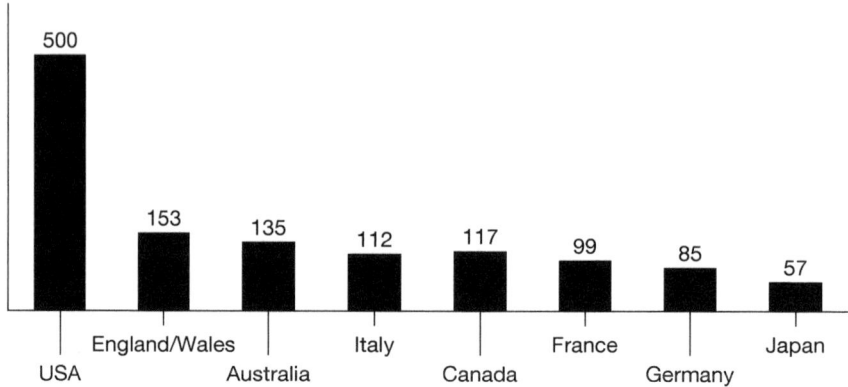

Figure 1.1 Imprisonment per 100,000, 2010, Eight Developed Countries.
Source: World Prison Brief n.d.; Bureau of Justice Statistics, (2011).

and Japan at 57 per 100,000 would look very large, and the English imprisonment rate also is about half again as high as the cluster of other European nations that average about 100 per 100,000: Germany, Italy, and France. This high-for-Europe English total (then 124 per 100,000 in 2000) inspired David Garland to see England and the United States as similar "high crime societies" in his major volume, *The Culture of Control*, in 2001.

But it would be much easier for any observer to take notice of England and Wales as distinct from the other non-US imprisonment rates if the hugely greater American bar were not a part of the figure. All of the other national patterns seem to cluster around 100 per 100,000 once the American total frames the distribution. The distance between England/Wales and Japan looks modest because of the elevated status of the American penal skyscraper.

This chapter is about when the extraordinary penal growth that led to the current level occurred and why the dynamic of growth in the United States was unexpected. Chapter 2 will then begin to describe how the unexpected explosion came about.

The Recency of American Mass Incarceration

One important element in the story of the epic dominance of American rates of incarceration is how much of the singular level of confinement has happened very recently. Figure 1.2 gives a graphic portrait of rates of imprisonment in the same eight nations that were profiled in Figure 1.1. but this time for 1970, two-thirds of the way through the twentieth century. Seven of the eight countries measured had the same governmental systems and

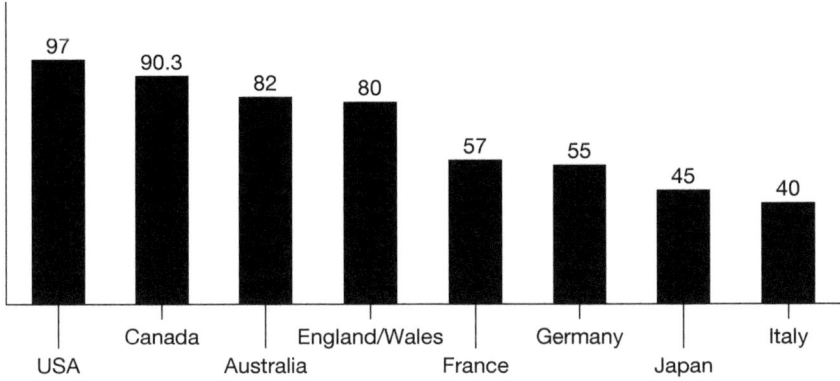

Figure 1.2 Imprisonment Rates in Eight Developed Countries, 1970.
Source: World Prison Brief n.d.; Bureau of Justice Statistics; Government of Canada 1982.

geography in 1970 and 2010, while the 1970 version of Germany excluded the eastern population then in a separate state.

The eight nations profiled in 1970 are much more closely clustered in reported rates, with the two lowest nations reporting just under half the rate of imprisonment as the highest nation. The difference in prisoners per 100,000 is 56 per 100,000 from the lowest to the highest reported rate. The United States has the highest reported rate at 96 per 100,000 but this is a rate just 7% higher than that of Canada and 20% higher than England and Australia.

There are significant history lessons when the United States is compared to other nations in 1970 and then again in 2010, and even more significant lessons when the United States rates in 2010 are compared to the same national rates in 1970.

Imprisonment in the United States was in 1970 on the high end of developed nation rates, but it was not what a statistician would characterize as an "outlier." Between 1970 and 2010, however, the distance between the United States and each of the other seven nations increased by more than 10-fold. England and Wales had the second largest expansion of prison population in the 40 years between the two profiles: their prison population grew from 80 per 100,000 to 153 per 100,000. By 2010, however, notwithstanding the almost doubling of Britain's imprisonment rate, the gap between the English rate and the American rate that had been 20% in 1970 became 227% in 2010. And the gap between the US and other national rates was larger than that for every other nation in the figure.

But the most sobering substantive insight about imprisonment in America comes when the country we have become is compared to the country we were in 1970. Nobody can doubt that 500 prisoners per 100,000 citizens is mass incarceration. But what about 97 per 100,000? That figure was on the high side in international comparisons, suggesting that some long-standing features in American society and government were associated with larger than average rates of incarceration, and many reformers found fault with the scale of imprisonment circa 1970 (Sherman and Hawkins 1983, 8–17). But the expansion of US imprisonment occurred in a single generation from 1974 to 2007, and this recency of onset has consequences both for the proper diagnosis and for the treatment of the current level of American imprisonment.

The natural tendency when discussing issues of what is called "American exceptionalism" is to search for the long-term structural and historical circumstances that distinguish the United States from European and developed Commonwealth nations. The first stop for students of American difference is more likely the pages of Alexis de Tocqueville's *Democracy in America* than the newspaper accounts of current events. And there are of course a vast and often troublesome list of social, demographic, and historical circumstances that set the United States apart from other modern states and might make it more vulnerable to substantial use of incarceration than other nations. But there is a world of difference between how such vulnerabilities played out in the middle decades of the twentieth century and the 400% increase in the scale of imprisonment that was concentrated in a single generation from 1974 to 2007.

A potentially useful metaphor here might be between chronic and acute disease processes in medical statistics. In the social and biological context, we may also encounter settings where long-term features like income distribution and food marketing and cultural preferences make one or more nations vulnerable to rapid increases in problems such as childhood obesity. But if the growth in the phenomenon is concentrated in a short historical period, the proximate causes of that growth during its volatile growth spurt are obviously important. The Centers for Disease Control and Prevention reports that using a consistent childhood obesity standard, between the mid-1970s and 2008 the percentage of obesity among US children increased from 5% to over 16%, so that more than two-thirds of the problem was generated in three decades (CDCP internet NCHS Health E Stat). Just as the search for proximate causes should start in the recent history of patterns of child nutrition, this book will argue that the most important place to focus on the proximate causes of the 500 per 100,000 imprisonment rate is in the 34 years that produced four-fifths of that concentration.

The Growth of Imprisonment in the United States

For most of the twentieth century the number of persons governments put in prison was not considered an important topic in criminal law or criminal justice policy discourse in the United States. The journals of legal scholarship were not greatly concerned with any aspects of American prisons and imprisonment. In the 100 years after 1910, the *Harvard Law Review* published a grand total of 27 articles with the terms "prison" or "imprisonment" in their titles. The *Journal of Criminal Law and Criminology* was an exception to this bypassing of prisons as a scholarly topic, publishing 155 articles in the century after 1910, including 70 titles on prison topics in the period 1910 to 1960. But even this specialized criminal justice journal did not focus on questions of what Gordon Hawkins and I called "the scale of imprisonment," which we defined as considering the "size of a society's prison enterprise in relation to other criminal sanctions and to the general population. How many prisoners? How many prisons? What criteria should govern decisions about how large a prison enterprise should be constructed and maintained?" (Zimring and Hawkins 1991, xi).

Even the specialized *Journal of Criminal Law and Criminology* published only a single article of the 70 on prisons in its first half-century that focused on variations in rates of imprisonment, a paper by Edwin Sutherland and C. C. Van Vechten Jr. on declining prison populations in England that was published in 1934.

There were two reasons why questions about the scale of imprisonment did not excite the interest of American criminal law and criminology specialists—one a feature of American government and the other an uneventful period in prison population trends in the United States. The detail of government that discouraged interest in variations in US prison policy is the federal system. When Professor Sutherland became interested in the scale of imprisonment in England, he could study rates of prosecution and punishment in a single government and collect data on a single (national) prison system.

In the United States, imprisonment is divided up into 50 state systems and a national prison system. Add to those 51 different penal systems thousands of regional, county, and municipal institutions for remand and short-term confinement. That national system is only for crimes and criminals within the limited jurisdiction of the federal government. Each of the 50 states in the United States has its own criminal code with its own schedule of criminal penalties, its own criminal court system, and its own prison system. The overwhelming majority of all persons incarcerated in prisons, traditionally over 90% and recently over 85%, are distributed over 50 state prison systems.

As a matter of formal law, since the United States does not have a single prison system, it also doesn't have a single rate of incarceration. So if Professor Sutherland had wanted to find out whether the number of prisoners had increased or decreased, he would have had to add up the 51 different prisons systems each year and then compare the two aggregates. And this decentralized authority is more than just a complication in obtaining and adding up data. In an important sense, there is no single scale of imprisonment or prison population but rather 51 different systems making decisions. In formal terms, there is no government in the United States that implements a policy of 97 prisoners per 100,000 in Figure 1.2 or 500 prisoners per 100,000 in Figure 1.1. Mass imprisonment in the United States is real, but a single rate of imprisonment of 500 per 100,000 is a fiction.

If the first reason why study of the scale of imprisonment didn't happen for a long time was the decentralized nature of imprisonment in the American system, the second reason why the topic was ignored for a sustained period of time was the lack of any conspicuous movement in the aggregate numbers of persons imprisoned in the United States over time. In the four decades from 1930 to 1970, the national imprisonment rate may have been a legal fiction, but it was a very stable fiction.

Using collections of prisoner data from both the state and federal government, Alfred Blumstein and Jacqueline Cohen published the first article on the scale of American imprisonment ever in the *Journal of Criminal Law and Criminology* and titled it "A Theory of the Stability of Punishment." The year was 1973.

The general theory being supported was that levels of severe punishment tend toward stability over time, and the previous four decades of imprisonment in America were Exhibit A in the Blumstein and Cohen case for stability. The stability of the national aggregate imprisonment rate between 1930 and 1970 was shown by their Figure 2, reproduced here as Figure 1.3.

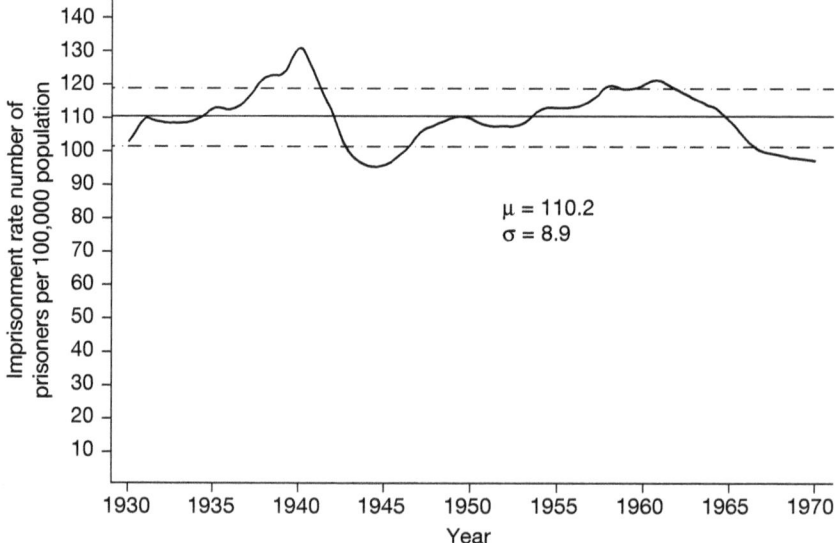

Figure 1.3 Imprisonment Rates in the United States, 1930–1970.
Source: Blumstein and Cohen 1973.

The authors report their statistical findings with economy: "It can be seen that over the period the imprisonment rate was reasonably constant, having an average value of 110.2 prisoners per 100,000 . . . and a standard deviation during that time . . . of 8.9 prisoners per 100,000 population" (Blumstein and Cohen 1973, 201).

The theoretical insight that the authors derived from the lack of any dramatic movements in rates of incarceration transformed a drab and unremarkable data set into an exciting statistical arena for debates about when and why the lack of variance could be attributed to a dynamic social process. But it was not to last long.

Blumstein and his associates published twice more in the 1970s in support of constancy or "homeostatic punishment process." But then the entire theoretical debate was overtaken by events that are the central concern of this book.

Figure 1.4, using data from the Bureau of Justice Statistics, shows yearly levels of aggregate imprisonment in the United States from 1926 until 2007.

What Figure 1.4 shows is two distinct patterns over 80 years of US imprisonment. The decades from 1926 to 1970 are the stable era that led to Blumstein's theories. But the year the "stability" article was published began a three-and-a-half-decade period of explosive and uninterrupted growth in rates of imprisonment. The contrast between the four decades after 1930 and the 35 years that followed is stark. The highest imprisonment reported for a year in the 1930–1970 period was 38% above the lowest rate reported for any year (131.5 versus 95.5), and there was no clear trend over time. In the 30 years after 1972 the aggregate national rate grew every year, and the rate of imprisonment by 2007 was five times the base rate in 1972. Mass imprisonment was essentially born in the dramatic increases of this discrete

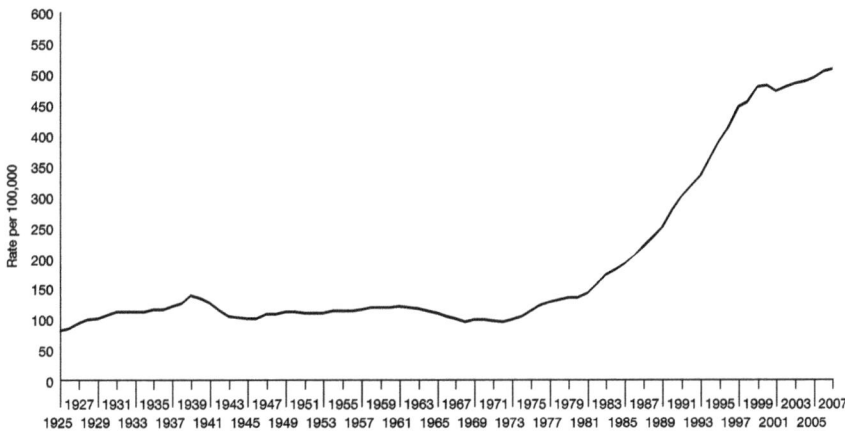

Figure 1.4 Imprisonment Rate per 100,000 Population, United States, 1925–2007. *Source*: Zimring 2010, Figure 2.

subperiod in American history. The central substantive questions behind the contrasting trajectories of 1930–1970 and 1972–2007 are obvious. Were there in fact homeostatic influences that reduced upward variations in imprisonment in the almost half-century before 1973? If so, what happened to them in the 1970s and why?

An Enormous Policy Surprise

Even in retrospect, the magnitude and sustained persistence of growing imprisonment after 1973 is a surprise to the most sophisticated observers and a mystery that must be resolved if those who wish to minimize the damages of mass incarceration in the twenty-first century are to do their jobs effectively.

There were five separate barriers to achieving a fivefold expansion of rate of imprisonment in a single generation in the United States, restraints so powerful in combination that even after the fact of its occurrence, the smart money might still wish to bet against its possibility. Here are the five restraining circumstances that make the tidal wave of increased imprisonment difficult to explain: lack of precedent, an environment of legal and political stability, decentralized powers to punish, insufficient penal capacity to accommodate extraordinary expansion, and the escalating pressure of penal expansion on state fiscal resources.

Lack of Historical Precedent

The prison was the primary punishment for the most serious crimes and most incorrigible criminals for the two centuries prior to 1973 in at least 100 countries, including every nation in what has been called "the rich world." In those two centuries, the number of nations that sustained a 400% increase was none, and the number of nations that expanded rates of imprisonment for 30 successive years was none. So both the magnitude and the consistency of the American prisoner expansion had never happened. All other things being equal, things that haven't ever happened are regarded as unlikely to occur. And the pattern in the United States was doubly unprecedented, in the level of increase and in the protracted duration of the imprisonment increase—a double black swan. And the variations observed in other nations during the period of the American explosion suggest that the penal environment in an increasingly global world was not providing or supporting extreme volatility in developed nations. So the US pattern from 1972 to 2007 was both singular and unprecedented.

Governmental Political and Legal Stability

While the growth of imprisonment might be called a "revolutionary" change in penal scale, the America in which it occurred was anything but revolutionary. The United States in the generation after 1970 was stable in four dimensions that should influence the prospects for radical change in imprisonment—the governmental system was stable, the political orientation of the population was stable and incremental in most policy domains, the structure and content of the criminal law was not substantially changed during this period, and the priorities and operating strategies of prison administration were also stable. So this was not case where the nation that experienced an unprecedented and revolutionary change in one policy area was also prone to major shifts in its other aspects of politics or government.

But surely a fivefold increase in rates of imprisonment must reflect changes in principles of criminal liability or the definition of criminal conduct or the type and length of criminal sentences provided by legislation. But this turns out not to have been true of the first half of the imprisonment boom in the United States, and therein lies an important story of the phenomenal breadth of discretionary power in American criminal law. During the period from 1973 to 1985, when the rate of imprisonment doubled in the United States, there was no general trend toward either increasing the number of behaviors made criminal or escalating either minimum or maximum terms of imprisonment. A few states shifted from indeterminate to determinant sentencing systems (including California and Illinois) in the 1970s, but there is no evidence that shift had any significant impact on the growth of imprisonment during that period. This first period in the uninterrupted generation of explosive imprisonment growth is decisive evidence that the extraordinary latitude for exercise of discretion in American systems of criminal justice can produce very large changes in rates of imprisonment with no important changes in the legal framework of criminal punishment. The addition of federal and state drug war legislation and "truth in sentencing" laws added substantial weight to increases in imprisonment in the 1990s. But the vast level of discretion meant that the legal structures in place in the United States when it had a prison population of 205,000 in 1972 were not greatly different from the legal structures that were responsible for 800,000 prisoners in 1991. But why? Stable systems of law and governance should be associated with more modest levels of operational change. But not in the imprisonment boom of 1973–2007. The system remained formally stable for the most part but operationally radically changed. Discretionary power made this transformation possible, but why were discretionary authorities who had presided over a four-decade period of operational stability in imprisonment themselves so powerfully transformed? Why wasn't the formal stability of the system a deterrent to radical change?

The Decentralization of Penal Power in the American Federal System

I have already emphasized that the delegation of the power to pass and administer separate criminal codes and justice system means that the national totals reported in all this chapter's graphs for the United States are actually an aggregation of 51 different systems making decisions about imprisonment independent of other state governments and most federal standards. Having a large number of governments each making separate decisions should produce a large variety of individual rates but with the aggregate average being a midpoint of the distribution individual states, so that adding them all together will moderate the extreme values of individual states. The diversity of crime problems, legal systems, and political preferences that are present in the federal system should produce a wide variety of outcomes in any year, but in any time series, having to add up 51 different systems each year should produce a single, national, year-to-year trend that averages away the extreme values in some units. A single decision-maker or decision-making body, if willing, has the power to push values sharply up or down. But a large number of systems averaged together should moderate the total year-to-year trend. Maine and Louisiana can each drag the trend only a slight distance toward their state's particular taste. So dividing penal power up into 51 shares and then averaging the result should reduce year-to-year changes in most situations. But that was not the case for prison populations in 50 states and the federal government for 1972 to 2007. Why?

The moderating influence of decentralizing decision-making depends on diversity among the many governing units. The reason why decentralized power didn't have much restraint on the growth of imprisonment was that all of the governments were shaping policy in the same direction. It is really diversity rather than decentralization that should moderate changes over time, and diversity at the state level wasn't much in evidence in the period of the imprisonment boom.

The dominant pattern of growth policy among the 50 states emerged in the mid-1980s. The "Scale of Imprisonment" analysis, published in 1991, noted:

> As of 1980 only eleven states reported rates of imprisonment higher than at any previous point in the century. But a cyclical hypothesis has been decisively disproved by prison population trends since 1980. Forty-six of the fifty states report rates of imprisonment between 1985 and 1987 which are at the highest level they have experienced in a century. (Zimring and Hawkins 1991, 152)

As a mechanical matter, we know why decentralized decision-making wasn't an insurance policy against explosive penal growth—it was lack of diversity. But *why* were 50 states and the federal government all pointing in the same direction and preferring high levels of growth? What were the concerns that operated that broadly, and how powerful were they? To what extent were the new broad social and political attitudes cyclical or permanent?

Limited Prison Capacity

The physical institutions that hold prisoners are expensive, distinctive, and long-lasting elements of the hardware of state and federal government. The received wisdom of the political economy of prison policy was that the relatively fixed "capacity to punish" was an important constraint on adding more prisoners as a policy option (see Pontell 1984). This aspect of what Pontell called "the ecology of crime and punishment" would slow down rates of prison expansion as the 51 different prisons systems in the United States bumped up against their limited number of cell spaces. But this moderating impact of rates of imprisonment should have been fully operative by 1987 when 46 of the 50 states had already locked up more prisoners than at any other time in the twentieth century, but most of the increase in rates of imprisonment happened after 1987 (see Figure 1.4). Why is this?

Does the rapid 22 years of growth after 1985 in the United States undermine the theory that exhausting physical places to house prisoners will restrain further expansion? Probably not. But the American case study does suggest that the dynamics of demand to imprison in this era overpowered the forces of fixed capacity as a deterrent. If so, it will be important to identify the nature of the pro-expansion influences and to determine the extent to which they continue to operate in current circumstances.

Increasing Costs of Imprisonment

The large capital cost of building new prisons is not the only financial constraint that should have argued against continued increases in prison population over the period after 1970 in the United States. All during the last half of the twentieth century, state prisons were more than 90% of total imprisonment, one of a relatively small number of functions where the primary responsibility was with state rather than federal and local government. The primary responsibilities for state government were in 1975 education and roads, which were a much more substantial fiscal demand than prisons.

The impact of imprisonment costs on state budget over the four decades after 1975 can be illustrated by a California case study. In 1975, the total of state expenditures was $8.82 billion dollars. The $200 million for prisons was less than 38% of the state's contribution to the University of California (Figure 1.5).

By 2016, the imprisonment share of the total state budget had expanded from 2.3% to 6%, an increase of share of almost three times. Meanwhile the state contribution to the University of California system had decreased from 6.2% of the state budget to 1.9%. While the University of California had almost three times the budgetary share of prisons in 1975, its state spending share in 2016 was now only one-third of corrections.

A sevenfold expansion in the number of state prisoners in any state would be expected to create at least a sevenfold increase in the constant dollar cost of operating state prisons in the United States unless there are major economies of scale in operating prisons. If prisons are already at or near capacity at the beginning of a period of growth, there are no obvious or substantial economies of scale on offer. Even a strategy of intentional overcrowding is not a likely money-saver because security problems may increase and the very major share of security staff to total budget may increase. And additional issues of identifying medical needs and providing medical care will also increase costs in overcrowded environments. Further, a rapidly increasing cohort of older prisoners as long prison terms enter their second, third, and fourth decades will increase medical costs. California prisons in 2017 had medical budgetary expenses equal in dollar value to the *total* prison budget for the state in the early 1980s.

So one further restraint on rational state governments continuing to expand prison populations for 30 consecutive years would be the extraordinary costs that they generate. Particularly in periods of tight financial pressure, so many increasing claims on what little new revenues are being generated by state government should be a substantial impediment to growing incarceration every year, given the new demands on the operating expenses of 50 states in the period 1972–2007.

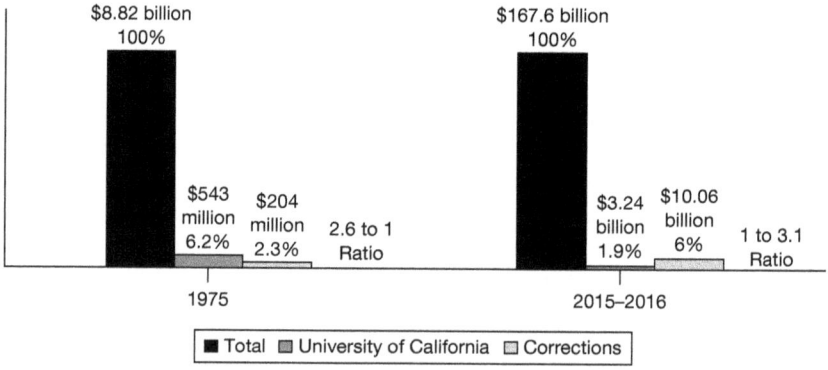

Figure 1.5 California State Budgets in 1975 and 2016 for Corrections and University of California. *Source*: Governor of California 2015; Brown 1975, 891.

Here again, whatever antigrowth momentum might have been generated by never-ceasing new budgetary demands were overcome in almost all states every year for a generation.

*****

Why so much time and detail on describing why the full generation of exploding growth in imprisonment shouldn't have happened when we all know it *did* happen? This is a study about repairing the damage of mass incarceration, not denying its existence. But the first section of this chapter showed that four-fifths of all the increase in prisoner population that we have come to call mass incarceration has developed only since 1973. And the second part of the chapter has shown five features of the American experience that make this nation in that era a very unlikely candidate for the correctional growth that happened. A high level of political and governmental energy was necessary to generate the large and sustained changes in practice that expanded the prisons without major legislative change. Which institutions changed penal practices and why? Who were the actors that kept the acceleration in place, and why did they act as they did?

These are important issues not only for understanding the history of imprisonment in the United States but also for designing plausible strategies to reduce the damages that the expanded scale of imprisonment has produced. The institutions and actors who created expansion will remain powerful in coming decades. What changes in incentives and criteria for success or failure might best influence the number and duration of prison sentences? What incentives and which actors might best minimize the harms suffered by the already sentenced and already released? Is a frontal attack on the main courses of penal expansion the best strategy for harm reduction, or would different institutions and actors, indeed different allocations of power, promise larger and longer-term benefits?

Two Fundamental Questions

The 35 annual entries in the national portrait of rates of imprisonment after 1972 in Figure 1.4 give the impression of a single national pattern and a continuous upward trajectory. But looks can be deceiving. This section addresses two fundamental questions about the character of the 35-year growth in rates of imprisonment. The first part of this section discusses whether the aggregate growth of imprisonment in the 50 states and the federal system is best viewed as (a) a single process with 51 different levels of government participating in essentially similar transformations of policy or (b) an aggregation of different levels or types of policy change. The second part of the section addresses whether the 35 years of increase were a single era of growth or are composed of two or three distinct and discrete eras with different causes and magnitudes.

One Process or Many?

The aggregate growth rates portrayed in Figure 1.4 are the sum of data from 51 different governmental systems. As a matter of political science and perhaps of logic, it is inaccurate to speak of the rate of imprisonment in the United States as a single measure or to speak of the growth rate of imprisonment in the United States as a unitary phenomenon. But noting the multiplicity of different components of policy in American penality is the beginning rather than the end of the analysis I am suggesting is required. Despite the large number of states and the diversity of their social and demographic composition, it is not unusual for nationwide trends to be evident in matters relating to crime and punishment. One recent example of a plenary national trend was the sharp decline in reported serious crime in the United States during the 1990s (Zimring 2007; Steiker 2011). Zimring and Hawkins noted in 1991, "One of the most puzzling features of recent decades is the way in which the many political units that share power in the American Criminal Justice system altered their policies in a way that increased prison populations at the same time and with similar intensity" (Zimring and Hawkins 1991).

The fourfold increase in imprisonment rate in the United States is obviously a broad trend to produce an aggregate impact that large. But there are two rather different patterns that can produce large growth in the aggregate. The large growth numbers can mask very large differences between highest-growth and lowest-growth jurisdictions where there are significant differences between one cluster of jurisdictions and another. In that case, aggregate growth levels are not the best way to study the causes of differential growth. The differences between states will be at least as important as national trends over time.

But the large number of states might all be more or less evenly participating in a national trend, in which case studying the factors associated with different rates of growth in different states will not provide an obvious key to the characteristics shared by the states that are the main causes of growth in all states. This methodological point was argued by Zimring and Hawkins:

> At stake . . . is the appropriate unit of analysis for imprisonment policy. To the extent that the United States is a single social system, approaches that view variations in imprisonment as an outgrowth of social and economic processes would emphasize the national scale of the unit of analysis. . . . To the extent that prison population is best viewed as an outcome of conscious governmental choice, the most significant political power over imprisonment is exercised at the state level and the state should be the significant unit of analysis. (1991, 137–38)

While Zimring and Hawkins spotted an important issue, their analysis jumps to premature conclusions about the appropriate level of government for studies of the scale of imprisonment. Even if the major influences on rates of imprisonment are political, the mechanisms that produce political change at the state level may be national in scope and might best be studied at the national aggregate level. If most states respond in relatively uniform ways to a national-level stimulus, interstate variation should not be the central focus of the search for causal factors.

Figure 1.6 shows the distribution of percentage growth in rates of imprisonment for the US federal system and the 50 states.

The pattern of state rate growth most consistent with a unitary national trend over the time period would show the largest concentration of states in the middle of the distribution, with very few states at both extremes. The model for this type of pattern is a normal distribution around a mean value. To the extent that extreme values are found, they should tend to be smaller states and there should not be any clear pattern of regional clustering in one part of the distribution. That pattern would be a distribution consistent with a unitary national trend.

A pluralistic distribution would not concentrate in the center of the growth rate scale, would have clusters of cases at some distance from the mean, and would produce clusters of cases with apparent similarities in geography, crime, or politics and different characteristic growth rates. To the extent that a distribution suggests a unitary pattern, the appropriate level of analysis is the national aggregate. To the extent that plural clustering is evident in the distribution, the explanation of patterns of state variation becomes an important focus of inquiry.

But which sort of distribution is shown in Figure 1.6?

A formal statistical analysis confirms the visual impression that the pattern of state growth rates over 1972–2007 is consistent with a normal

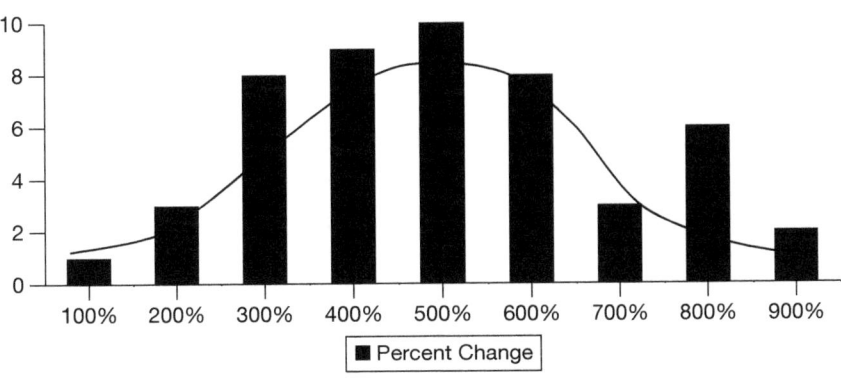

Figure 1.6 Distribution of State Imprisonment Growth Rates, 1972–2007.
Source: Bureau of the Census (1970); Bureau of Justice Statistics (2000).

distribution. I use the 50 different state growth rates as the sample set because they were produced in the same fashion. The federal data are excluded from this analysis. Two statistical tests analyze how often a distribution of 50 outcomes (in this case percentage growth in state imprisonment rate) like that shown in the figure would be likely to occur as chance variations from a normal distribution. They are the Shapiro-Wilk and Shapiro-Francia tests, each named after its creators. Table 1.1 shows the 50 state results for the growth rates reported in Figure 1.6.

The smaller the probability that this is a 50-case sample from a normal distribution, the more likely the pattern of difference observed is not normal, with a probability of .05 or less a usual benchmark for strong statistical evidence of non-normal distribution. But using a Shapiro-Wilk test produces a probability of normal distribution of .31151, and the Shapiro-Francia test probably is .46612. The question these tests address is "how likely" it is that a distribution like that being tested could be the outcome of sampling 50 readings from a normal distribution. The answer is "pretty likely." There are thus no strong indications in these analyses of anything other than 50 different outcomes of a uniform process.

One Policy Era or Three?

When trends in national rates of imprisonment are charted over time in Figure 1.4, the visual image is of two discrete trends—a flat and relatively stable period from 1930 to about 1970 and a second continuously upward period of uninterrupted growth. While the upward trajectory of increased rates of imprisonment moderates as the base rate of prison population increased in the 1980s and early 1990s, the number of prisoners added to the US population remained between 300,000 and 437,000 for each five-year

Table 1.1

The Probable Normality of Distribution of Imprisonment Growth Rates of 50 US States

Test	Observations	W	V	Z	Probability > Z
Shapiro-Wilk	50	0.97322	1.259	0.492	0.31151
Shapiro-Francia	50	0.97985	1.045	0.085	0.46612

Sources: Growth rates, Bureau of Justice Statistics; tests: Royston, P., "A Simple Method for Evaluating the Shapiro-Francia W Test of Non-Normality," 32 *Statistician* 297-300 (1983); Royston, P., "Estimating Departure from Normality," 10 *Statistics in Medicine* 1283-1293 (1991); Shapiro, S.S. and R.S. Francia, "An Approximate Analysis of Variance Test for Normality (Complete Samples)," 67 *Journal of the American Statistical Association* 215-216 (1972); Shapiro, S.S. and M.B. Wilk, "An Analysis of Variance Test for Normality (Complete Samples)," 52 *Biometrika* 591-611 (1965).

period between 1985 and 2000 (see the comparison of growth rates and numbers in Zimring 2007, 50, Figure 3.5). So the visual temptation in a graph like Figure 1.4 is bifurcation into a single era of stability and a single era of growth.

It is, however, one thing to note that a growth rate has been constant over a long period of time and quite another to assume that the substantive influences that were driving increases in prison population in the late 1970s are the same as those that were operating in the 1980s and remained stable in the 1990s. There are some indications that policy emphasis changed over the generation of growing rates, with higher rates of commitment for a wide range of felonies being more important in the period prior to 1986, greater proportionate growth in drug and sex crimes being of greater significance from the mid-1980s to the mid-1990s, and legislative increases in prison terms and longer prison sentences showing a more important role in the decade after 1995 (Zimring 2005).

Without a doubt the changes in emphasis and priority over time during the different eras make generalization over the entire growth period about causes of imprisonment growth a hazardous occupation. The sharp growth not only in drug prisoners but in the percentage of state prisoners sentenced for drug crime between 1987 and 1991 (see Figure 3 in Zimring and Harcourt 2007, 219) suggests somewhat different causal paradigms for earlier prison growth than during the drug war's peak years. The distinct skyrocketing of sex offenses other than rape after 1986 is another example of a major substantive shift halfway through the 30-year expansion.

But there may be more unity in the process of prison growth than preoccupation with the changing characteristics of crimes and sentences would allow. To the extent that a relatively fixed expansion of imprisonment might be either desired or tolerated in the years after 1972, the crimes or sentence lengths that are added to reach that level may not be an overwhelmingly important influence on the motivation or tolerance for prison growth. To the extent, then, that the relatively constant growth of imprisonment before and after the peak emphasis on the war on drugs indicates that drug offenders simply crowded out marginal property offenders or restrained longer prison sentences for street criminals when they took priority in the late 1980s, the drug panic may not have been itself a primary cause of change in the growth rate of imprisonment. To the unknown extent that the pace of national prison expansion operated independently of the categories of cases that were given emphasis in filling the new space, the conception of the post-1972 growth of imprisonment as a unitary trend across 35 years is plausible.

On the general issue that introduced this short discussion, "One Policy Era or Three?," the most attractive answer is "both of the above." There were major shifts in emphasis over the course of the 30-year expansion, from the seven offenses with victims regarded by the FBI as "index crimes" to drug crimes and nonrape sex offenders, and there was a shift in emphasis from increasing prison admissions to lengthening sentences. And these distinctions should be carefully noted when sorting through measurements of the character of policy changes and the impact of those changes on crime and on communities.

Yet, in its essence, the expansion was a single policy framework: while the particular criminal topics or types of behavior varied over time in the expansion era, the preferred official response elected was always the same. The questions varied from robbery and homicide to repeat offenders, to child molesters, to crack users and dealers. Yet whatever the question of the day, the answer was always prison. Probation and conditional release increased substantially. But these were only techniques for deferring the only credible and serious penal response in the American arsenal—the prison. This was the unifying and distinguishing characteristic of American criminal justice for a generation. The drug war after 1985 was not so much a cause of the prison expansion of the 20 years thereafter as it was a result of the monopoly of prison as the only policy choice considered during the prison expansion era. If drugs were a serious problem, prison could be the only option to be considered in this era of American crime policy.

"One Process" as a Research Strategy

The first of the two basic issues just discussed—"one process or many"—demands a general approach to how empirical questions on prison trends should get asked and answered in this book. Since 50 different states and the national government have separate penal systems and vary both in how many persons per 100,000 are imprisoned at any one time and in how big an increase occurred during the expansion era, a basic research strategy could be to compare high-growth to low-growth states to determine why some places increased imprisonment more than others and with what effect. The movement in the national aggregate is not an important aspect of this research strategy, and the implicit assumption is that most of the many important choices that should inform future policy in the United States should be contained in the variations between states in the expansion era.

The study of the causes, character, and impact of different policies in the cross section of American states is a hardy perennial in correlational studies of state policy impacts. If the important changes are cross-sectional rather than over time, and if the differences in state policy are very large and easy to explain, this strategy of analysis is quite plausible. For examples of this type of cross-sectional analysis and emphasis in the study of levels of imprisonment, the reader can consult the first major installment of my adventures in imprisonment policy, *The Scale of Imprisonment*, especially Chapter 6 (Zimring and Hawkins 1991).

But the major change this book hopes to examine is the huge expansion of imprisonment over time in the 50 states and the federal government. And if the appropriate measure of imprisonment growth in each state is the percentage increase in each state from its base rate of imprisonment (I think this is the best choice), then the analysis in the section "An Enormous Policy Surprise" suggests that the changes in American state rates look quite like 50 different entities participating in the same general pattern.

For this reason, Chapter 2 profiles shifts in crime, law enforcement, and criminal punishment in the national aggregate. The imprisonment changes in the generation after 1970 were a national expansion, with 50 different states and the federal government fully participating.

2

Crime, Law Enforcement, and Sentencing in an Era of Prison Expansion

THE AIM OF this chapter is to profile the standard statistical dimensions of extraordinary change in imprisonment. To what extent do measures of crime, of arrests and convictions, of prison admissions, and of parole look like business as usual during the generation of high imprisonment growth, and to what extent do any trends in standard measures of crime and punishment provide clear advanced warning of large shifts to come in prison numbers? If there are leading indicators of changes in prison populations during the generation-long upcycle of imprisonment rates, what do those leading indicators tell us now about what is likely to happen in the coming decade?

The chapter is divided into three unequal sections. The first section outlines the type of statistics the chapter will emphasize and will explain the aggregate level of measures that were selected and analyzed. Which crimes are important in studying the levels of reported crime and why? Why are national aggregates more important than state-to-state comparisons over time of crime numbers, arrests, and prison admissions and sentences? How frequently should the national numbers be compiled and compared?

The longer, second section of the chapter provides an analysis of trends in crime, law enforcement, and punishment over the 45 years after 1969 in the United States. The third section of the chapter discusses the implications of the second section's data for deciding how much of the growth of imprisonment was attributable to changes in US population and crime rates and how much resulted from changes in policy.

Two preliminary observations may help readers prepare for the proliferation of statistical presentations and interpretations this chapter demands. The first point to emphasize is that each stop on this statistical train ride produces information of importance in understanding past trends and predicting future developments. The detailed analysis in these pages is hard work but not wasted effort. The second preview of the chapter's analysis is that almost all of the vast changes in imprisonment during the generation after 1970 were produced by policy changes rather than changes in crime or criminal offenders. Mass incarceration was a policy choice by those who held discretionary power in local government.

Methods and Measures

There are two basic styles of attribution that one hears in accounts of how imprisonment rates increased. One way of telling the story of the changes in prison population is as a series of things that happened to governments, increases in crime, a shift toward more repetitively violent offenders on the streets, and greater public demand for incarceration and for longer terms of incarceration. In this passive version of how governments instituted larger levels of imprisonment, the real initiating causes of changes in policy are nongovernmental. The more active story that is often told by governmental actors is that getting tough was a deliberate governmental strategy to reduce crime or reassure crime victims, something that holders of governmental power did on purpose. The passive account puts distance between police chiefs, prosecutors, and legislators and overcrowded prisons. It is protection from blame that comes at a cost because the policy actors in the system are not authors of its success.

Why Aggregation?

But one very difficult issue for arbitrating between passive and active criminal justice agents in telling the story of mass incarceration is this chapter's decision to pour the decisions and outcomes of 50 states and the federal government into a single story. The range of political orientations one can find in American state and local government since the 1970s is truly staggering. Sheriff Joe Arpaio of Maricopa County in Arizona conducted as flagrantly punitive a program of jail administration as any twentieth-century administrator, and even he would fight the notion that his style or his tactics were typical of American local government (Arpaio 1996; Wong and Gambino 2017). Progressives like Lee Brown and Patrick Murphy were big-city police chiefs in the late twentieth century, and so was Philadelphia's pugnacious Frank Rizzo (Meriden Journal 1967). There was a similar range in ideologies and temperament among prosecutors in the thousands of counties across the United States. And there were of course red states and blue states with very different political values and orientations to criminal justice.

This is precisely the type of variable that this chapter's aggregation of US governments will not investigate and measure. To some extent, this is a real limit on the comprehensiveness of the inquiry. But the justification for analysis of the nation as a whole to the detriment of assessing individual jurisdictional difference is that the pattern of increase was so general in its timing and relative magnitude that the contribution of individual variations to the size of the general increase are relatively small. Frank Rizzo and Joe Arpaio didn't help matters much in their state's upward spiral of incarceration late in the twentieth century, and Patrick Murphy and Lee Brown didn't slow things down much where they held office; they are minor figures in the basic process. The numbers in this chapter are national because the scope of the increase was national.

Yet the close-to-uniform rates of growth is a surprise because the variance from state to state in the United States in criminal justice policy and prison population is substantial in 2020 and has been substantial throughout the prison expansion. In an earlier volume, *The Scale of Imprisonment*, Zimring and Hawkins reported differences in rates of imprisonment that were 10 to 1 when the highest state (North Carolina) was compared with the lowest state (New Hampshire) in 1980, and the cross-sectional differences in 2016 were at the same magnitude (Zimring and Hawkins 1991, 149; Bureau of Justice Statistics 2016). The earlier volume titled its chapter of interstate variations "51 Different Countries" to emphasize the huge cross section. The highest reported level of imprisonment per 100,000 population for a state in 2016 was Louisiana at 777 while the lowest level was Maine at 132. But the increase in rates of imprisonment measured against each state's 1970 rates of imprisonment show much more similarity than difference.

Which Crimes, Which Arrests?

The next section of the chapter will discuss trends in crimes and in arrests in the United States over time. But which crimes and arrests are important to study? The answer to this question is best determined by the central pattern being investigated—a large increase in prisoners. A tiny minority of all reported crimes lead to criminal charges, and most of those charges will result in nonimprisonment sentences should a conviction be obtained.

Table 2.1 compares the percentage of all arrests for the seven traditional index crimes in 2014 and contrasts that distribution with the percentage of state prison inmates who were in prison in 2014 as a result of a conviction

Table 2.1
Percentage of All Arrests, Seven Index Crimes and Drugs and Percentage of State Prisoners, 2014

	Percentage of arrests (2014)	Percentage of state prison inmates (2014)
Murder	.09	12.5
Rape	0.18	12.5
Robbery	0.84	13.7
Burglary	2.12	10.5
Assaults	13.00	10.0
Larceny	11.00	3.8
Auto theft	0.6	0.8
Drugs	13.93	15.7
Total arrests	100% 11,205,833	100% 1,325,305

Source: Uniform Crime Report (arrests) and Bureau of Justice Statistics 2014 (state prison inmates).

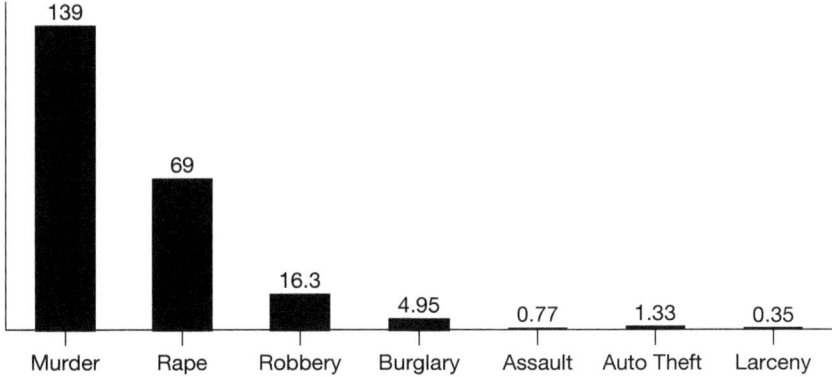

Figure 2.1 The Rate of Prison Impact for Each of Seven Arrest Categories, 2014. *Source*: Table 2.1.

for that crime classification. I add one nonindex crime category, drugs. And all of the arrests and prisoners profiled in Table 2.1 are for state and local police and the state prisons, which are more than 85% of all prisoners.

Figure 2.1 shows the degree to which persons in prison for a listed offense are a larger or smaller share of prisoners than of arrests. If a relatively small number of arrests (for example, murders 0.09% of total arrests) produce a large concentration of prisoners (12.5% of the total), Figure 2.1 shows that persons convicted of that offense are 139 times more overrepresented in the prisons than in arrest populations. For larceny, by contrast, a much larger share of arrests are for this crime (11%) than the corresponding share of prisoners (3.8%). So the relative prison risk in Figure 2.1 is low (0.35).

The way in which "imprisonment impact" is measured in Figure 2.1 combines two different elements that determine the number of offenders in prison on any given day—the chance of conviction and prison sentence *and* the length of a prison sentence. If those convicted of murder and manslaughter receive sentences 10 times longer than burglars, there will be 10 times as many of them in prison for that reason alone in any day's percentage of prison inmates as are reported in the offense-specific arrest categories reported in the left-hand column of Table 2.1. This is why such large differences show up in Figure 2.1's offense-specific profiles.

One of seven index crime categories reported in the figure and the table combine Part One "index" and less serious "Part Two" arrests. The Uniform Crime Report separates the huge number of assaults in police statistics into "aggravated assaults" and other assaults, and most of its reported assault arrests are not in the aggravated category (74% in 2014 of the almost 1.5 million assault arrests). The chance of imprisonment for Part Two arrests for assault is probably much smaller than for Part One assaults, but the exact difference in risk is unknown. The risk ratio reported as 0.77 in the table might be as high as 3 if confined to aggravated cases only but cannot be determined. Since 10% of all persons imprisoned have been sentenced for nonfatal assaults, the crime category is an important part of what generates prison admissions. Omitting the nonaggravated cases from the left-hand column of Table 2.1 would overestimate the prison risk for assaulters, while including all of them as I do will underestimate the risk of prison for an offender in the aggravated category.

The reason for this kind of detailed analysis in this chapter is to construct a measure of both crime and arrest rates that connects meaningfully to the likelihood of imprisonment. There were more than 11 million arrests reported in 2014 in the United States, and most of them carried a low or nonexistent risk of a sentence to a state prison. But the six index crimes other than larceny in Table 2.1 account for 60% of all prisoners and when drug arrests are added account for more than 75% of all prisoners in 2014. The rest of the analysis in this chapter will use variations in reported crime rates for these six index felonies as a prison-impact-related measure of crime and of arrests. I will not include larceny, a huge category of arrests that outnumbers all the rest of index crime arrests combined but only accounts for 3.8% of all prisoners (and even that conviction total will also include many original burglary charges).

The main analysis will also not include the omnibus "drugs" category because it is bottom-heavy and impossible to subdivide into high-risk (sales, hard drugs possession) and very low prison risk categories (possession of marijuana, etc.).

But if the defining character of the crimes and arrests to be counted is imprisonment impact, the relative impact of a single arrest on imprisonment varies by a factor of 100 from 139 in Figure 2.1 for murder and non-negligent manslaughter to 1.33 for auto theft and 0.77 for assault. That is too heterogeneous a range of prison impacts for a single category. The best method to subdivide the prison-relevant offenses is to separate the "top three" offenses (homicide, rape, and robbery), which range from 139 times more prevalent in imprisonment than in arrest down to robbery, which is 16.3 times more concentrated in prison custody groups than in arrests. The other index offenses included in the national aggregate are the "bottom three"—burglary, auto theft, and assault—and they range from 4.95 times more concentrated in prison than in arrests (burglary) down to the assault aggregate (at 0.77), but really at least twice as high for aggravated assaults.

Statistical versus Attitudinal Crime Effects

The ups and downs of offense and arrest rates provide one objective measure of crime and its impact on citizen attitudes. And the natural method to test citizens' reactions is to see whether state sentencing officials react to citizen concerns. But citizen's fears and attitudes toward crime also vary over time and may restrain or accelerate prison population policies in legislation and in the decisions of public officials. The next section will test variations in arrests and criminal sentences, a straightforward and mechanical test of whether one year's changes in crimes influence the next year's imprisonment and sentence length.

The indirect and subjective responses of citizens to crime may take longer to have maximum impact and may also linger in emotions and attitudes. These are no less important just because they are harder to measure.

Trends in Crime and Arrest

Figure 2.2 begins the examination of crime trends as a potential explanation of systemic responses by reporting the volume of reported "top six" offenses in the FBI index crime reports in the reports starting at 1970 and for every fifth year thereafter until 2015. The figure reports the aggregate of the six traditional offenses in the index other than larceny, which is excluded because of its large numbers and typically nonserious nature. Arson is also excluded as often not discovered.

The six types of crime that are aggregated into a single volume for each year are not further distinguished in the figure because reported crime is relevant here not as a measure of the workload of either law enforcement or

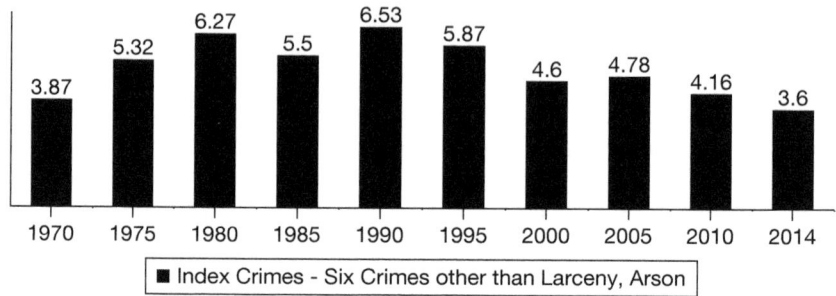

Figure 2.2 Volume of Six Index Crimes, 1970–2014 (Millions). *Source*: Federal Bureau of Investigation n.d.

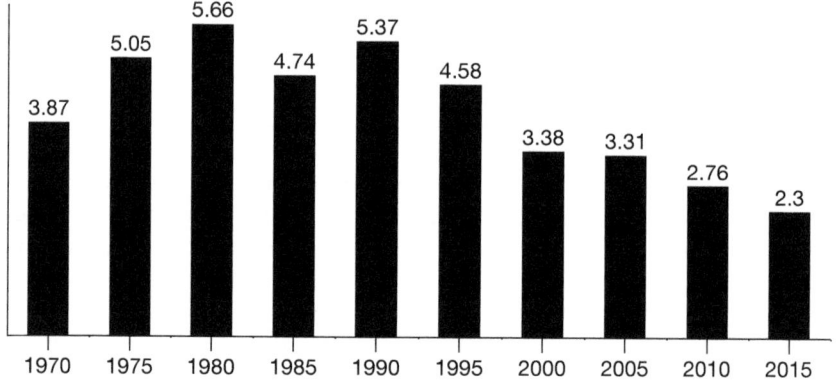

Figure 2.3 Population-Adjusted Crime Rate for Six Index Offenses (Millions). *Source*: Bureau of the Census n.d.a, n.d.b, n.d.c (population); Federal Bureau of Investigation (crime).

the justice system but rather as a measure of how citizens and officials view crime as a problem. Only a minority of reports provoke police investigation, but the fact that a crime is reported is a strong indicator that a victim or witness regards the event as problematic.

The volume of crimes reported is also an incomplete number in the FBI statistics because many offenses go unreported to or by police. And the volume of crime in Figure 2.2 is also not yet reported as a rate per 100,000 citizens. Figure 2.3 will provide those numbers and is thus a better index of variations in personal risk of becoming a crime victim.

The volume of reported index offenses excluding larceny and arson increases substantially from 1970 to 1980, then drops between 1980 and 1985, only to climb by almost 20% in 1990 to the highest total anytime in any period, a 71% increase in crime volume over a two-decade period. Then during the 20 years after 1990, the volume of reported offenses for the top six index crimes drops back all the way to the volume level noted in 1970. If reported offenses are a good measure of police and prosecution workload, there were modest to moderate increases for two decades and then a complete return to 1970 crime volume.

The news is even more cheerful when the crime volume is adjusted for increasing population to measure citizen risk. Figure 2.3 adjusts the total top six Uniform Crime Report crime volumes recorded so that crime volume is adjusted to reflect the expansion in number of citizens.

When adjusted for increases in the nation's population, the crime rate of top six offenses still goes up for 10 years, down from 1980 until 1985 and then returns to just under its highest crime level adjusted to population for 1990. At its peak, the risk of crime for the average citizen was up 49% in 1980, and the per capita rate of these most serious offenses had already fallen below the 1970 start rate by 2000. By 2010, the citizen's crime risk for the top six offenses was 28% lower than the 1970 crime rate.

The volume of reported crimes, which is a rough measure of trends in the number of persons who commit crimes and one factor in determining the number of persons who might be sent to prison, cycles up, then back down to 1970 levels by 2010 and 2015. The crime rate also goes up—but never more than 49% and then is under 1970 rates by year 2000.

One final measure of the importance of crime in a political democracy is how serious citizens believe the crime problem is at various different times. With respect to citizens' fear of crime, one question to explore that issue that has become a standard in survey research is to ask about whether respondents are fearful of walking after dark in their own neighborhood. Figure 2.4 shows the level of concern over time from 1968 to 2016. The pattern over time reflects the ebb and flow of crime volume as observed in

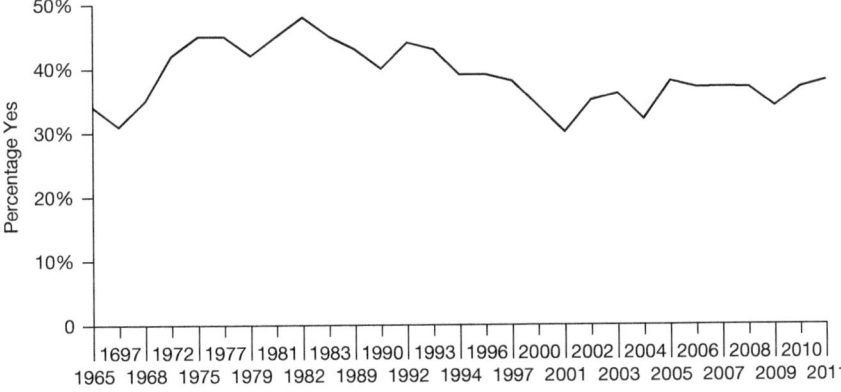

Figure 2.4 Percentage of Persons Afraid to Walk at Night in Local Neighborhood, 1965–2011. *Source*: Gallup n.d.

Figures 2.2 and 2.3 until 2000 but then rises in the period after 2001 and stays relatively high while the crime rates reported in Figure 2.3 continue a steady drop.

But if personal fear was supposed to be the central motive for increasing prison commitments, both the magnitude of the increase in neighborhood fear and the failure of elevated levels in 1992–1997 to stay in place do not match well with the results in imprisonment trends.

There is, however, a second and somewhat distinct element of public sentiment on crime and criminal justice that might match up better with changes in justice policy and involve different groups and different sentiments. When researchers ask whether the punishments and legal processes currently used in the criminal justice system are too lenient, too harsh, or about right, they are measuring not public fear of crime or feelings about their own neighborhoods but public anger or satisfaction with the criminal justice system as a governmental operation. The "too lenient" judgment is about hostility and will often involve persons with strong feelings about government who are in demographic groups, community areas, and ages not closely tied to high rates of crime. This aspect of the politics and ideology of crime policy in the United States was an important element in legislative initiatives like three strikes and you're out in California (Zimring, Hawkins, and Kamen 2001, ch. 9) and the federal Crime Control Act of 1994 (Windlesham 1998).

Arrests

The formal beginning of a criminal prosecution is usually an arrest by police that is referred to local prosecutors and results in the initiation of a formal criminal charge. Variations in the rate of arrests, particularly for offenses of high seriousness, should be important leading indicators of rates of criminal convictions and the referral of convicted offenders to prison. So variations in the rate and the seriousness of arrests by police should be an important indicator of subsequent rates of sentences to prison.

But only some of each year's most serious of the more than 11 million arrests reported by the Uniform Crime Report in 2014 lead to imprisonment. So the most prudent examination of the role of arrest trends in explaining rates of imprisonment should carefully restrict the rate of arrests to offenses likely to provoke imprisonment sentences and to persons who are fully responsible for the criminal conduct for which they are charged.

Figure 2.5 shows trends in rates of arrests with relatively high risks of imprisonment in two respects. The arrests included in the count are for the six index offenses with the highest reported risk of imprisonment in 2014, homicide, rape, robbery, burglary, assault, and auto theft. Only persons over the age of 18 when arrested are counted in Figure 2.5's tally because only a

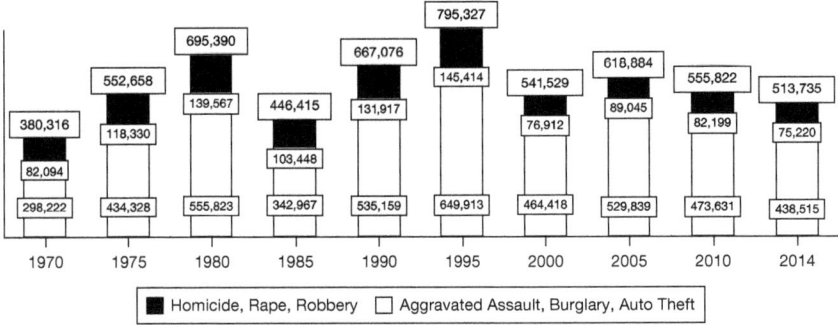

Figure 2.5 Arrests of Persons over 18 for Six Index Crimes, 1970–2014. *Source*: Federal Bureau of Investigation, Uniform Crime Report (1970–2015).

tiny number of juveniles arrested stand serious risk of prison. These adult arrests for those six crimes account for only 8% of reported arrests in 2014 but are 60% of the arrests that lead to a prison sentence. Because the top three charges produce almost 40% of all prisoners with just over 1% of all arrests, those offenses are separated in reporting from the next three of assault, burglary, and auto theft.

The volume of the top six adult arrests is about 10% of the reported top six offenses in Figure 2.5, and arrests over time in our every-five-years sample show a cyclical pattern not dissimilar in trend from the reported crime volumes in Figure 2.2. Because I will be using the volume of arrests to project impact on prison population, no adjustment for population changes is prudent and none is offered. The number of top six adult arrests starts at 380,000 in 1970, then climbs to 795,000 in 1995, doubling in 25 years. The next 20 years show a drop of 35%, so that the number of top six adult arrests at the end of this 45-year period are about 35% larger than the volume of top six arrests in 1970, just keeping up with the 36% increase in population.

For the three most serious crimes—murder, robbery, and rape—where just over 1% of all arrests produce 38.7% of all state prisoners, the volume of arrests goes up 77% in the 25 years up to 1995 but then drops to under the volume of top three arrests by 2000 and stays close to there for every measurement in the new century.

The largest volume of new prison admissions that the arrests measure would predict if mechanically applied would be a doubling increase by 1995 and then an almost immediate drop back after that. By 2000, the volume of homicide, rape, and robbery adult arrests was *under* the volume of such arrests 30 years before in a nation that was smaller in population by 78 million citizens during the earlier period. For the top six adult arrests, the volume of new imprisonment due to increases in felony arrests should be about 40% when 1970 is the base year.

There is, of course, one obvious missing piece to the current calculations of adult arrests that is an important leading indicator of imprisonment admissions and prison population. Drug crimes and drug offenders were a modest segment of state prisoners in 1979 (6.4% of prisoners) and grew by 1986 to 8.6% of state prisoners. Then, while the total prison population was growing very quickly, the drug offense proportion of that expanding total also almost doubled, to 15.7% in 2014. The federal prison system has an even larger share of its total population convicted of drug charges. So why can't the volume of drug arrest reported by the FBI also be used as an explanatory leading indicator of imprisonment rates from 1970 to 2015?

One problem is that the data collected and reported on drug arrests by the FBI are not clear about the severity or nature of the offense leading to the arrest. Each of the six index offenses reported in Figure 2.5 has a clear definition for reporting agencies. But drug offenses cover all state and local laws banning possession, use, or sale of any one of a wide variety of substances. The 1.52 million "drug arrests" profiled in Table 2.1 are probably a "bottom-heavy" aggregation—80% or 90% of the arrests are for possessing or using small quantities of rather soft drugs. What can variations in this bottom-heavy aggregate category tell us about the likely impact of trends in prison population? Not much, it turns out.

Three decades ago, in a chapter titled "Five Theories in Search of the Facts," Gordon Hawkins and I described the apparent impact of variations in drug arrest volume on total prison population: "The only substantial illegal drug abuse indicator available over the full time period 1950–1989 is rates of drug arrests by police as reported by the FBI. We presented a figure, reproduced here as Figure 2.6, that contrasted trends in drug arrests with prison population over the period 1950–1988.

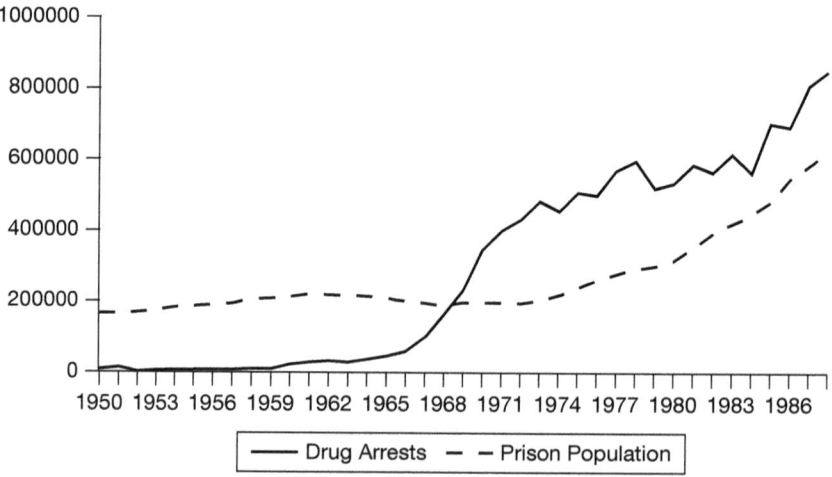

Figure 2.6 Total Number of Drug Arrests and Total Prison Population in the United States, 1949–1988. *Source*: Zimring and Hawkins 1991, Figure 5.7.

Drug arrests fluctuate without clear trend through the 1950s and then explode from 10,500 in 1959 to over 480,000 in 1973, a 47-fold increase in 15 years. The volume of arrests then fluctuates between 450,000 and 616,000 per year for the next decades before further significant increases after 1984. The lack of fit between patterns of drug arrests and prison population is startling. As arrests increase at compound annual rates close to 30%, the aggregate prison population (for all offenses) is stable. When the prison population starts to increase, the volume of drug arrests stabilizes. It is only in the mid-1980s that drug arrests and prison populations grow together" (Zimring and Hawkins 1991, 135).

But what of the period after 1985, when aggregate drug arrests and prison population both expanded substantially? This was a dramatic shift from prior patterns over the decades after 1950, and this change in pattern is a clear signal that it was changes in criminal justice *policy* rather than just changing numbers of drug arrests that forged a new link between drug arrest volume and prison population.

While it might seem that most variations in rates of arrest are not policy driven, this is almost never true for vice crimes not reported by victims. Policy is also important when a police determination of seriousness makes a substantial difference, as with the classification of assaults as "aggravated"; even the volume of arrests in any given year can be driven by changes in policy priorities.

A dramatic demonstration of how changes in policy can influence index crime rates reported by police, as shown in Figure 2.5, is how police seem to be finding a greater proportion of reported assaults to be "aggravated assaults" in recent years, so that these qualify for inclusion in index crime numbers. In 1970, the Uniform Crime Report reported 16,000 killings and 335,000 nonfatal "aggravated assaults," a ratio of 21 nonfatal assaults for each fatality. By 1995, however, while the volume of homicides had gone up 35%, to 21,606, the number of nonfatal but "aggravated" assaults classified by the police had increased 228%, to 1,099,207. So the ratio had increased from 21 assaults per reported homicide to 51 assaults per reported homicide. Either the death rate from serious assault had fallen by far more than half or the police had become much more likely in close cases to call an assault "aggravated." The reclassification hypothesis seems much more plausible.

This kind of policy-driven reclassification of close cases can mismeasure crime trends. The aggravated assault volume reported in 1970 was 45% of the total volume of index crimes of violence, but added additional assaults were no less than 72% of the increase in violent crime over the next quarter-century. To the extent that changed classification was responsible for 27% of the additional crimes reported in 1995, the 1995 violent crime total had been inflated by more than 200,000. So even the modest partial attribution of increased prison population to changes in crime rates rather than policy, suggested by Figure 2.4, may well be an overestimate.

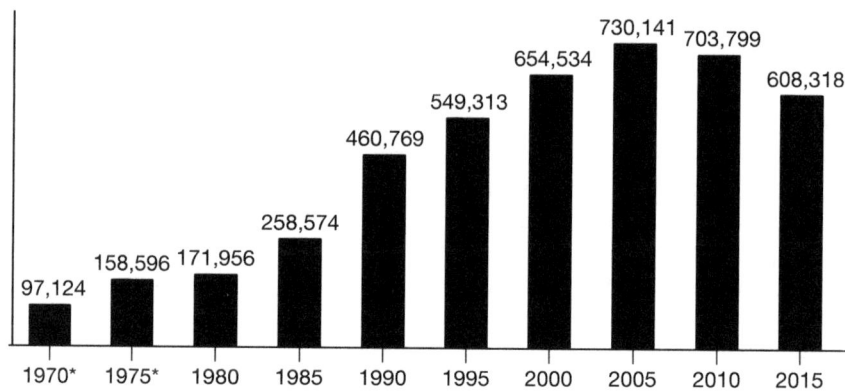

Figure 2.7 Prison Admissions in Federal and State Prisons, 1970–2015.

Note: The 1970 through 1977 statistics for prison admissions only reported direct commitments from courts. The Bureau of Justice Statistics then added all other prison commitments for 1978 onward. We calculated the ratio of direct commitments to total commitments for 1978, 1979 and 1980. The three-year average was .817 of the total. So we then multiplied the direct commitment numbers for 1970 (79,351) and 1975 (129,573) to obtain the estimated total prison commitments for those years in Figure 2.7. *Source*: Bureau of Justice Statistics (1971, 2016).

The variation in criminal charges by police over the 45 years of the great prison expansion played a very small role in explaining the prison boom. And even the modest rate that arrests have played is not clear evidence that either increasing crime or greater police efficiency increased prison numbers. The same impulse toward penal severity that operates with courts, prosecutors, and probation and parole authorities can also increase the volume and the severity of arrests by police.

Prison Admissions

There are no comprehensive statistical summaries of felony judicial proceedings or convictions in the United States for the period of the prison expansion, so nationwide statistics covering the period from 1970 to 2015 jump from data on arrests to information on the volume of prison admissions in the United States, and for the period under study, it's quite a jump. Figure 2.7 profiles the total volume of prison admissions for the every-five-year entries used earlier in the chapter for crime rates and arrest rates.[1]

---

[1] The 1970 through 1977 statistics for prison admissions only reported direct commitments from courts. The Bureau of Justice Statistics then added all other prison commitments for 1978 onward. For Figure 2.7 I calculated the ratio of direct commitments to total commitments for 1978, 1979, and 1980. The three-year average was 0.817 of the total. So I then multiplied the direct commitment numbers for 1970 (79,351) and 1975 (129,573) to obtain the estimated total prison commitments for those years.

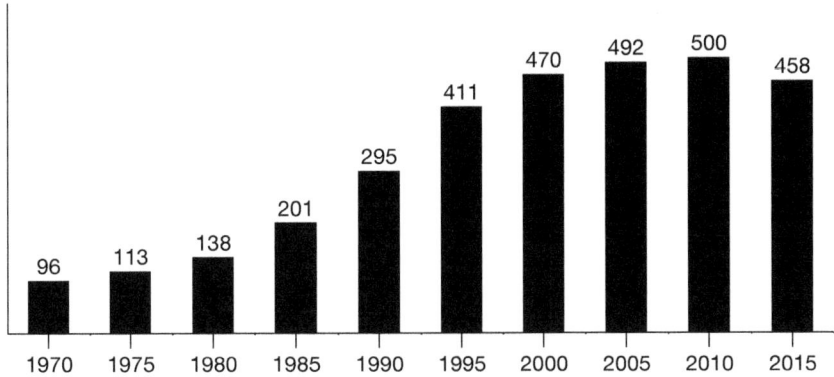

Figure 2.8 Combined Federal and State Rate of Imprisonment, per 100,000 Population, 1970–2015. *Source* data: Bureau of Justice Statistics.

The scale of the increase in prison admissions is vastly greater than the increases we observed in reported crimes and arrests, and the increases in prison admissions persist much longer than for crime and arrests. Prison admissions almost double in the first decade of the time series, then almost triple between 1980 and 1990. While crimes and arrests peak, in the first two decades of expansion prison admissions increase by 374% and then keep growing. By 2005 the volume of prison admissions is 7.5 times the 1970 rate, while crime rates reported in Figure 2.3 decline somewhat from the 1970 level. So sentences to imprisonment were increasing at least six times as fast as crimes or arrests and also kept increasing for at least a decade after crime rates turned down in the mid-1990s.

For state prisoners, the growth of prison admissions was also both earlier and larger than the growth in aggregate prison populations, which is shown in a rate per 100,000 in Figure 2.8.

The data in Figure 2.8 have been adjusted for changes in population, as were the international comparisons earlier in the book. The data in Figure 2.7 are not yet adjusted for changes in population, so this somewhat magnifies the comparison between similar time periods. But correcting for the 45% increase in population on the volume of prison admissions produces an estimated growth in admissions equal to that of total prisoners. Figure 2.9 shows the two rates by year from 1974 to 2015 with all population adjustments made.

With all the population adjustments in place, prison admissions take off earlier than total prison population, and stay closer to their high than does the total prison population. As far beyond the old level of US total prisoners as we are by 2015, and in spite of the declines in the rate of prison admissions, the recent level of prison admissions is still much further ahead of 1970s rates and 1980s rates than is the total prison population, and that suggests that total prison numbers will stay high.

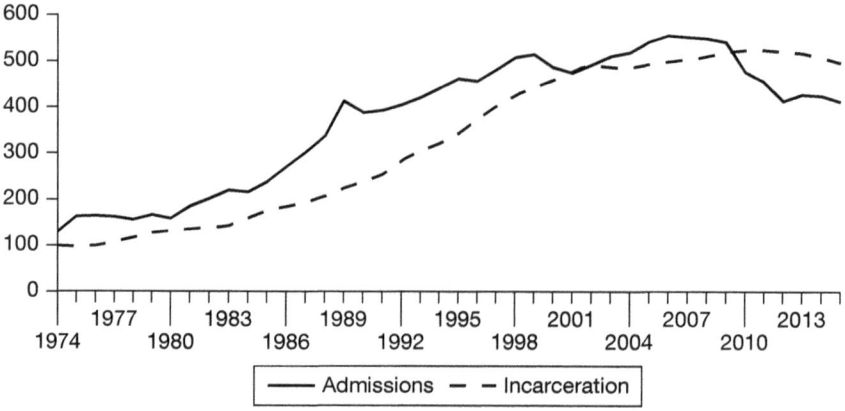

Figure 2.9 US Prison Admission and Incarceration Rates Normalized to 1974 Rate. *Source*: Bureau of Justice Statistics Annual Reports.

Time Served to Release

The final element that is a major determinant of the number of persons in prison at any given time is where and when persons sentenced to prison get released. The term used to determine this concept is "time served to release," which in most state criminal justice systems is a mix of the criminal sentence that produced the original commitment to prison as modified by statutory provisions in both the criminal law and prison administration. In many states, parole boards review prisoners and may grant parole release earlier than the formal end point of the original sentence, but parole release is subject to supervision and is conditional, and those on parole often are returned to prison for violations of conditions imposed.

There are two methods used to estimate trends in time served by prisoners. The first is to sample only those persons released from prison and use that as an estimate, for each type of offense, of how long all persons sentenced for that type of offense will stay in prison. The problem with this measure is that not all persons sentenced to prison are released in any given year, and the prisoners who are *not released* in any given year tend to have longer sentences than those released. That means the average derived by this method will always underestimate the time to be served by all prisoners in any specific offense group and also in the aggregate prison population.

A second approach is explained by Allen Beck and Alfred Blumstein in a 2012 paper prepared for the National Academy of Sciences prison committee of inquiry:

> The other most common approach is based on the ratio of stock population to admissions. . . . This approach works ideally if the admissions rate is sufficiently stationary over time. . . . This admission-based ratio permits us to estimate total time served. (Beck and Blumstein 2012, 24)

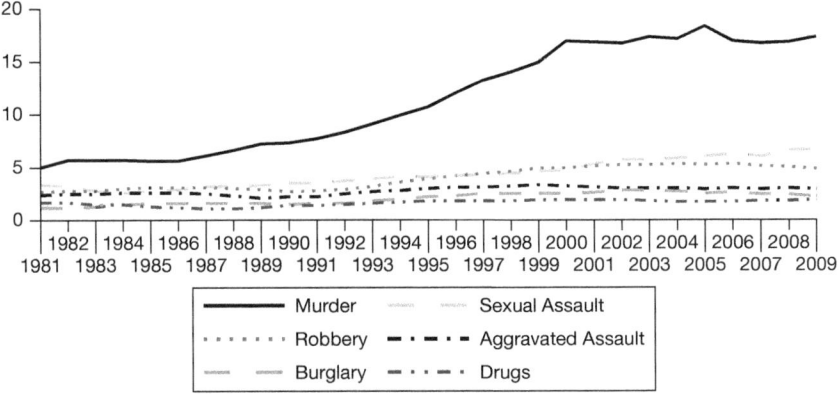

Figure 2.10 Estimated Time Served (Years) in State Prisons. *Note*: Includes parole violators with new sentences; three-year averages for admissions. *Source*: Beck and Blumstein 2012.

Beck and Blumstein provide time served in prison estimates for murder, assault, sex assault, robbery, burglary, and drugs in their Figure 18 for state prisons for the three decades 1980–2010.

The method they used in Figure 2.10 (taken from Beck and Blumstein 2012) is in essence an average of the two methods just reviewed. While imperfect, this is the best estimate that can be provided.

The time-served estimate for murder more than doubles in the period studied, and sexual assault and robbery also increase significantly in the years after 1990. The precise contribution of those increases to the net level of imprisonment is difficult to measure on the 2017 total prison population. Further, the long, often all but unlimited, terms for murder convictions might provide a legacy population that will grow in number and also magnify the difficulty of maintaining prisoners in a prison environment over time.

The Federal System

The focus so far in this chapter has been on state criminal justice systems. The admissions and total population figures provided in this section have included federal admissions and prisoners but have not contrasted federal with state systems. Beck and Blumstein compare state versus federal rates of incarceration by expressing the state rates per 100,000 population and federal rates per million national population in their Figure 4, which is here reproduced as Figure 2.11.

For the first 20 years of the period after 1980, the federal prison rate, while growing, was never even 10% of total imprisonment. But federal prison populations grew even faster than state rates and passed the 10%

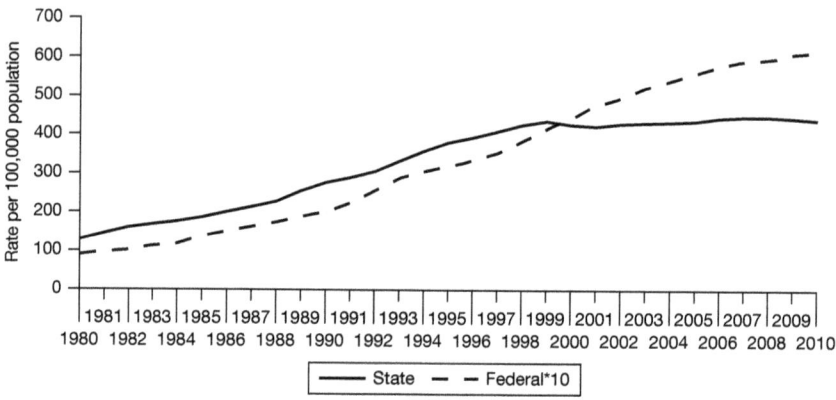

Figure 2.11 Trends in State and Federal Incarceration Rates, 1980–2010.
Source: Beck and Blumstein 2012.

threshold of total prison population in 2000. There were two important reasons why federal prison rates grew even faster than state rates. The first was the much larger share of all federal prisoners who were convicted of drug crimes, so that when both state and federal systems greatly increased their drug prosecution rates, that increase had a greater impact on total federal prison volume because of the larger role of the dynamic drug sector to the total. The other change that boosted the federal prison numbers even faster than the states was an expansion in prison terms for drugs, weapons, and robbery (Beck and Blumstein 2012, Figure 25). During the George W. Bush administration, federal prosecution of weapons and drug crime to produce high federal sentences was considered a type of aid to states by transferring the costs of protracted imprisonment from state to federal budgets. In addition, the federal prison policy changes that happened after 1975 were much more closely linked to the creation and policy preferences of a new federal sentencing commission and to legislation on drug offenses than were the patterns in the states. And the impact of deliberate expansion of sentence lengths was more substantial in the late 1990s and early in the twenty-first century.

What Lessons from These Data?

What can we learn about the causes of the growth in imprisonment from the quick tour through national statistics on crime, law enforcement, and imprisonment? And what do the patterns observed so far tell us about what is likely to happen over the next decade or so in the United States?

The statistical patterns of reported crime and of arrests over the generation after 1970 show moderate movements that cycle up for a decade, then down, then up again for half a decade, and downward for at least a decade. The cyclical nature of crime trends and the absence of high-magnitude crime increases don't fit with the one-directional and high-magnitude expansion of imprisonment. And one measure of citizens' fear of crime, being afraid to walk in the one's neighborhood at night, showed only moderate movement upward, then fell back to earlier levels, which fits nicely with the actual expansion in crime rates and their subsequent decline. There is in crime data and the fear of neighborhood crime no close fit with soaring rates of imprisonment.

But these two cyclical and relatively moderate findings are not convincing evidence that public opinion did not change in the 1980s and 1990s or that changes in public opinion were not important in motivating shifts in crime policy. The earlier discussion in this chapter distinguished between a citizen's fear of crime and a citizen's attitude about the effectiveness and appropriateness of the criminal justice system. Whether or not they are afraid, citizens can get angry about institutions of criminal justice. There are clear indications that whenever citizens are asked whether criminal punishments are sufficiently severe, there is substantial sentiment that the system is too lenient. Using National Opinion Research Center data, belief that punishment for criminals is "not harsh enough" was always a view held by a substantial majority in the United States between 1972 and 1989 and in the years after. But dissatisfaction with the courts seems to be a chronic condition rather than a novel feature of opinion in the 1970s and 1980s. As Zimring and Hawkins argued in 1991, "If negative public views causes [sic] increases in prison population, that population would be ceaselessly spiraling upward" (1991, 129). What was it that caused a chronic public dissatisfaction to motivate the huge policy changes in the period after 1975?

Perhaps the key variable here that translates public opinion into political action is the increasing salience of the crime issue in public opinion. The Zimring and Hawkins hypothesis:

> It may well be that the public always thinks that criminal offenders are treated too leniently. But this attitude is likely to be far more politically significant when crime is the number one or number two public concern than when chronic dissatisfaction with the operation of the criminal justice system is not a preeminent concern. (Zimring and Hawkins 1991, 136)

The appropriate way to measure the salience of crime issues is to find out how important the public judges crime to be relative to other national problems such as the economy, global warming, and smog. And there have certainly been periods in the decades of prison expansion when violent crime or urban crack cocaine was a very high public priority. But these are much shorter periods of intense concern than the sustained upward spirals of prison admissions that persisted for decades. It would take a modified version of the salience hypothesis to fit the 30-odd years of constant growth—a theory that salience was a necessary condition to launch an upward spiral in imprisonment but that once the process was underway, it could be sustained without consistent and intense public concern.

So variations in crime rates and in the fear of crime don't link persuasively with the major shift in imprisonment under scrutiny, but public hostility to criminals and criminal courts might have helped launch increases in the use of prison in the political and legal processes. Yet there is no plausible theory of public opinion that can account for the sustained dynamic of expanding imprisonment over the era after 1975.

There are also no strong clues to be found in patterns of police arrests and the initial crime classification of the persons the police delivered to the front doors of American criminal courts. The volume of arrests for crimes likely to produce prison sentences didn't increase much prior to 1995 and then quickly fell back to the rates found in the early 1970s. If patterns of arrest were the primary driver of increases in the rate of imprisonment, the increase in rates of persons behind bars by 2007 would be closer to 40% than to 400%.

The fundamental cause of the explosion in prison populations in the United States is a huge increase in prison commitments from local governments in the 50 American states. All by itself, the increasing volume of prison admissions can explain about 90% of the growth of state imprisonment. Trends in prison admissions are also efficient leading indicators of trends in total imprisonment. The logical foundation for this is far from rocket science—the principal determinant of how many people will be in prison next year is how many were sent to prison this year and last year. But this means that reformers should pay close attention to admission rate trends.

The dominant role of increasing prison admissions as an explanation for the huge prison increase also identifies both the level of government and the branches of government that have been the primary moving parts in prison expansion. Criminal convictions and prison sentences are produced by local governments—usually county government—and the two branches of local government that unequally share power in criminal sentencing are executive branch prosecutors and criminal court judges. In court systems where the vast majority of felony case dispositions are the product of negotiated guilty pleas, the defendant's criminal sentence is usually determined long before the judge who issues the formal sentence is involved in the case. Prosecutors are the central power players in local criminal justice.

The dominant role of local government is obvious in two of three mechanisms that produce prison admissions. Criminal convictions that produce prison sentences are wholly the function of local criminal courts, as are convictions for new offenses by persons back in the community on parole.

But what of person sent back to prison (readmitted, in formal terms) because of violations of conditions of parole? Since parole supervision is a function of central state government, any shift in the proportion of persons on parole who get returned to prison might be a policy change produced by an agency of state government. Since many persons who do get returned to prison are sent back for parole violation, it is important to see whether there have been major changes in the percentage of parolees returned, which might signal a state-level policy change. That is the function of Figure 2.12, adopted from the Beck and Blumstein report (2012).

The rate of parole subjects who are returned to prison per hundred prisoners on parole is stable throughout the 30 years Beck and Blumstein examine, so that there are no indications of state parole policy changes that influence the number of prison admissions for parole violation. The primary determinant of the number of parolees returned seems to be the number of persons on parole, and this in systems of extensive parole release is a function of the number of persons sent to prison. So local government has a dominant influence on all three sources of rates of prison admission.

But what of the power of central state government to write criminal laws and specify criminal penalties? What about mandatory minimum penalties passed by draconian legislatures? Since prosecutors have discretion not to prosecute and can always accept pleas to lesser offenses, there is no such thing as a mandatory minimum penalty for prosecutors. It is judges whose discretion is constrained by such laws.

The fact that the primary architects of the nation's massive prison expansion are local prosecutors only compounds the mystery of why so many units of government intensified policies at the same time. Instead of

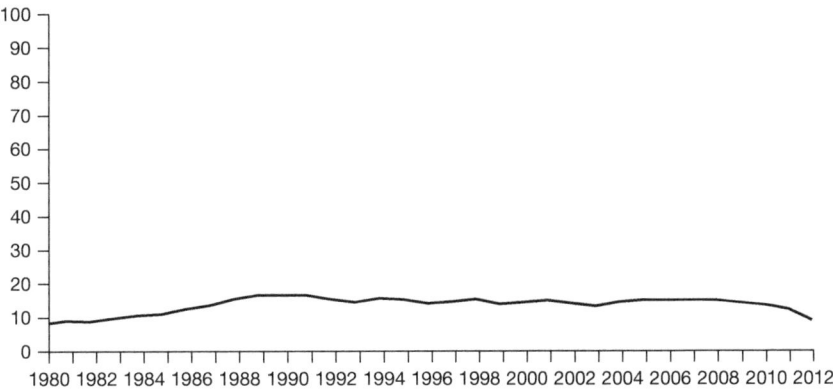

Figure 2.12 Parole Revocation Re-admissions to Prison as a Percentage of Total Persons in Prison, 1980–2012. *Source*: Bureau of Justice Statistics, Annual Probation Survey, Annual Parole, Survey, Annual Survey of Jails, Census of Jail Inmates, and National Prisoner Statistics Program, 1980–2015.

puzzling about why 50 different states made large changes at the same time, we now have to wonder why 3,000 prosecutors made extraordinary changes in the same direction at the same time (see Pfaff 2016).

If county government has been the center stage for the changes that produced the growth of imprisonment, knowing the location of the primary causes might also help measure the motives and priorities of the primary actors in creating the policy shifts. The next chapter will explore why prisons became the dominant method of punishment policy changes in the 1970s and 1980s. But the search for motives for increasing levels of imprisonment should focus its main efforts on those levels and branches of government that were the primary moving parts in the penal expansion. It is the attitudes and motives of prosecutors rather than legislators that is most closely linked to the changes in behavior that expanded imprisonment. Discussion of the question "Why prison?" in the next chapter will focus on the appeals that were important to the local prosecutors who were the primary cause of the increase.

It may also be that the same institutions that were powerful forces for increasing imprisonment are good targets for efforts to reduce imprisonment. Certainly, if the proportion of felony charges that produce prison commitments was the major cause of increased imprisonment, then altering preferences at the local level of government may be an efficient means of reducing the number of persons sent to prison.

One other value of trends over time in prison admissions is as a leading indicator of future fluctuations in total prison population. The logical foundation for prison admissions as an indicator of total population trends is obvious, and admissions data work well as a leading indicator of total population trends at the national level in Figure 2.9, beginning to decline earlier than the population total. There is no reason why admissions trends shouldn't work well as a prediction of population trends at the individual state level as well.

With the national data we have already examined, we do not yet know what level of prison admissions is necessary to maintain a certain level of total prison population. The fact that total imprisonment declined after prison admissions dropped from a three-year average of 738,000 in 2005–2007 to an average of 638,000 in 2008–2010 and that this decline preceded a decline in the rate of imprisonment from 2009 to 2015 does *not* mean that an admissions rate of 638,000 each year is not sufficient to maintain a prison population close to 500 per 100,000. Changes in prison release policy may also have contributed to the decline in total prisoners and the total imprisonment rate per 100,000. It will take a state-by-state analysis of admission rates and subsequent changes in total imprisonment rates to establish what levels of admissions—all other things being equal—will maintain total prison populations at their current high levels.

And the modest drops in national prison admission rates to date are not yet terribly encouraging as a preview of substantial declines in imprisonment.

The three-year average volume of prison admissions in 2013, 2014, and 2015 was 621,000, the same volume recorded for 1998, 1999, and 2000. The rate of imprisonment for both these three-year periods was also similar, and imprisonment rates went up after 1998–2000.

There are in the patterns to date of prison admissions trends no indication of larger declines than the modest numbers already on record. Adding more than 600,000 prisoners each year to state and federal prisons is only a decline from the astronomical volumes of the earliest years of the twenty-first century.

3

Why the Prison-Boom Generation?

Imprisonment is one of several alternative punishments available for persons convicted of serious crimes but also the most serious of commonly used punishments in most modern criminal justice system. This chapter will focus on a comparison of imprisonment to other sanction measures available in the American criminal justice systems under study, but the attempt will be made not merely to explain the appeal of prison commitments as a general matter but also to discuss why prison commitments were regarded as a more attractive choice by governmental actors at the time and in the places where prison commitment expanded from the mid-1970s onward. Instead of simply outlining the characteristics of prison versus nonprison sentences as an abstract proposition, I will try to identify what made prison sentences attractive in the era of their great growth—1975 to 2010—and in the levels of government and branches of government where the prison decisions were being made.

Prison and Other Punishments

While detailed and comprehensive statistics on criminal justice outcomes have not been available for the period 1970 to 2015, there are several features of American criminal justice in this era that are not controversial. The first is that a wide variety of sentencing outcomes were available in state and federal justice systems after conviction for a felony. In most state systems, one major distinction in the sanctions available is between public custodial institutions (prisons for lengthy terms, jails for shorter terms) and programs and conditions of restitution, home or electronic monitoring, or participation in treatment or training programs. In state systems, a majority of persons convicted of felonies are not sent to prison. In the federal system, a majority of person convicted of felonies now do serve some time in secure confinement.

The second obvious fact of the period since 1970 is that the rate at which persons charged with crimes are sent to prison (and to jail) has increased substantially and has continued since 2007 at close to the post-1970s high.

Two Methods of Comparison

While the extent to which imprisonment has increased is difficult to determine precisely, the general magnitude of the expansion is quite large.

Table 3.1 uses available profiles by the offense leading to commitment for all persons admitted to state and federal prisons in the United States in 1970, prior to the great expansion, and in 2006, when prison admissions were at their highest level.

There are three major limitations to the information available in the table. The first is that the report covers prisons only and not the total of persons locked up in prisons (usually for one year or longer) and jail (shorter sentences and pretrial detention). The second important limit is that only those sent to prison are counted. So we can't know from the table, for example, what percentage of all persons convicted of robbery and burglary are sent to prison in 1970 or in 2006. The third limitation is that by focusing on persons admitted rather than all persons in prison, we count persons with long prison sentences the same as those with shorter sentences.

There are some significant differences in the offense profile of new prisoners in 2006—three times as many are drug offenders and a larger share of new prisoners are property offenders in 1970 (45%) than in 2006 (25%). But the bulk of new prison commitments involve the same mix of violent and property crimes. The percentage distribution over the two different periods resembles the description announced by the police commander in the classic film *Casablanca*, "Round up the usual suspects."

But any similarity between the two eras in Table 3.1 was produced by eliminating the huge difference in the rate of prison admissions between 1970 and 2006. Figure 3.1 tells a much different story by comparing the estimated volume of prison admissions for each of eight offense groups in 1970 and 2006.[1]

---

[1] The offense volumes for 1970 were estimated by multiplying the Bureau of Justice Statistics report of the percentage distribution of offenses leading to prison admissions by the total reported court commitments to prison in 1970, 97,124. The offense volumes are estimated for 2006 by multiplying the reported volume of admissions by the percentage of each

Table 3.1

Percentage Distribution of Offenses Leading to Commitment, 1970 and 2006

	1970	2006
Violent		
Homicide	6.3	2.1
Assault	6.0	8.5
Rape	3.0	4.9[a]
Robbery	14.4	6.6
Property		
Burglary	16.7	9.9
Larceny	18.8	9.5[b]
Forgery, fraud	9.5	5.5
Drugs		
Drugs	10.3	32.3
Morals, order		
Liquor	1.3	3.1[c]
Weapons	0.4	3.5
Draft	0.8	—
Contempt, etc., other public order	2.4	5.0
All other	12.0	9.1
	100%	100%
	(50,632)	(537,658)

[a] Sex offenses in 2006.
[b] Includes auto theft in 2006.
[c] Includes DWI in 2006. *Source*: Cahalan 1986 (1970 data); Carson and Golinelli 2014, Prison Admissions 2006.

The method for estimating offense-specific rates of admission is straightforward but not precise. For each year, I have multiplied the percentage the Bureau of Justice Statistics reports for each offense by the total the agency reports for prison admissions.

The pattern in Figure 3.1 is that huge increases in the volume of persons sent to prison are *absolutely pervasive*. There are no crime categories where the volume of prison admissions does not expand by an extreme multiple that has only occurred in the United States. Homicide, where imprisonment has always been a consistent policy, more than doubles, and robbery

offense reported by the Bureau of Justice Statistics. The 2006 volume of "other" violent arrests was distributed among assaults, sex crimes, and robbery in the same proportion as these three categories were reported (10.75% of violent crimes were not specified). For property crimes, the 14.51% of other property crimes were also distributed in the same pattern of the three reported categories of offense.

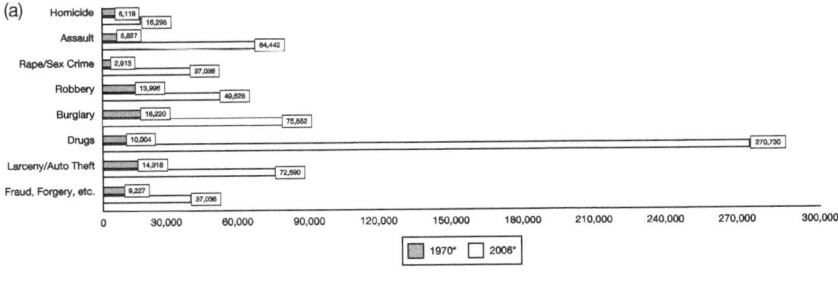

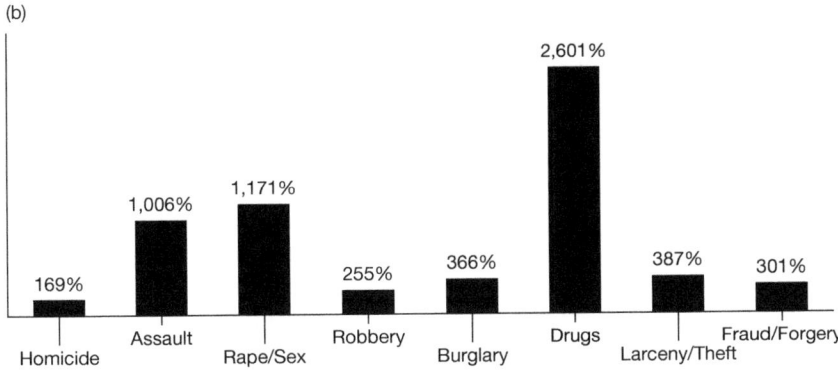

Figure 3.1 Volumes of Prison Admissions by Offense, Eight Crime Categories. *Source*: Bureau of Justice Statistics, 1970–2019.

expands by a factor of four. Burglary admissions increase by a factor of five. The sex offenses included in that category have expanded somewhat since 1970, but the volume of prison admission goes from under 3,000 to almost 40,000, an increase that is much more than expanding categories would explain. Drug offense prison admissions are an outlier, even against the stupendous scale of the other increases, increasing more than 20-fold. (Much of the difference between drugs and conventional crimes with victims may reflect different investments by law enforcement.)

The exponential growth of prison admissions is vastly higher than the 47% increase in the US population over the period from 1970 to 2006. Homicide prison admissions grow at more than three times the rate of population increase, and every other offense category experiences an expansion of prison admissions at least five times as great as the growth of population.

Two substantive conclusions can be drawn from Figure 3.1 that are of importance to this chapter's main concern, the appeal of prison to local government in the generation after 1970. The first and most important finding is that the changes manifest in Figure 3.1 are not specific to a particular crime or crime category but rather indicate a general policy of increasing emphasis on imprisonment. This wasn't a war on drugs only, or a war on violence, or a crusade against sex offenders, although the policy being pursued was all those things. Decision-makers in criminal justice at a retail level had a forceful and general desire for imprisonment, short terms or terms of intermediate length. No matter what the question was, prison was the answer. There is in the 36-year two-point comparison in Figure 3.1 no suggestion of a priority concern with any particular problem. And, at least for state imprisonment patterns, there is a little evidence of any willingness or felt necessity to reduce either prosecution or punishment levels for non-drug offenses to facilitate more penal resources for drug offenders. Prison was evidently not considered a scarce resource in this era of state and local criminal justice.

The second obvious lesson of Figure 3.1 is that patterns of prison admissions tell rather different stories about the criminological and social bite of penal policies than an analysis of imprisonment that focuses on the population of prisoners in any given day, when offenses with long sentences have much more impact on total population. In 2014, for example, the percentage of prisoners in custody for murder, rape, and robbery was 38.7%, while drug offenders were less than half that population, at 15.7%. It is this kind of total prisoner comparison that is customary for those trying to argue against the emphasis on drug policy prescriptions for prison overcrowding (see Pfaff 2016, 32–33; Forman 2017). But while those convicted of murder, rape, and robbery are more than twice the volume of prisoners on any given day (see Table 2.1), what Figure 3.1 tells us is that for 2006, persons sent to prison for drug offenses were more than twice the number of those sent to prison for murder, rape, and robbery combined.

Which is a better measure of the costs of mass imprisonment—prison admissions or prison population totals? A respectable argument can be made for prison admissions as equally important to any day's percentage of total prisoners. The drug offenders going to prison may well get out sooner than do robbers and killers, but the harm of their having been in prison done to them, their families, and their communities may still be very substantial. What Figure 3.1 tells us about 2006 is that penal policy toward drugs is producing twice as many prison convicts, many more than twice as many ex-prisoners, and twice as many families of prisoners as homicides each year. Certainly one cannot read across the bar charts of Figure 3.1 and conclude that mass incarceration is *only* a matter of misguided drug policy. But the vast expansion of drug-related imprisonment has played a major role in the destruction of offenders' lives, harm to offenders' families, and damage to the communities that they are removed from.

The contrast between the expansion of long sentences for robbery and assault and the vast expanses of short sentences for possession and sale of drugs tells us one further aspect of the pro-imprisonment orientation that we are considering—it is also a general preference as to sentence length. The personal preferences and policies that produced the explosion of prison admissions were not solely focused on long prison terms but rather pursued and obtained a mix of long and short terms. What was so attractive about sending people convicted of crime to prison, for sentences long or short? Does this preference link to a clear theory of the purposes of imprisonment that took off in the United States in the period after 1970? What theory or theories might explain the enthusiasm for all sorts of prison terms for all kinds of crimes?

The Classification of Penal Purposes

The central issue of this chapter is a peculiar subcategory of the hearty perennial question: Why do governments punish? For what I want to know is why prosecutors and other actors in local government wished to increase imprisonment for all serious crimes beginning in the late 1970s. What changes in objectives, priorities, or levels of information can be associated with the locations and periods of the great prison expansion?

One obvious starting point for a survey of penal purposes is the customary listing of community and state motives for punishing those guilty of crime: deterrence, incapacitation, and retribution. Did any or all of these become much more powerful dynamics in the litigation of criminal cases in the last decades of the twentieth century?

Deterrent threats are intended to prevent crime by persuading persons who are tempted to commit crimes not to do so to avoid the pains of punishment. But if the threat of punishment is supposed to do the job, why would this motive ever require actual increases in levels of imprisonment by local government? The answer, of course, is that imposing sanctions is necessary to make the threats to potential criminals more credible (Zimring and Hawkins 1972, 160–67).

Deterrence is always a positive aspect of penal sanctions from a prosecutor's eye view of the justice system, but strong belief in the power of general deterrence by prosecuting attorneys wasn't easy to find in the 1980s and 1990s, because general deterrence is thought to require that potential offenders weigh costs and benefits. This is always a hope when long sentences of penal confinement are sought, but there is no evidence that the pursuit of general deterrence was a major priority in changes in penal practice in the United States, at least through the mid-1990s. Economists who regard penalties including imprisonment as costs imposed on offenders and advertised to potential offenders always place heavy emphasis on deterrence (see Zimring 2008), but most prosecutors would regard primary reliance on deterrence as unduly optimistic because it relies on potential offenders making rational decisions and all of the offenders they encounter are failures of a deterrence policy. Further, there is, from a prosecutorial perspective, a more attractive moral logic to punishment that is intended to restrain the criminal behavior of the person punished.

Zimring and Hawkins identified this as a general rhetorical advantage for the second purpose of prison—incapacitation:

> [Incapacitation] will commonly appear morally fitting and appropriate because it involves punishing particular individuals to prevent *them* from committing further crimes. In the case of general deterrence, the reason that certain individuals are imprisoned . . . is to prevent the commission of crimes *by other people*. The apparent [moral] justification [of incapacitation] is that [it] represents the pursuit of crime prevention by locking up the right people. (Zimring and Hawkins 1995, 15)

So both its ethical appeal and the capacity of secure confinement to restrain crime even if offenders are irrational have particular appeal for prosecutors. The timing of increased interest in incapacitation is also a good fit, at least with the first two decades of the post-1970s penal expansion.

What of the notion of penal desert as retribution? Retribution as a motive of punishment is probably as old as the formal criminal law. Punishment is, after all, distinct from other acts of a government not at war because it is intended to do harm to its subject. There is typically in criminal law no direct connection between retribution as a purpose and any particular type of punishment. But any substantial increase in the demand for retribution would increase the proportion of prison sentences because prison is the most severe of frequently available criminal sentences. In the rhetoric of the 1970s and 1980s, however, commentators like James Q. Wilson also seemed to merge claims about incapacitation effects with retributive claims that were framed as specific to incapacitation. "Since society clearly wishes its criminal laws more effectively enforced," he wrote, "this means rising prison populations, perhaps for a long period" (1975, 173).

Retribution was typically discussed as a claim that a certain minimum level of punishment was a necessary good in a functioning system of criminal justice, but retributive theories also recognized that excessive punishment would be unjust. Retribution is in this sense a contrast to a later variation on these traditional notions of punishment as a normative virtue that imagines the punishment decisions made in criminal justice as a status competition between victims of crime and those who offended against them. In this rhetoric, *any* increase in the punishment of an offender is approved as an enhancement of the social status and statute of crime victims (see Zimring, Hawkins, and Kamen 2001, 223–24). The implicit assumption of positing a symbolic zero-sum competition between victims and offenders was that "anything that is bad for offenders must be beneficial to victims. Once every policy question becomes a status competition, the appropriate result is a foregone conclusion. . . . The rhetorical versatility of this conception is quite astonishing. No punishment seems too extreme if anything that hurts offenders benefits victims" (Zimring, Hawkins, and Kamen 2001, 223–24).

This sort of assumption was more important in political dialogue and legislative rhetoric in the 1980s and 1990s than in the attitudes and priorities of prosecutors and other agents of local government. The only extensive use of status competition logic in criminal prosecution was in the appeals used in death penalty trials by prosecutors.

The same pragmatic mindset that motivated plea negotiations and willingness to allocate scarce resources in such decisions made prosecutors poor candidates for unlimited claims of retributive necessity.

So the major new appeals of increasing imprisonment for prosecutors in traditional "purposes of imprisonment" terms were clustered around the promise of crime reduction through incapacitation. And the publicity around statistical claims for incapacitation that came into play in the mid-1970s provide a good fit with the early stages of the increasing emphasis on prison admissions (see Wilson 1975; Shinar and Shinar 1975).

But the general emphasis on prison admissions—for serious crimes as well as for those of intermediate severity—seems broader than selecting a specific group of very active offenders for restrictive confinement. In addition, the entire conceptual framework of incapacitation probably doesn't apply to drug commerce and indeed to most drug crime, yet the phenomenal growth in prison sentences was if anything larger for drug offenses than in any other major crime category. So the impetus for massive expansion in prison commitment involved ambitions much broader and far less selective than the expansion in perceived opportunities to incapacitate. Some priority much broader than incapacitation created the pervasive expansion documented in Figure 3.1.

Operational Features and Incentives

Not all the concerns that influence the behavior of prosecutors and judges in local government can be found in textbooks on the philosophy of punishment. Budgetary incentives and disincentives are one important dimension of decisions by government agencies of substantial impact to prison population. And the way in which units of government define their goals and measure their success or failure can have impact on both the number of persons they send to prison and the length of prison terms.

This section of my analysis will focus on two issues in the political economy of incarceration in the United States, the incentives of local units of government to use custodial facilities they don't have to pay for and the use and importance of prison sentences as indicators of adversarial success by public prosecutors. Each of these was an important part of why local governments embraced prison sentences during the generation of uninterrupted prison growth after 1970, and each operational incentive must be diminished if levels of imprisonment are to be substantially reduced.

The "Correctional Free Lunch"

The first operational incentive to local government to choose prison was a function of the fact that prisons in the United States are paid for by the state level of government out of state correctional budgets, but prison populations are determined by the number of prisoners sentenced to prison by local prosecutors and judges and the length of prison sentences these local officials impose. This is not, in a formal sense, an incentive for local prosecutors to choose prisons rather than nonsecure criminal sanctions, other than the absence of any financial disincentive to do so. However, this perception of prison as a costless option does become an incentive to use prison when alternative sanctions, such as local jails or county probation, are paid for in part by local government. At that point, the county prosecutor can minimize costs to county government by choosing sanctions that substantially increase costs at the state level of government.

This problematic allocation of the power to make punishment decisions and the responsibility to pay for them can be remedied either by reallocating sentencing power to the bill-paying branches of state government or by imposing costs on local government for using prisons or providing payments to local governments who reduce prison use.

There is some circumstantial evidence that the cost-free status of imprisonment to local governments played a role in the growth of imprisonment because prison populations which don't involve local expenditures grew more quickly than jail populations (Sentencing Project 2017, 2).

But why should this economic problem suddenly generate mass incarceration growth after 1970? While there were reductions of central state parole authority in some states in the 1970s, for the most part both the power of local governments to determine prison volumes and the "free lunch" lack of any financial consequences to county governments have been features of American government throughout the twentieth century, including the decades when there was no sharp expansion in prison numbers.

It seems unlikely that the cost-free character of prison commitments by local governments was at any time in the twentieth century the dominant cause of sharp increases in rates of imprisonment. But when other motives for increasing either the number of persons sent to prison or the length of prison sentences become important, the absence of any financial cost to local government removes whatever restraint might otherwise moderate prison expansion. More than the free-lunch phenomenon in state government produced the prison boom after 1970. But the cost-free environment that greeted penal expansion increased the magnitude of expansion and encouraged trends to continue over a sustained period. The need to rationalize cost incentives will be an early necessity in effective reform programs.

The Hazards of Adversarial Ambition

One distinguishing characteristic of criminal justice in the United States and other national descendants of British rule is an adversarial system of criminal justice, as contrasted with the inquisitorial systems that evolved on the European continent. The United States, along with Canada, Australia, and the United Kingdom, makes the public prosecutor into the state representative trying to convict persons charged with crime and advocating for the application of strict penal measures after conviction. In the United States, the office that prosecutes criminal charges is usually an agency of county or sometimes city government, and the chief prosecutor in such an office is usually an elected official. Elected provincial advocates of punitive outcomes are always natural candidates for policies that produce increases in imprisonment, but what might explain the emphasis on prison in the generation after 1970?

There are two changes in criminal processes that fit well with an acceleration process that began in the 1970s: first, an intensification of adversarial competition as a result of constitutional requirements imposed in the 1960s on criminal prosecutors and restrictions on police investigation, and, second, the creation of management systems that measured prosecutorial effectiveness by convictions and prison sentences.

The series of defendant-centered changes in the constitutional rules governing the criminal process imposed by the Warren Court were intended to level the playing field of criminal investigation and litigation and thus to benefit criminal defendants, but some critical observers have suggested that the reactions that rulings in *Miranda, Mapp v. Ohio*, and *Gideon v. Wainwright* provoked may have put defendants at a net disadvantage.

Professor William Stuntz of Harvard argued this "net disadvantage" thesis in his book *The Collapse of American Criminal Justice*. Stuntz proposed three separate latent impacts of the due process cases that may have put most criminal defendants at hazard. The first was a complication of criminal cases that put poor defendants at particular risk:

> By making defense lawyers more central to criminal litigation than they already were and by dramatically enlarging the range of legal claims they could raise on their clients' behalf, Warren's Court *increased* the gap between rich and poor defendants even though the decisions were intended to narrow that gap. (2011, 218)

The second prejudicial change, Stuntz proposed, was a shift from substance to procedure:

> Warren and his colleagues continued and exacerbated a long-term trend: They proceduralized criminal litigation, siphoning the time of attorneys and judges away from the question of the defendant's guilt or innocence and toward the process by which the defendant was arrested, tried and convicted. (2011, 228)

The third prejudicial effect and the most directly relevant to increasing levels of imprisonment was the diversion of cases to informal methods of outcome. "The Warren Court's decisions made arrests and prosecutions, hence also prison sentences, more expensive; that is the natural consequence of adding new restrictions on evidence gathering and new procedural claims to criminal litigation" but, Stuntz argues, "The consequence was a more streamlined criminal process—one designed to yield the most convictions at the least cost—than the one that existed before Earl Warren" (2011, 234). "Constitutional law establishes procedural hurdles the state must clear—but also creates cheap alternatives if clearing those hurdles seems too costly. The net result is to make searches, interrogations and criminal prosecutions cheaper, not more expensive" (238).

One problem with evaluating these arguments as a major explanation of changes in imprisonment is the uncertainty that state criminal processes prior to the Warren Court were really more protective of defendants or less punitive. A second problem is why even the cheap and easy paths to criminal convictions should lead to substantial expansions in prison commitments. Why wouldn't the easy victory of a conviction obtained through the plea negotiation process be a sufficient indicator to prosecutors and to their superiors of their success in the adversarial process?

Perhaps guilty pleas are too easy to obtain to ever function as a meaningful measure of the prosecutor's professional accomplishment. If guilty pleas are a dime a dozen in the post–Earl Warren universe of criminal justice, what types of outcome can be used to measure the effectiveness of a prosecutor in the adversarial contest? In plea bargaining, the real currency of the struggle is what punishment the defendant will agree to. Defense attorneys and their clients wish to either avoid imprisonment or, for very serious crimes, minimize the term of imprisonment. What does the prosecutor want?

IMPRISONMENT AS AN INDICATOR OF ADVERSARIAL SUCCESS

In the reality of felony-level plea negotiation, avoiding a prison term is defense attorneys' measure of success for two reasons. First, that is usually the most important objective of their clients. Second, it is usually the best outcome that is achievable on the facts of the case and the record of the client.

But if avoiding prison is a clear win for the defense attorney, what outcome in criminal process is a clear victory for the assistant district attorney (ADA) who bargains with the defense? As both an operational matter throughout a prosecutor's office and as a personal motive for the ADA, sending an offender to prison seems an obvious indicator of adversarial success. The ADA who comes home after obtaining a guilty plea that results in a sentence of imprisonment has had a good day, and these punitive outcomes can also become measures of productivity for supervisors if they become visible in the administrative offices of prosecuting attorneys. Good prosecutors send people to prison.

But the adversarial process is not a recent invention, so one important issue in considering the role of adversarial incentives in explaining the generation of expanding imprisonment after 1970 is whether there were changes in the mid-1970s that might plausibly explain why a potential adversarial incentive of such long standing suddenly started elevating prison admission rates. There are three candidates available to consider: the increased salience of public concern about crime, the intensity of adversarial interactions after the Warren Court decisions, and the invention and widespread adoption of detailed prosecution management systems to generate quick and accurate statistics on prosecutorial outcomes in each criminal case. One motive for increasing prosecutorial efforts to generate prison sentences is as a reaction to larger levels of public concern about crime. The increased salience of the crime issue discussed in Chapter 2 might have launched more prosecutorial effort to obtain prison terms in the late 1970s and 1980s, and that initial push might have become self-sustaining. Particularly since the crime decline of the early 1980s was followed by increases and another period of high-salience concern in the United States from 1986 to 1995, there were high levels of public concern for 10 of the 15 years after 1975 to captivate the attention span of public prosecutors.

A second factor that might have produced increased emphasis on prison sentences as measures of adversarial effectiveness was the intensification of adversarial dynamics in prosecutorial activities after the Warren Court constitutional changes. Defense attorneys were a larger and more important part of the fabric of prosecutorial activity in the post-Warren era, so prevailing in adversarial competition also might become a more important element in evaluating prosecutorial performance. The more intense and more important the adversarial competition, the more attention will be paid to prison sentences as a measure of prosecutorial success. This link between adversarial activity and incarcerative sentences might be a plausible way in which Professor Stuntz's list of latent consequences of the due process cases got translated into a boom in imprisonment.

But all of these metaphorical references to measuring success and keeping score assume methods of measuring success and failure in individual cases as well as an interest by administrators and litigators in monitoring data on adversarial effectiveness. Until quite recently, however, county district attorney offices were among the least data-centric and statistical operations anywhere in American government. District attorneys are, after all, lawyers, far removed from a culture of statistical categories and often believing that each individual case they litigate is unique. Schools of business taught courses in management and statistics. Law schools did not. And prosecutors went to law schools.

The pioneering efforts to bring gathering and analyzing data on case processing and case outcomes to prosecutor offices took place in the 1960s, very late in the evolution of data management in most other areas of commerce and governance but also just before the explosive growth in prison admissions began. In the late 1960s, a project funded by the Law Enforcement Assistance Administration created for federal prosecutors the Prosecutor's Management Information System (PROMIS), a tool to monitor cases and to document outcomes, including not only acquittal or conviction but the nature of the sentence imposed. The capacity to keep score rather quickly became a standard element of the management of prosecutor offices of any size, and the nature of the criminal sentence, jail or prison or not, became a prominent feature measured by the new management technology.

When the experts at a workshop called "What's Changing in Prosecution?" were asked in 1999 to identify significant recent changes, the first important heading in the report was "scientific and technical advances" (Heyman and Petrie 2001, 12) and the first technical change on their collective list was "the development and use of office computers and new software systems" (12). "Before the introduction of this computer technology, the ability to analyze and, in many jurisdictions, even describe what was happening in criminal litigation was virtually nonexistent. *There also was no means of establishing accountability for decisions, case processing delays or case outcomes*" (Heyman and Petrie 2001, 13; emphasis added).

The importance of these technical innovations was that "using new management or investigative tools" might well have impact on policy (Heyman and Petrie 2001, 12). The timing of the introduction and proliferation of computerized data and management systems is close to a perfect fit with the pervasive increase in prison admissions and apparent emphasis on prison sentences for every variety of felony offense. Brian Forst, writing in the late 1990s, documented several steps in the rapid introduction and use of these systems:

> Prosecution was significantly influenced by these developments in the 1970s with the advent of prosecution management information systems. . . . Federal funding to encourage the introduction of this technology accelerated its acceptance by prosecutors. . . . Large prosecution offices hired computer specialists to manage these information systems in the 1970s and 1980s. . . . Prosecutors became increasingly computer literate in the 1980s and 1990s, largely through their personal acquisition of more user friendly desktop personal computers at home. (Forst 2000, 28)

Suddenly, assistant district attorneys and their supervisors had computers and software that could compare convictions and penalties in the ADA's last 10 cases with the track record of other ADAs in the office. If a sentence of imprisonment was regarded as a measure of adversarial success, it soon became a much more visible measure of adversarial success.

PROMIS AS SABERMETRICS?

An illustration of the potential impact of such measurements on the selection of policy objectives can come from a much more statistically sophisticated activity than criminal prosecution: the world of baseball. Mathematics and simple statistics have always been important elements in the cultural life of American baseball. Generations of usually male children grew up with batting averages and the earned-run average of pitchers as their primary motivation to acquire mathematical literacy. But the invention of what came to be called sabermetrics late in the twentieth century created much more complicated compound statistics to use in comparing the competitive value of individual athletes and has had some real impact on how players are valued and traded. Sabermetrics and its first cousin, Moneyball, have become case studies of how a change in evaluative procedure in baseball soon had impact on how players were valued and traded.

And the saga of sabermetrics may suggest ways in which the scorekeeping of sentencing outcomes in prosecutor management systems reinforced the value that managers and front-line litigators saw in prison sentences as evidence of prosecutorial effectiveness.

Would this more visible form of scorekeeping have produced significant increases in prison sentences even without the increased salience of crime and punishment in public opinion and the larger emphasis on adversarial competition produced by new due process standards and more defense attorneys? It is by no means far-fetched to suppose that a greater emphasis on statistical measure of prosecutorial success could function independently to increase prison commitments, but the history of the period is too crowded with other adversarial pressures to test a wholly independent measurement effect. The only evidence that we have from the complicated multiple-cause changes of the 1970s and 1980s is that a variety of doctrinal and systemic changes jointly produced much larger emphasis by local prosecutors on prison sentences for a wide variety of crimes.

And the unusually wide impact of the imprisonment increases—more imprisonment for every type of felony crime—is consistent with prosecutorial ambitions that were not limited to particular crimes or particular offenders. This was not prison for repeat offenders or for violent offenders or for drug offenders. This was prison for crime and prison for criminals of all varieties—it was, in short, a policy of prison emphasis almost as wide as the adversarial system in which the modern prosecutor functioned. And the generality of the policy is circumstantial evidence that adversarial considerations rather than more specific concerns or priorities were the primary motives for shifts in prosecutorial emphasis.

But even assuming that all three of the proposed pressures on prosecutors were operating and interacting, there is a gap between the modest intensity of the shifts in prosecutorial emphasis and the huge impact on the system. Sabermetrics management systems can focus more attention on increasing imprisonment outcomes, but should this cause a 650% jump in prison admissions? And the increased salience of crime as a concern made more compelling the chronic complaints by citizens about the leniency of criminal sentences, but why should this generate a 400% increase in rates of imprisonment over a 35-year period? Why do such modest causes have such major effects?

THE WRONG KIND OF ACCOUNTABILITY?

To the extent that management systems and improved data on case outcomes contributed to massive increases in imprisonment, it would be an ironic example of problematic unintended consequences. The architects of prosecution management systems wanted to make individual prosecutors more accountable to management by supervisors and more susceptible to evaluation, but their conception of efficiency and accountability didn't emphasize substantial increases in penal severity or greatly expanding the percentage of defendants sent to prison. The emphasis of the system designers was on consistency and adherence to principles (see Forst 2000).

But the adversarial values of both prosecutors and their managers made an emphasis on punishment an entirely foreseeable priority for individual prosecutors and their supervisors. In retrospect, a concern about the uses of management systems to elevate penal outcomes should have been a more visible element of the design and evaluation of prosecutorial management systems than it evidently was in the 1960s and 1970s. The development of management systems in criminal prosecution was inevitable in the United States. The risk that such systems would intensify the pursuit of higher levels of punitive outcomes in the adversarial arena of criminal justice should have come as no surprise.

A Dual Dynamic?

None of what I have called adversarial influences in the 1970s and 1980s can by itself plausibly explain the massive changes in imprisonment that were generated from 1975 to 2005—there is too little cause and too much effect. But the accident of political economy that was identified earlier as "the correctional free lunch" might help explain both the duration of the impact and its scale.

An increase in citizens' concern about crime in 1975 can be expected to soon appear on prosecutorial radar screens, but why should that type of stimulus last more than the two or three years that public concern is a visible active ingredient? This question introduces the consideration of what I want to call a "dual dynamic" explanation of the prison expansion.

The previous discussion of the free-lunch phenomenon identified one reason why it could not function as a primary cause of the growth of mass incarceration after 1975. The cost-free character of prisons to county governments in the United States was a long-term characteristic of state and local government rather than an invention of the 1970s. How could this long-term characteristic explain an effect that was substantially confined to the generation after 1975? This still seems a dispositive objection to any account that has the cost-free character of prison to county officials as the singular primary cause of prison growth.

But a dual-dynamic account of prison growth is less vulnerable to quick dismissal. In this version of the story, increased public pressure on crime and punishment and heightened attention to prison sentences as prosecutorial success stories begin the increase of prison commitments in the later 1970s. The cost-free character of prison terms to prosecutors has little influence on when and why the increased commitments begin. But the cost-free consequences for prosecutors and county governments generally ensure that there are no negative consequences felt by the agencies of government that produced the expansion. Adversarial pressures step on the prosecutorial gas pedal. The correctional free lunch means that nobody puts on the brakes. Without any negative feedback, even modestly motivated punitive initiatives can be self-sustaining, and this produces larger impacts and longer periods of expansion than would have been expected if the original impetus for policy were acting alone.

The bad news about this kind of dual dynamic is that very modest levels of punitive pressure can produce very large effects, out of proportion to their original energy levels because they were not counterbalanced by the responsibility for the change agents paying for the institutional changes in prison capacity that were necessary to accommodate the changes in policy that were put in place. When there are no local costs to continuing increases of penal confinement, the expansion we can expect to observe will be much greater than what might have been the net effect if cost consequences restrained the enthusiasms of penal expansion. In a very real sense, the failure of cost allocations to restrain the size and length of penal expansion is a distortion. But might this also be good news from the perspective of reformers who hope to reverse mass incarceration?

Usually, when democratic governments generate large changes in policy, it makes sense to assume that extraordinary discontent produced them. But the run-up in American imprisonment might be an exception to this rule. To be sure, there was political support for an expansion in prison population, but the magnitude of the expansion was neither a conscious objective nor a strongly desired outcome. The state governments that projected correctional growth were almost powerless to control prison admissions and often would issue correctional population forecasts not as normatively supported policy but rather as events outside the control of state government—more resembling weather forecasts than planned and desired policy outcomes.

So the particular scale of prison confinement that topped 500 per 100,000 for prisons early in the new century was more a product of superficial and nonspecific penal objectives than a hard target where advocates had strong preferences for either numerical levels of confinement or for continued growth. And even the local governmental actors who were the primary causes of state imprisonment growth could have been superficially motivated to continue expansion. The more that the scale of expansion was a nearly accidental outcome, the more receptive state and local governments might be to reductions in the scale of imprisonment.

4

How American Institutions Encourage and Sustain High Rates of Imprisonment

THE PRISON IS a universal feature of criminal justice in modern nations. It operates as the top rung of the ladder of penal responses to crime everywhere, and rates of imprisonment vary over time in many different nations. But no nation has ever experienced an expansion of prison population on the scale of the United States—a sevenfold expansion of prisoners and a fivefold increase in the imprisonment rate per 100,000. The central concern of Chapter 3 was to explain why American justice systems placed such heavy emphasis on imprisonment as a desirable outcome in the generation after 1975. Why did analysts, planners, and criminal prosecutors emphasize imprisonment in this era? This chapter explores the broader but related question of why an expansion of prisoners that started in the 1970s could grow so much more in the United States than in any other place during any other era. While Chapter 3 focused on changes that took place in the 1960s and 1970s, this chapter addresses the broader issue of what elements of American society, government, crime, and economy created an environment where penal expansion could be so large.

While Chapter 3 paid special attention to the particular history of the second half of the twentieth century, this chapter must consider a wider variety of elements that have set the United States apart from other nations over the long term. When searching for what provoked the push toward more prison sentences in the 1970s and 1980s, I argued that the longer-term historical trends and social values that Tocqueville discussed in *Democracy in America* were poor candidates as the proximate causes for a trend that started more than a century after the book was published. But when the subject shifts to exploring what features of American government and society provided an environment that could produce penal expansion of such magnitude starting in the 1970s, a much longer list of circumstances and values demand attention.

Indeed, the list of plausible explanations for the penal expansion is too long to allow any hope of testing which features of US governance and society are of greatest importance in explaining the scale of penal growth. But even without a realistic prospect for a detailed account, a discussion of important elements of an environment that facilitated high-magnitude growth is a necessary start to considering how much of the current circumstances of mass incarceration can be reversed, as well as which aspects of policy and sentiment are most likely to reduce incarceration and the harms it imposes.

The objective in this chapter is first to identify some of the characteristics that magnified the impact of the increase in incarceration and then to consider the extent to which the environmental conditions discussed in the first section will also inhibit the effectiveness of efforts to reduce imprisonment levels and the harms associated with imprisonment. The final section of this chapter will address the changes in structure and sentiment that might best reduce the impact of incarceration. Much more detailed analysis of harm reduction strategies will then become the focus of Part II of this book.

Some Conditions That Exaggerated the Scale of American Penal Expansion

The United States was one of three nations where rates of imprisonment increased in the period 1970–2010. Italy reported the lowest imprisonment rate of the eight nations surveyed in 1970 at 40 per 100,000, and that rate more than doubled to 112 per 100,000 in 2010, a rate close to the average for the seven European and Commonwealth nations. England and Wales had a smaller 40-year percentage growth than Italy but their 89% growth produced the highest total imprisonment rate—151 per 100,000—of the seven non-US nations profiled in Chapter 1. But the scale of American imprisonment growth in the post-1970 era was so far removed from the Italian and English experience that it appears a totally different dynamic of penal growth.

A short list of the characteristics that might explain how the United States became the host of this unprecedented growth includes the following:

1. Features of governmental organization and resources
2. Adversarial and politically responsive criminal punishment decisions
3. The retributive insufficiency of noncustodial punishments

4. Public fear of life-threatening violent crime
5. Public confidence in the crime-preventive efficacy of incarceration

Governmental Organization and Resources

Three aspects of how governmental policy has been organized and administered may increase the likelihood that increases in incarceration might be larger in scale and longer in duration than in national systems with more centralized power over crime and punishment:

1. Provincial dominance of criminal law and punishment
2. Redundancy in criminal jurisdiction and enforcement resources
3. Substantial public wealth

PROVINCIAL POWER

Provincial control of crime and punishment in the United States is more extensive than in any other rich nation. Each of the 50 states has its own criminal code with separate definitions of crimes, separate scales of authorized punishments, and near-total administrative control over the state's prisons. Many criminal justice functions are further decentralized, with jails for short-term and remand confinement centered in county government; prosecution and criminal courts are usually agencies of county government, and police and sheriffs are typically the responsibility of municipalities (police) and county government (sheriffs).

Chapter 1 reported on one way in which the decentralized nature of crime policy should have made the extraordinary growth of the national prison population less likely in the United States—with 51 different power centers, we would expect to see variations in policies in different states so that there would be less substantial variation over time in the national aggregate.

But there are also a number of characteristics of the provincial jurisdiction, its politics, and its proximity to local law enforcement that made state governments more hospitable to prosecution and punishment and more difficult environments for downsizing of penal systems and budgets. State governments tend to be less diverse in population characteristics, less cosmopolitan, and more susceptible to one-party dominance than national governments.

The number of primary governmental responsibilities at the state level is also more limited—roads, education, crime and punishment—than in the plenary portfolio of national governments, and this smaller inventory of primary responsibilities makes it more likely that crime issues can become centrally important in political contests—one reason why the crime issue became salient at the state level is that it had less competition than it would face in a political market at the national level, which has primary powers in economic policy, national defense, and international affairs.

Not only is the range of governmental authority more limited in state government, but the interests and backgrounds of those who govern is also usually more restricted and often parochial. In the early years of the twentieth century, law enforcement posts were common proving grounds for the governorship. Thus nearly 20% of governors ... had held law enforcement positions (Ferguson 2006). The attitudes as well as the expertise of local district attorneys and assistant attorney generals are not irrelevant to the choices persons with such backgrounds later made in state legislatures and state executive government.

One obvious impact of dominance of state government in crime and punishment concerns the death penalty. In most nations, the presence or absence of execution as a criminal punishment is an issue decided at the national level. In the United States, both the national government and state governments have legal power to invoke the death penalty. Both the federal government and a majority of US states have authorized a death penalty for some serious crimes, but the distribution of actual executions is an extraordinary case study of provincial dominance. All but three of the first 1,300 executions in the United States were conducted by state governments—through 2016 the states were responsible for 99.8% of the combined state and federal total. What seems obvious in that extraordinary distribution is that the power that states have to conduct executions has been a major influence on the total volume of executions in the United States (Zimring 2003).

The provincial power to imprison almost 90% of all prisoners may also be a partial explanation for why total rates of imprisonment in the United States could rise as quickly as they did. The lower volume of competing priorities and the higher vulnerability to law-and-order sentiments are two plausible biases at the state level. But the shorter distance between state governments and local governments may translate as well into a larger capacity of local officials like police and prosecutors and local governmental interests to carry influence when resources are allocated by state decision-makers. And the same features of provincial dominance that may increase patterns of growth of prison populations may also reduce the impact of efforts at the state level to reduce prison populations.

REDUNDANT JURISDICTION AND ENFORCEMENT RESOURCES

In theory, the distribution of power to prohibit and punish criminal behavior among two different levels of government need not increase either the total amount of resources committed to criminal enforcement or the total

Table 4.1
Drug Prisoners in State and Federal Prisons, 1985 and 2002

	Drug offenders in prison	
	1985	2002
Federal	7,200	63,898
State	38,900	252,249
Total	46,100	316,147

amount of punishment that the two systems deliver. If there is a strict division of labor between levels of government, either in which behaviors are prohibited or in the total level of resources devoted to law enforcement and punishment, the duplication of jurisdiction need not expand total impact. But in the United States, there is extraordinary overlap between the targets of federal and state penal prohibitions and also substantial redundancy in the resources invested into criminal courts, prisons, and—most importantly—agencies to investigate and enforce criminal laws. The overlap in criminal prohibitions and enforcement covers a wide variety of crimes, including crimes of violence, firearms possession and use, and child pornography, but the major impacts of redundancy in enforcement and punishment concern drugs. At all times, this redundancy has contributed somewhat to increased levels of imprisonment in the United States but never to the extent displayed in the crusade against drug crime that was launched in the United States in 1985. Prior to 1990, the population of offenders in federal prisons was persistently under 10% of total prison population, so the maximum impact of redundancy on total imprisonment was correspondingly limited.

The total volume of drug prisoners increased almost sevenfold in 17 years from under 50,000 to over 300,000, and the expanded contribution of the federal system to the growth in drug prisoners was far from trivial. The number of added federal drug prisoners—when the 1985 total is subtracted from the 2002 total—was 56,648, an additional increment of federal drug prisoners alone by 2002 that exceeded by 10,000 the total number of drug offenders in *all* prisons in the United States in 1985. So the impact of redundant increases in enforcement effort, prosecution, and punishment during the drug war was substantial.

But will redundancy in jurisdiction always tend to increase levels of imprisonment, or might not two operating systems responding to changing fashions at the same time also magnify downward trends in prosecution and punishment? What makes the likelihood of such two-sided impact remote is the institutional influence of redundant law enforcement resources on criminal prosecution and conviction. The drug war provides a textbook case of the expansion of special purpose law enforcement at the federal level. Figure 4.1 is adopted from an analysis by a Syracuse University project to

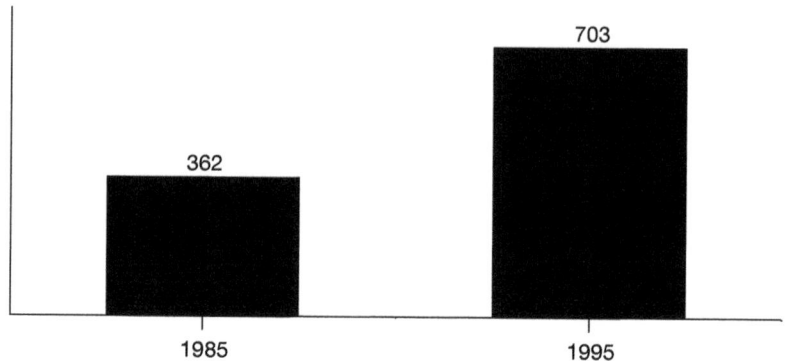

Figure 4.1 Inflation-Adjusted Estimates of Federal DEA Budget (Adjusted to Nearest Million). *Source*: Drug Enforcement Administration n.d.; Bureau of Labor Statistics n.d.

analyze the inflation-adjusted budget of the federal Drug Enforcement Administration during the drug war expansion.

The inflation-adjusted budget almost doubled in less than a decade, and once this type of growth has occurred, it is difficult to reverse. The Justice Department Management Division reported that both the inflation-adjusted budget and the level of authorized manpower at the Drug Enforcement Administration (DEA) continued to grow from 1995 to 2002 (Management Division 2002, 100–103). That much sustained enforcement machinery devoted to a specialized criminal justice function puts consistent upward pressure on drug crime detections, prosecutions, and punishment. To the extent that redundant jurisdiction creates and sustains larger levels of enforcement and prosecutorial manpower, it exerts upward pressure on levels of punishment and inhibits reductions in prison population.

Redundant law enforcement and punishment in federal and state criminal justice has been a chronic condition of moderate importance for a long time in the United States, but its impact was moderated by the relatively small scale of federal law enforcement and imprisonment. The changes that came with the war on drugs in drug enforcement and the scale of federal imprisonment make the much larger redundant federal institutions now in place a more pronounced influence on the total scale of imprisonment in the United States.

GOVERNMENT WEALTH

A final characteristic of federal, state, and local governments in the United States that makes them more likely to support increases in imprisonment is public wealth. The United States is and has been a rich country by world standards for well over a century and the richest nation on the planet per capita for more than half that time. The most direct measure of what I want to call public or governmental wealth is the amount of taxes collected by the various levels of government, although taxes are only one form of governmental access to money, along with public debt and the income from publicly owned enterprises. Income from taxes has been a substantial majority of noncapital spending at all levels of government in the United States most of the time, and by comparison with other nations or earlier historical eras, public income was plentiful in the United States throughout the post–World War II era.

The most significant level of government for considering the public capacity to support prisons is the state level, and the critical era for imprisonment growth was the four decades from 1970 to 2010 (see Chapter 1, Figure 1.4). The most appropriate measure for state taxes as real income for public purposes is derived by correcting the income from taxes by adjusting, first, for expanding population and, second, for the changing purchasing power of the dollar. After these adjustments, the inflation-adjusted per capita tax income to the states almost doubled between 1970 and 2010.[1] This relatively high level of prosperity was a source of reassurance to those in government worried about the demand of prisons on the public purse. Particularly in the early stages of penal expansion in the late 1970s and 1980s, the budgetary impact of prison administration was relatively modest (see Zimring and Hawkins 1991, 141). As the prison populations expanded, the impact on total state budgets got more visible and more worrisome. And during the prolonged recession of 2007–2010, the cost of prison expansion became a major concern in many jurisdictions.

The larger visibility of questions of cost when public revenue is under pressure suggests that just as relatively high growth in tax revenue invites larger levels of penal expansion, real scarcity of public funds can be an important motive for attempts to reduce levels of publicly funded imprisonment. The size of public income and the demands from by other areas of primary responsibility for state governments are important influences that both can restrain growth when public money seems tight and subsidize penal growth when the public purse-strings loosen.

Localized, Political, and Adversarial Determinations of Criminal Punishments

In all eight of the national systems profiled in Chapter 1, the determination of guilt or innocence in individual criminal cases and the punishments,

---

[1] In 1970, state tax revenue totaled $47,905,000,000 (see Bureau of the Census 1970). In 2010, state tax revenue totaled $514,326,256,000 (see Bureau of the Census 2011). The inflation adjustment is $5.73 to the 1970 dollar (see Bureau of Labor Statistics n.d.). The 2010 total divided by the inflation adjustment is $89,760,254,101, or 1.87 × the 1970 revenue.

if any, to be imposed are the joint responsibility of government lawyers serving as prosecutors and legally trained criminal court judges. But there are three aspects of criminal court prosecutors and judges in the United States in the 50 state systems where most prison sentences are imposed that make prosecutors and judges more prone to impose prison sentences and to resist efforts to reduce levels of prison sentences.

LOCALIZED PROSECUTION AND SENTENCING

The first aspect of both state trial court judges and of prosecutors is that they are localized—they begin their careers in a single locality and typically stay there as long as they remain trial-level legal actors. It is also typical that the local settings where they practice professionally are communities where they have residential histories and identities. This emphasis on local origin and identity for both judges and prosecutors is a sharp contrast with the training and career patterns for judges and prosecutors in European systems and Great Britain. And it is a normative feature of American state government.

But it is a normative feature with problematic implications for local influence on law enforcement, prosecution, and punishment. Strong local histories are associated with personal relationships to persons in local law enforcement and government. There is widespread suspicion, for example, that local prosecutors and judges are inclined to believe police officers and administrators when evaluating claims about police use of deadly force (Zimring 2017, 167–76, 180–95). The personal relationships a judge or prosecutor has with others in government interact with the ways that the criminal courts depend on police cooperation to make conflicts in testimony or ambiguities about the intention and beliefs of police likely to be resolved in favor of the police. To the extent that most opportunities for advancement require continued success in a single local environment, the desire to favor the interests of local opinion leaders is also an obvious influence on the decisions made by local prosecutors and judges.

The influence of local identities and career opportunities on the attitudes and choices of prosecutors and judges is compounded by a second important feature of local criminal courts—the political selection and retention requirements for many judges and virtually all chief district attorneys in the United States. Where judges must either run for office or (more frequently) stand for voters to favor or oppose the judge's retention, the potential influence of the electorate will put upward pressure on sentence severity if it has any influence on judicial sentencing tendencies. What is less clear, however, is how often and with what strength the prospect of electoral review generates independent influence on the discretion of judges when making sentencing decisions or influences whether and when judges reject proposed punishments recommended by prosecutors in favor or greater or lesser punishments.

When more than one nonincumbent runs to be elected district attorney, any real contest between candidates will frequently involve competitive claims to be tough on crime. But when incumbent prosecutors run for reelection, there are rarely genuine contests, and this reduces both the visibility of the electoral process and its potential influence on the incumbent's aggressiveness in pursuing visibly punitive case outcomes. So the less important the electoral contest, the smaller the probable influence on both the rhetoric and reality of prosecutorial penal severity. But the direction of any influence of democratic local politics on punishment severity is easier to predict than its magnitude. Nobody would propose that local elections of judges and prosecutors reduces the influence on sentences of frequently punitive public fears and reactions to criminal events that achieve public notice. How much additional pressure and under what circumstances are not easy to determine.

The final aspect of local prosecution and sentencing that generates pressure for prisons as punishment is the adversarial context in which punishments are determined. Prosecutors are usually advocates for harsh sentences in legal and public discourse about criminal sentences. Local judges often encounter sentencing questions not as individual decisions they make without the involvement of other actors, but instead as the outcome of a contest between advocates for leniency and severity as the adversary process carries over to issues of punishment. So judges (themselves not infrequently former prosecutors) must decide a sentencing outcome as in large part a debate between lawyers. When the presence or absence of a prison sentence becomes the judicially determined outcome of a status competition between prosecutors and defenders, the personal and professional aspects of the status competition may become as important as any of Chapter 3's list of purposes of imprisonment as a punishment when the ultimate decision is made. So the importance of a status competition between advocates can infiltrate the process of making punishment decisions.

And there is one further potential status competition that may provoke imprisonment sentences as symbolic currency—the prosecution's argument that prison should be the judge's method of recognizing the social importance of a crime victim's suffering. So recognizing the suffering of victims becomes a less obviously self-centered appeal that prosecutors can use to secure the punishment outcome that they also desire as a status reward for their efforts.

The adversarial context in which punishment decisions are selected puts special pressure on punishment decisions that appear to serve public opinion and the victim's symbolic interests in severe punishment as a status reward. While public opinion and crime victim status have an impact on criminal punishment in all governments, the adversarial and local setting in which punishments get decided in the United States make public fears and status needs of much more importance in the choice of sanctions.

THE RETRIBUTIVE INADEQUACY OF NONCUSTODIAL PUNISHMENTS

There are, in all major nations, two types of institutions that lock up persons in secure confinement as a deliberate punishment. The prison typically confines persons for periods of one year or more, although on occasion former inmates who have been paroled from previous prison terms will return to a prison for a shorter stay. The jail, usually administered by local rather than state governments, combines persons detained while awaiting trial and persons sentenced to shorter terms of punishment, typically less than a year.

For all developed nations, these institutions of penal confinement are the most serious forms of criminal punishments that are imposed with any frequency by the criminal justice system. And in all developed nations, there is a substantial gap between the severity of these forms of custodial confinement and all other common penal measures. Financial penalties, best designed as day fines so that ability to pay is a determinant of the amount of the fine, can only appear highly punitive if the offender has sufficient property to pay a very substantial financial penalty. The most common alternative to penal confinement is a sustained period of supervision in the community with restrictions on privileges such as driving, drinking alcohol, or social relations with known co-offenders or gang members. But such regimes of supervision are frequently regarded as most important by members of the community and by the offenders subject to them for what they are not. The principal feature of a probationary sentence is that it is not incarceration.

The large perceived gap in penal severity between incarceration and everything else is not a recent phenomenon, nor is it a circumstance restricted to public opinion and criminal justice in the United States. Canadians and Italians are also inclined to regard a nonincarcerative criminal sentence for serious crime as lenient to the point of objection. But the gap between incarceration and anything short of incarceration is much less visible in systems with less concentrated local actors, and publicity about lenient outcomes is much more likely with extensive adversarial involvement in the process of punishment decision-making. So all of the local, political, and adversarial aspects of criminal justice in American states makes the gap between incarceration and anything less more visible and more problematic when local prosecutors object to alternative measures short of incarceration.

The visibility and political vulnerability of nonincarcerative punishments has, with two exceptions, made the search for what have been called "alternatives to imprisonment" in the United States into a high-failure enterprise even in the context of the huge growth of prisons.

The two exceptions to the problematic prospects for alternative programs have been (1) drug treatment as a compulsory but not expressly punitive alternative to prison and (2) jail as an incarcerative alternative to prison. The push toward drug treatment as an alternative to imprisonment came late in the huge run-up during the war on drugs, but avoided the cynical public judgements that other community-based alternative innovations had encountered. Proposition 36, a California ballot initiative, essentially required that persons convicted of nonsale drug felonies be offered participation in drug treatment programs as a preferred alternative to imprisonment (Zimring and Harcourt 2007, 432–72).

There are two features of hard-drug users that make nonincarceration more acceptable to a normally punitive public. For addictive drugs, a therapeutic approach to ending the offender's addiction is presented as an alternative strategy of crime prevention, not merely as a choice not to incarcerate like probation. And there are no clear victims when drug use and possession are the only basis for criminal liability. There is good reason to believe that this therapeutic strategy would have general appeal for drug-dependent defendants in most of the United States unless they have committed crimes with obvious victims.

The other successful "alternative" to imprisonment is simply a lower dose of the same penal medicine. The shift from prisons to local jails in the California realignment that will be analyzed in the second section of this book is a demonstration of the near-monopoly that secure confinement has as a first option as a serious punishment. The principal genuine alternative to imprisonment is not locking offenders up. And this has little rhetorical appeal in the adversarial discourse in most branches of American criminal justice.

Public Fear of Life-Threatening Criminal Violence

Fear of crime, particularly violent crime, is an important element of public policy toward crime in all democracies, but probably more important in the United States than in other developed nations. It is widely assumed that crime is a more important issue in the United States because crime rates are higher there than elsewhere in the Western world. In the colorful language of Morris and Hawkins, "American may or may not be the land of the free but it is certainly the home of the brave" (1970, 57).

It turns out, however, that the true status of US crime rates and the role of crime rates in influencing public attitudes are more complicated than commonly assumed. To be sure, there is a clear connection in the United States between trends in crime rates over time and levels of public fear of crime as measured in surveys. This was discussed in Chapters 2 and 3. But rates in the United States of most common types of crime are no higher than in urban

Western nations. Rates of burglary and theft are higher in London than in New York City, and most property crime rates are just as high in Sydney, Australia, as in Los Angeles, California (Zimring and Hawkins 1997, ch. 3). But life-threatening criminal violence is far more prevalent in the United States, between two and nine times more common, in American cities and towns than in Western Europe or Canada and Australia.

The level of public fear and concern about crime also seems to be somewhat higher in the United States than in other Western nations even when, as is true of the period 2000–2017, levels of crime are low by historical standards. This could be a function only of higher American levels of homicide (including robbery homicide) without any social or political complications. But the provincial and adversarial dominance of crime policy and the overlap between race-based attitudes and fear of robbery homicide by black offenders may also contribute to crime fears and criminal justice concerns.

Whatever the linkage of public crime concerns to political and social attitudes, the consistent importance of concerns about violent crime remains an influence on the low level of public support for most alternative-to-imprisonment sanction innovations and will be a formidable obstacle to broad-based efforts to reduce prison populations.

The most dramatic demonstration of the importance of public attitudes toward violent crime for sentiments about prison is the visible exclusion of violent offenses and violent offenders from proposed reforms designed to reduce prison populations (see Pfaff 2016; Forman 2017; Obama 2017).

But public fear of life-threatening violence limits the effectiveness of reform efforts to reduce prison population in both direct and indirect fashion. The direct effect of trying to exclude violence offenses and offenders from reductions in prison commitments and the reduction of prison terms is that this strategy removes a very substantial share of current prisoner populations—up to half, depending on the definition of violent crime and the degree to which prior record is used to exclude a once-violent offender from current leniency for a current conviction for a nonviolent offense.

The indirect effect of public concern about life-threatening violence is to reduce support for all efforts to reduce prison sentences and to increase skepticism about all regimes of reducing prison populations. To the extent that the violent criminal offender becomes a dominant image in discussions of penal reform, it not infrequently produces skepticism about any programs designed to reduce incarceration

Public Confidence in Incapacitation

If high levels of crime produce high levels of public fear, then sustained periods of low crime rates should be regarded as a positive environment for trying to engineer substantial reductions in prison populations. With one important exception, this hypothesis is probably correct. The exception is that many of the functionaries associated with punishment policy during the huge run-up in confinement have argued that the increased imprisonment has been a major cause of the crime reduction. There is widespread belief that a share of the reduced crime of the period after 1994 is in large part the product of the incapacitative impact of increased prison numbers. Where this becomes part of the dialogue about prison policy, it both supports expansion of imprisonment and restrains widespread reductions.

MISSING PIECES

The list of structural features and prison-specific attitudes in this section is, of course, a small sample of the elements that make the United States importantly different from other places and that also might influence levels of imprisonment. And it is also impossible to assess how important each factor individually or all of them collectively have been in contributing to the actual size of the prison expansion of the post-1970 era. But each of the elements outlined has played a role in the expansion of the period, and it is therefore useful to consider to what extent the elements outlined in this section will be an influence on future imprisonment policy.

So my objective now after briefly acknowledging a few of the missing dimensions of American difference that can influence imprisonment policy is to turn my attention to the likely impact of the influences that have been identified on the impact of efforts to reverse the growth of imprisonment that is the current condition of American life.

A wide variety of the distinctive cultures, religions, and attitudes about race that distinguish large parts of the American nation from other places may be associated directly either with attitudes toward imprisonment or associated statistically with variations from state to state in rates of imprisonment. There are also theories linking economic conditions with cross-sectional variations in state-level rates of imprisonment, though not yet with the explosive growth of the prison population after 1970. My failure to address such matters in this chapter is not an assertion that the cultural baggage of American history is not important in explaining the magnitude of recent prison growth.

One peculiar feature of the preceding discussion is how loosely linked the characteristics of US government and crime policy are to social and demographic factors that might be discussed when searching for the causes of variations in crime. Variations in crime rates over time have played a relatively minor role in explaining variations in imprisonment, so a detailed search for changes in the population and the economy that might influence crime rates are not high on the agenda of things that might have major impact on rates of imprisonment. Of course, very large shifts upward or downward in rates of serious crime should have some influence on resulting prison populations, but there have been no projections of demographic or economic futures over the past half-century that powerfully predicted major variations in levels of crime (Zimring 2007, 56–69). Just as changes in age structure in the population and of economic trends have had little influence on crime rates or imprisonment, there is no reason to expect this loose linkage to abate in the foreseeable future.

The Influence of American Environmental Circumstances on the Prospects for Reducing Prison Populations

This section discusses the likely influence of the environmental factors and attitudes identified in the previous outline on whether efforts to reduce the prevalence of imprisonment can succeed and on the scale of reduction that can be expected in the three decades after 2020. The division of labor between this chapter and Chapter 5 should be stated at the outset. This chapter does not attempt to generate a comprehensive prediction about how much imprisonment is likely to be reduced in the proximate American future. That is the task of Chapter 5. This chapter has focused on one piece of the puzzle—the environmental elements that help explain why prison growth, once started, grew by so much for so long. And one important issue relating to this short list of environmental conditions is whether they are likely to continue and if so with what effect on the attempt to roll back the level of imprisonment.

In one important respect, the topics being considered in this chapter are a biased sample of influences and attitudes that, considered by themselves, produce an even more pessimistic perspective than my rather gloomy general forecast in Chapter 5. Recall that the list of features isolated in this chapter were selected because they are suspected of promoting penal escalation. It is thus to be expected that unless there have been extraordinary changes, this chapter's features will function in the future as restraints on the effectiveness of efforts to downsize incarceration.

But while a careful survey of the likely influence of these features in the policy choices of the coming decades is not a cheerful task, it is a necessary one. Careful planning to minimize the punitive impact of these circumstances will enhance the effectiveness of efforts to reduce rates of incarceration. As important, bumping up against the limits of the reduction of incarceration also should motivate reformers to diversify their reform objectives. Much more than reducing the number behind bars may be necessary in the United States in large part because both the number of prisoners and the harmful impacts that prison now generates will stay at high levels even with best efforts aimed at decarceration.

GOVERNMENT ORGANIZATION

The federal system of government and the dominance of state government as the primary system of administration of criminal justice will not change in the foreseeable future. Perhaps the federal courts or Congress could impose regulatory standards of living conditions for prisoners or access of prisoners to nonprison people and institutions, but there is no strong trend in that direction in recent years. So state and local governments are set to be the major power centers for imprisonment policy in the immediate future of the federal system.

The distribution of power among so many different governments should produce much greater diversity in the coming decades than it did during the prison boom years. This will provide an opportunity for several individual states to produce substantial declines in imprisonment rates, but a diverse distribution of trends in the individual states after the 2007 peak will probably push aggregate levels of imprisonment reduction closer to zero rather than deepen the aggregate level of decline. Just as the rare unanimity of increases during the high-growth era magnified the increases, a return to diversity will probably moderate the level of decline.

And every other aspect of what I called provincial dominance will probably impede substantial reductions in imprisonment. The crime policy atmosphere of state-level politics and the close proximity to local law enforcement and decision-makers certainly played a role in the high magnitude of the prison increase, but there is no good evidence of the extent to which provincial influence added prisoners. That same level of uncertainty obtains when we guess about how much resistance to lowering levels of incarceration is built into the circumstances of local dominance. Case studies of individual state efforts can help us start to measure how and why local factors complicate the process of reducing prison crowding.

A separate obstacle to decarceration is what I called the jurisdictional redundancy of federal and state criminal law. While the total federal prison population had traditionally been substantially lower than 10% of the national total in prison, the explosive growth in federal prisoners outstripped even the state growth rate after 1985 (Blumstein and Beck 1999). The Obama administration under Attorney General Holder made efforts to reduce federal drug imprisonment.

During the first 15 years of the prison boom, the substantial overlap between federal and state prosecutions and punishment produced some extra prison growth, but the impact of added federal punishment was limited by the relatively small size of federal prisons. From 1985 to 2002, the increases in federal drug prisoners documented in Table 4.1 increased both the size of federal prisons and the tendency of duplicative federal prosecution and punishment to add to the national imprisonment growth that was a direct result of redundant criminal laws and punishment.

The major issue in the era after 2020 is whether the tendency of federal charges, convictions, and imprisonment to keep total imprisonment high will be modest (as in the era before 1985) or more substantial (as during 1985–2002). The case for a smaller federal add-on is that the sweeping pressures associated with the war on drugs is long gone. The problem, however, is that one legacy of the war on drugs is a large federal law enforcement bureaucracy. The Drug Enforcement Administration (DEA) is a highly specialized and substantial police force that delivers most of its enforcement products to the US Department of Justice. The volume of its criminal charges tend to rise and fall with its staffing levels; and the staffing levels remain pretty close to their drug war highs. In June 2002, there were 4,256 DEA agents on duty (Reaves and Bauer 2003), and the DEA's 2017 budget request reports 4,026 agents in 2016, a reduction of only 6% from 2002 (Drug Enforcement Administration 2017). In 2015, when the federal prison population dropped by 14,000, the number of federal system prison admissions (46,912) was actually 3,000 *greater* than the 43,732 admissions reported from 2000 (Carson and Anderson 2016, Table 7; Guerino, Harrison, and Sabol 2011). Under these conditions, it seems prudent to assume that the upward pressure from the continuation of drug enforcement and other federal law enforcement efforts adding additional inmates will stay close to its drug war maximum impact.

The one aspect of state-level influence that might help reduce prison populations is the financial impact of imprisonment on state budgets. The great recession of 2007–2010 generated substantial losses of state and local revenue from income and property taxes. At the same time, prison costs had expanded with the large increase in prison populations. Prison crowding meant that capital costs were also on the near horizon if public penal facilities couldn't absorb new additions. In California, crowding generated large additional costs to bring medical care up to constitutional standard and to mitigate some of the toxic impact of extreme crowding (Simon 2014).

The competition for scarce financial resources in state government will continue into the middle-range future in most states in the federal system, and serve as a motive both to reduce prisoners and to scrutinize proposals that might increase imprisonment. For prison systems down from peak populations, some additional prisoners may be added without immediate capital costs to expand prison capacity. But the variable costs of expanding levels of imprisonment will be well worth avoiding even in states that have recovered from the recession. And with large state-level demands on the horizon for public pensions and infrastructure maintenance and improvement, any fiscal savings from downsizing state confinement levels will be a major attraction to state governments.

But the fiscal rewards of downsizing prison populations are often less substantial than had been hoped. In systems like New York and California, the fixed costs of facilities and staff often reduce the budgetary benefits that fewer prisoners deliver to correctional budgets. Still, the financial costs of any prison expansion will be quite large, and the eventual savings of significant downsizing might be of real importance to many state governments. Whether these fiscal consequences will carry impact to the branches and levels of government where many decisions about prison sentences are made is another question.

LOCALIZED, POLITICAL, AND ADVERSARIAL PUNISHMENT DECISION-MAKING

Judges and prosecutors will remain the primary decision-makers about individual criminal sentences in the middle-range American future, and their decision-making is likely to remain localized, political, and adversarial in ways that encourage high rates of prison sentences and tend also to produce longer terms of confinement than different decision-making structures would produce. To the extent that these local institutions continue to monopolize individual sentence determinations, significant reductions in prison populations will be harder to achieve, smaller in magnitude, and more prone to reversal of trends after short periods.

There are three distinctly different strategies of countering the biases of local and adversarial decision-making. One is to change the attitudes and role definitions that make local prosecutors and judges punishment prone. A second is to alter the institutional determinants of sentencing power so that different actors and different levels of government take more power in determining rates of imprisonment and actual time served. A third strategy is to transform the economic consequences to local government of sending people to prison to impose costs on imprisonment and benefits on sentencing decisions that avoid prison. All three strategies will be necessary to effect any stable and substantial change in rates of imprisonment.

Institutional realignments can take place both at the front end of the sentencing process (with sentencing commissions generating guidelines that create presumptive punishments for particular criminal violation/offender record combinations) and at the back end of the prison term (with parole release authorities decoupling the formal sentences of an offender from when he or she can be conditionally released). Both of these institutional innovations not only change the *branch* of government making decisions but also remove some power to different *levels* of government. A system that has both a sentencing commission and a parole board with substantial powers is less local (these are state level), less political (no electoral determinations), and less adversarial (fewer lawyers) than a system where prosecutor and judge are effectively the last word in punishment determination. Chapter 7 will discuss strategies to effect such changes.

Economic incentives are also necessary to reverse the overkill that is all but determined when the local level of government does not pay for prisons. These are the sine qua non of policies that can consistently reduce prison populations and sustain lower levels of imprisonment. (Raphael and Stoll 2013, Pfaff 2017, and Zimring and Hawkins 1991 all emphasize this priority.)

RETRIBUTIVE DEMANDS, INCAPACITATION, AND PUBLIC CRIME FEARS

Retribution, the desire for incapacitation, and fear are all public attitudes that provide support for imprisonment and are also frequent themes that legislators and prosecutors invoke in support of imprisonment. Such sentiments are not good news for those trying to soften imprisonment policy, but it is hard to gauge the separate power of public belief in these themes in determining levels of imprisonment. Fear of life-threatening violence almost certainly made crime policy and punishment into more salient topics in national and local politics. It was an important influence and may remain important. The sentiment that only incarceration qualifies as a credible punishment for serious crime is a powerful and attractive argument for prosecutors and legislators, but it doesn't have the independent capacity to make crime policy a much more important topic for citizens, so it probably plays a less dynamic role in the politics of punishment. I would guess that only fear of crime can independently sustain public pressure for more punitive priority. So any trends or events that generate broad fears about life-threatening violence will make reducing prison populations more difficult.

The Lessons of Adversity

The main arena for penal reform in the United States will be the same country that produced the epic increase in incarceration after 1975. The current structure of government and distribution of authority in punishment have not changed importantly from the governmental and justice systems that invented mass incarceration. The analysis in this chapter has identified several features of the hardware and software of American criminal justice that facilitated the prison boom.

This final section of the chapter will briefly outline three lessons from the survey of the peculiarities of American penality for the aims and means of reducing the harms of mass incarceration. In the real world of American crime and punishment, how much of a reduction in imprisonment is likely to be sustained? How might the pro-incarcerative aspects of provincial power and adversarial priority be controlled? What do the limits of decarcerative impact suggest will be necessary reforms in terms of penal confinement and in the destructive consequences of confinement for inmates, families, and communities? The first topic I address here is the likely range of the prison population in the coming decades. The second brief analysis will focus on strategic priorities for reversing the provincial and adversarial vectors in American criminal justice. And the final heading in this section addresses strategies of harm reduction for the multitudes who will remain in prisons and jails even after reforms have run their course.

Imprisonment and Jail in 2050?

Isn't this also the same United States of America that reported a prison population of 97 per 100,000 in 1970? Why couldn't reformers consider a return to 97 per 100,000 as reasonable target for reform? Both the statistical data reviewed in Chapter 2 and the analysis of local government and prosecution in Chapter 3 and this chapter suggest that the United States of 2020 is *not* the same nation at the front end of criminal prosecutions that generate prison admissions. The United States in 1970 reported slightly fewer than 100,000 new admissions to state and federal prisons. In 2013, with a population base that had increased by 51%, there were 630,000 new admissions to state and federal prisons, a per capita new imprisonment rate that is more than four times the 1970 rate. A major long-term reform effort would have to be regarded as a great success if it cut the prison admission level to half the 2013 rate, but that magnitude of new admissions could still sustain an American prison population of around 300 per 100,000. How likely is a reduction of greater than that?

This is not to say that an American system with a substantially smaller prison population wouldn't be safe or prosperous, merely that it is unlikely as a matter of political and governmental operation. A United States with only 350,000 of its citizens locked up would be a very nice place, but it is unlikely that I or my children will have the opportunity to live in that nation. And if the upper limit of reducing prison populations still leaves close to a million persons in the federal and state prisons of 2040, that suggests the necessity of expanding the scope of penal reform priorities to make prison less destructively punitive and to downsize the costs of the experience to prisoners, families, and communities.

Priority Concerns for Downsizing Imprisonment

Cutting American imprisonment in half from its current levels is a tall order even in the long term, but not an impossible one. Reducing the power of local governments in determining whether and for how long persons serve prison terms is not an extreme or costly practice. Sentencing commissions and parole authorities are modest but positive steps. The unprincipled but clever "truth in sentencing" state laws—which essentially reallocated discretion about prison terms to local government—should be candidates for quick and bipartisan repeal. It would greatly facilitate sharp declines in prison terms if imprisonments could cease to function as symbols of prosecutorial success in the adversary system. But even if prosecutorial hearts and minds resist correction, creating substantial economic incentives for local governments to reduce use of state facilities is an absolute necessity for rational resource allocation in state and local criminal justice. What Raphael and Stoll call "skin in the game" is a sine qua non for penal reform (2013, 258–63). The most appropriate methods of implementing such strategies and the impact of putting them in place will be addressed in later chapters. The central point of this mention is that this chapter's review of the environmental influences that promoted prison growth and the last chapter's discussion of how prison commitment was costless to local government make it obvious that correcting the "free lunch" character of prison to county governments is a necessary reform.

A less obvious example of how this chapter's discussion should influence the choice of policy priorities concerns the way in which redundant federal and state criminal prohibitions and enforcement added massive new cohorts of drug prisoners in both federal and state systems. When considering whether the tendency of this redundant jurisdiction to add to total imprisonment might abate now that the moral panic phase of American's drug war is ancient history, I was skeptical because most of the thousands of drug enforcement agents in the DEA are still on the job—and drugs are their only business. Yet there are several strategic alternatives that can reduce the impact of this group of agents on criminal cases and federal prison populations. One method is budgetary reform to cut the number of DEA agents from 4,000 to 2,000. A second alternative is to focus enforcement effort on high-value international targets. A third possibility is to put DEA agents to work on noncriminal or low-case-yield regulatory efforts in opioid use that involve medical prescriptions. But the point of this example for present purposes is that nobody would think to start discussing the DEA budget as relevant to deconstructing imprisonment rates without the analysis of redundant drug jurisdiction and enforcement in the first two sections of this chapter.

A final example of budgetary relevance concerns one controversy about the role of sharp reductions in the rate of confinement in state mental health institutions during the 1950s and 1960s as an influence on the subsequent growth in prison populations. Bernard Harcourt suggested that the decline in medical health facilities might be linked to the later expansion of prisoners (Harcourt 2006). Steven Raphael and Michael Stoll discount much direct spillover from the populations involved in state mental health institutions to the new inmate cohorts in the prison expansion (Raphael and Stoll 2013), and their critique is compelling. But both mental health institutions and most prisons are the financial responsibility of state government. So the reduction of the mental health institutional expenditures might well have created budgetary space for an expansion of the scale of imprisonment.

Expanding the Objectives of Reform

If there are a million or more Americans behind bars in prisons and jails in the United States in 2040, it can be considered a significant failure of American government and a threat to individual liberty and to the largely disadvantaged minorities from which prisons and jails draw inmates. And the million or so in jails and prisons will lead to millions of former prisoners and their families with legacies of stigma and disadvantage. Despite the best efforts of reform in the proximate future, this is the likely profile of the United States of 2040 and 2050.

Under these circumstances, efforts to reduce the population of Americans behind bars becomes a necessary but not a sufficient objective for penal reform. The services, opportunities, and living conditions of prisons must be improved in a million-prisoner nation. The local jails that become incarcerative alternatives to prisons are closer to the communities from which inmates are drawn, but in other respects are often worse than America's prisons. The larger our irreducible minimum of persons behind bars, the more important it will be to improve the conditions of confinement for those who cannot benefit from downsizing prisons and jails.

5

What Happens Next?

THE SUBJECT OF this chapter is what the experience of the last half-century suggests about future rates of penal confinement in the United States over the next generation. Predictions of all future social and governmental events is an art, not a science, and the margin of error in even midrange estimates of correctional policy is substantial. But if the margin of error for peering into a criminological crystal ball is so large, why should the effort even be made in an analysis of historical trends that can be described with greater precision? Why not ring the curtain down on the first half of this study at the end point of the known history of prisons and jails in American life? What is the value added in a short chapter rich in guesses and contingencies about a history that hasn't happened?

There are two reasons why a more systematic discussion of likely futures than ended Chapter 4 belongs in this study. The first reason is that the data and analysis in the previous four chapters provide valuable information about how criminal justice policies are likely to evolve in the proximate future. Many of the environmental circumstances discussed in Chapter 4 will continue to influence policies in the coming decade, as will the attitudes and economic incentives of state and local criminal justice addressed in Chapter 3. So the historical materials in the first part of the book should help us to reduce the epic margin of error that prediction inevitably encounters. The next 30 years are still a guessing game, but the guesses should improve in two respects—the assumptions about which features of the governmental system should influence the variability of prison population will be explicit, and they will be visible to a skeptical reader. I *hope* that the guesses produced in this analysis are closer to the real outcomes than less informed estimates, but I am *confident* that they will be transparent. When the projections discussed are wrong, it should be possible to link my mistakes to particular assumptions about crime and punishment discussed in these pages. So this chapter is a test of the value of the detailed statistics and insights produced in earlier chapters for predicting the future operation of institutions of punishment.

The central value that plausible projections of future correctional populations can have is on constructing an appropriate agenda for reforms for the circumstances that penal reformers are likely to encounter in 2030 and 2040. One set of important priorities comes from understanding the historical causes of increased incarceration and does not require further population projections. If the "correctional free lunch" was one important incentive for massive increases in prisoners, its reversal should be an early priority for reformers. If increasing the number of defendants sent to prison has become an important token of successful prosecutorial advocacy, then judges and administrators should disavow imprisonment as an indicator of litigation success and disregard sanction severity as a major criterion for promotions and prizes. A good analysis of the major upward vectors becomes a list of effective changes that reformers should seek to achieve. We don't require this chapter's statistical analyses to construct these obvious reforms.

But there are many priorities for reform that come into sharp focus when we face the likely future of crime and punishment in the coming decades. Comprehending the likely limits of decarceration in the coming decades clarifies both the human and material costs of prisons and jails as a lived experience that damages inmates and families. One million prisoners in 2030 is 10 million *former prisoners* in 2040 and 30 million family members impacted. If the scale of imprisonment cannot be reduced, then reducing the stigma from imprisonment and its prospective economic and social harms become more important. Prisons should also become less destructive and less isolated from families and communities. If we continue to lock up three times as many people as we should, then we must minimize the pain and damage we cause prisoners.

The chapter is organized in five installments. The first section discusses the problem of predicting the aftermath of unprecedented changes in policy. If there are no precedents for a change, what experience can observers draw on to predict the nature and magnitude of trends after the period of unprecedented policy? Are there significant changes in other settings that help us understand what trends in imprisonment are likely after a generation of explosive growth? So analogies and metaphors are pressed into service where the known history of imprisonment cannot instruct. The second section uses the historical record in the first decade after the peak rate of imprisonment in 2007 to explore the magnitude and distribution of imprisonment. The third section discusses the special circumstances of California and their implications for predicting trends in other states. The fourth section contrasts transformative shifts away from institutions in Europe with the current and probably future trends in state prisons. And the conclusion to the chapter provides a brief summary of the evolving trends in US prison population.

Is There a Law of Penal Gravity?

With all the difficulties of data and method, there can be no straightforward predictions of levels of imprisonment in the short- and middle-range future. What we usually read instead is a mixture of advocacy and alarm, an outline of punishment levels that observers hope are possible with reforms rather than what can be expected in the absence of significant changes in rules. This mix often creates a reform target that by definition returns American experience to its previous, more moderate levels of imprisonment; in the words of criminologist James Austin, "The solution lies in simply returning to the same sentencing and correctional policies that existed a few decades ago" (2010, 9).

To speak of "simply" returning American penal practice to its earlier patterns may reflect a belief in a law of penological gravity—that what goes up in imprisonment must come down. But what aspects of the criminal justice systems in the United States remain fixed over long periods of time? Certainly not the fixed plant of penal facilities or persons employed in prison administration, courts and criminal litigation, or law enforcement. The policies of the last generation have greatly expanded the institutions that investigate, prosecute, and confine. A metaphor of penological gravity imagines that penal outcomes vary over time but the universe that produces them is a constant. However, it is difficult to imagine a fixed penal universe that has survived the state and federal trends portrayed in Chapters 2 and 3. A return to 100 prisoners per 100,000 citizens would in some respects be a more radical alteration of institutional operations and expectations than the expansion that preceded 2007.

The problem with the assumption that future trends will incorporate reforms is that it provides no information about what policies are likely if the reforms don't succeed. In addition, realistic estimates of likely trends in prison and jail populations are important to reformers who want to protect the interests of the multitudes of Americans at risk of incarceration and its aftereffects. If your most desired reforms are baked into your only model of future crime and punishment policy, then you have no basis for advocacy if Plan A isn't realized. There is no foundation for a Plan B. This does not seem a prudent strategy in the current conditions of American government and society.

The central problem with assuming that all of the past generation's growth in imprisonment can be reversed is that we may fail to change the costs and consequences of high continuing levels of incarceration. A realistic perspective on future penal trends may be a necessary tool for effective protection of human rights in American criminal justice.

But where to look for realistic assumptions when there are no historical precedents to consult? An injunction against wishful thinking is an important but essentially negative lesson. What sorts of assumptions should be made about American penal policy in 2030 and 2040 and 2050?

The next section outlines some alternative assumptions about how the major expansion in 1970–2005 might influence patterns of incarceration. The section after that examines patterns of change in state and federal imprisonment during the ten years after the peak rates were reached in 2007.

Prediction without Precedent?

This chapter considers what is likely to happen to prison populations and criminal justice policy after a 35-year span in which rates of imprisonment jumped by over 400%. The technical problem is finding a methodology for predicting the aftermath of an event that has never before occurred. With no previous experience of such a substantial movement, what assumptions should be made about the influence of a large increase of imprisonment on trends in the years after the consistent growth has stopped? There are at least three contrasting assumptions about prison population trends after major increases that should be considered: (1) business as usual because variations in future imprisonment should be independent of past trends, (2) increased volatility because major historical shifts signal that prison populations are likely to vary more substantially in the future, or (3) regression toward long-term historical mean levels. A business-as-usual model would guess that future variations will be smaller than those in the immediate prior history but would not predict the direction of change. The second set of assumptions—volatility—differs from a business-as-usual model because it assumes that the circumstances that produced historically large changes in the immediate past are also likely to produce larger than historically normal changes in the future. But neither the business-as-usual nor the volatility assumption predicts the directions of change. Building volatility into future projections will increase the size of anticipated changes but will not predict whether imprisonment levels will increase or decrease.

The third assumption, regressing toward long-term mean levels of imprisonment, predicts that after big increases in incarceration to very high levels, the tendency for future trends will be to lower levels of prison population. While the direction of variation is clear in this assumption, the magnitude of the anticipated decline is not obvious, and there are problems of definition. What, to begin with, would the "long-term mean" level of incarceration be in a nation where 35 consecutive years of increase have elevated totals by 400%. The 1972 low point seems an implausible long-term mean value, but where in the steady increases should mean values be calculated? What is a long-term mean when values are changing so rapidly and so steadily in one direction?

A second issue concerns the magnitude of a regression toward the mean. If we could identify in the total growth a mid-point that was a long-term mean, how much of a movement back in that direction should be expected? If the prison rate grew from 100 to 500 in 35 years, should we expect a drop back to 400, 300, or 200?

There are two further complications of importance that should be considered before any assumptions about statistical patterns can be used to predict changes. The first is the decentralized power to imprison in the United States. Should a single national aggregate be the unit of analysis, or should 51 different systems be used to project populations that might be summed to project a national total? If the assumptions being used are based on how individual penal systems are supposed to behave, then 51 different projections should be produced.

The second complication that undermines the plausibility of any assumptions about future correctional population is that policies can (and should) change in ways that can influence prison populations. The business-as-usual assumption essentially denies that important changes will accrue since business will not be conducted as usual if major changes in penalties and procedures are introduced with the express intent of altering punishment levels. The competing assumption of continued volatility may well provide room for reforms to influence rates because one reason we might think that large jumps in prison population might predict higher levels of future change is that the unstable outcomes of past policy might provoke changes in the system that are intended to alter outcomes.

And the assumption of regression toward long-term means seems not only to anticipate reforms in state and federal punishment policy but to invite them. What, after all, will be the moving parts in any tendency of imprisonment rates to drop back toward prior levels? How many of the 51 different penal systems will attempt reforms designed to reduce imprisonment, and with what range of outcomes?

The next section of this chapter attempts to learn from the relatively short experience of US penal systems after the peak rate of imprisonment was reached in 2007 and to use that data as a baseline for projecting patterns and rates of imprisonment over coming decades. The analysis of the recent trends in this section shows that one state, California, was responsible for almost half of all the reductions that occurred from 2007 to 2017. The third section then discusses four lessons from the singular pattern of imprisonment levels in California. The fourth introduces case studies of charges in some American institutions and sharp declines of institutional populations

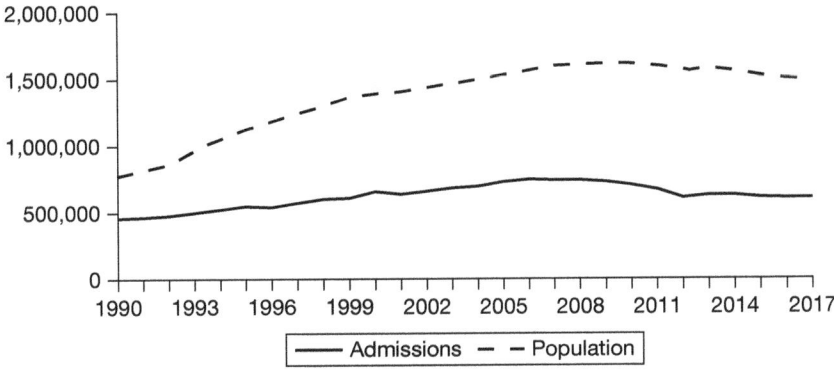

Figure 5.1 Combined Federal and State Prison Population and Admissions, 2007–2017. *Source*: Bureau of Justice Statistics.

in foreign nations and their long-term implications for future prison populations. The following section concludes the chapter by analyzing the likely impact over the next 30 years of current trends.

The First Decade after the Peak

The 35 years of every year increases in national imprisonment rate lasted from 1972 to 2007 and resulted in a peak rate of 670 per 100,000 for the US population 18 years and older. The best evidence of what is most likely to happen after the imprisonment boom is the ten years currently on record after 2007. Figure 5.1 begins the analysis with national trends in both prison admissions and imprisonment rate from 1990 through 2017.

The first 17 years covered by Figure 5.1 were the second half of the uninterrupted increase in imprisonment and the next ten the first period after its completion. In the aggregate, the trend after 2007 for both prison admissions and total prison population is downward, but the slope of the decline is quite modest compared to the uptrend that preceded 2007. The aggregate decline over the post-2007 decade is much smaller than the pace of the increase. Were this modest national rate decrease in 10 years maintained consistently for 36 years—or one year longer than the 35 years that caused the 400% increase—the rate of imprisonment in the United States in 2043 would be well over 300 per 100,000, so that well over half of the gains registered during 1972 to 2007 would have been retained four decades later.

To use the vocabulary of possible projected trends expected in the wake of the 35-year run-up, the national numbers for the first 10 years look like a mix of "business as usual" with some elements or regression toward the mean. If these trends continue, patterns of imprisonment a quarter-century after 2020 will look more like the rates of the 1980s and 1990s than like the national pattern in the years before the great expansion. Why?

One important reason why there was only modest downward movement in rates of imprisonment was the modest level of decline in rates of prison admissions after 2007. The number of new prison admissions reported in 2017 was 606,571. That was 19% fewer new prisoners than were reported in 2006—an all-time high of 747,000. But over 600,000 new admissions is still a substantial annual addition to prisons, on the high side of the stunning growth during the prison boom. The 606,571 admissions recorded in 2017 are more than the 603,000 reported for 1998 and just under the 611,000 in 1999. But the rate of imprisonment in 1998 was already 463 per 100,000 and still growing. So every indicator in the aggregate national numbers during the ten years after the all-time high suggests that modest declines from historic highs are the most likely pattern in the foreseeable future.

Comparing the States

What patterns emerge when the available data on prisoners are analyzed state by state? Table 5.1 starts this analysis by contrasting the pattern across 50 states during the first decade of growth in the United States (1972 to 1982) with the state-by-state contrast for the 10 years after 2007 (2007–2017). The table reports for each period the median value for the states as well as the amount of growth or decline in the state with the 12th-highest and 12th-lowest state in each period.

During the first decade after 1972, all 50 states reported growth in prison populations, with the median growth rate being 91.4%. States in the *bottom 25%* of prison growth reported growth up to 63%, which is more than seven times the percentage of the average decline in the 10 years after 2007.

Table 5.1 shows the two major differences from the baseline period to the more recent trends: consistent direction and very high magnitude. After 1972, each of the 50 states increased its rate of imprisonment—the pattern was universal. After the 2007 national high, no fewer than 15 states reported increasing rates of imprisonment from 2007 levels in 2017, and the decline reported by the median state was only 8.6%. So the variations from state to state that would be expected with 50 independent policy determinations are evident after 2007, variations not evident during the 35-year rate escalation. In this sense, the period after 2007 is a return to the business-as-usual pattern.

And even though 35 of the 50 states had some reduction in imprisonment rate, the size of the decline was small compared to the scale of the previous increase. The average increase in rate was 91% in 1972–1982, while the median 10-year decrease was only 8.6% in 2017—a 11 to 1 differential.

Table 5.1
Comparing Patterns of Growth and Reduction One Decade after Low Points (1972) and High Points (2007) in Rates of Imprisonment

	25th percentile	Median	75th percentile
1972–1982	+63%	+91%[a]	+128%
2007–2017	–21%	–8.6%[b]	+2.7%

[a] New Mexico (90.7%) was 25th and Washington (92%) was 26th.
[b] Indiana (8.7%) was 25th and Illinois (8.5%) was 26th.

Indeed, there is an important contrast between the 8.6% decline noted by the median American state and the significantly larger 13% decline in aggregate national prisoner levels. This suggests that one or more states might have had exceptional performances during the postpeak years that deserve special attention. And when we inspect the states at the extremes in the 50-state distribution, the pattern of exceptional performance is confirmed. When sorting through states at the extremes over any period of time, we expect to see small states at the top or bottom of the distribution. For the 1972–1982 period, this expectation is confirmed—the highest increases are Delaware, Alaska, Montana, and Vermont, ranging from the fifth smallest to the smallest in total population. But the largest state, California, reports the fifth highest percentage decline in prisoners in the 2007–2017 period—a 30% decline, which is more than three times the reported national total for the period and three times the decline reported by states in the middle of the 2007–2017 distribution (30.4% versus 8.6%).

The combination of the size of California and the magnitude of its drop in rate of imprisonment has a substantial impact on the aggregate national statistical profile reported in Figure 5.1 and Table 5.1.

Figure 5.2 illustrates the "California effect" on the aggregate national pattern by comparing California to the United States without California.

With respect to the outcomes during this period, California and the rest of the United States look like two different countries. The California reduction is eight times as great when adjusted for population and deserves sustained attention in any discussion of strategies of reducing incarceration, and California is one of the three substantial states (along with New York, New Jersey, and Connecticut) to have experienced significantly greater reductions in prison population than most other American states. These high-achieving states can serve as models for change if other states are motivated to seek substantial policy shifts.

But the very thin total of 48,000 fewer prisoners for the 49 states other than California suggests that there is no substantial tendency to shrink prison populations at work nationally in the first decade after 2007. There are almost as many states that have experienced no reduction in the number of persons in prison between 2007 and 2017 as there are states that have

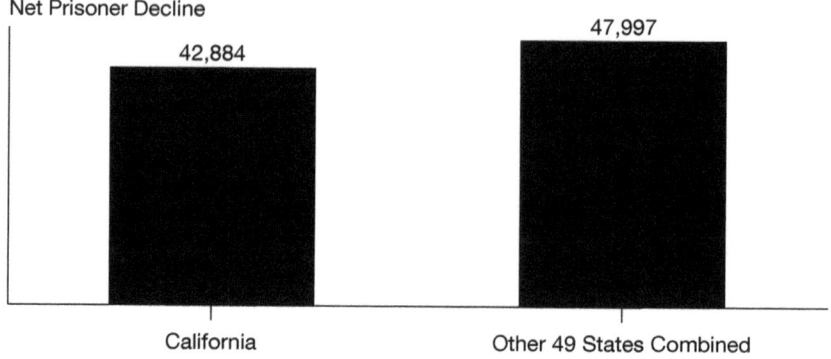

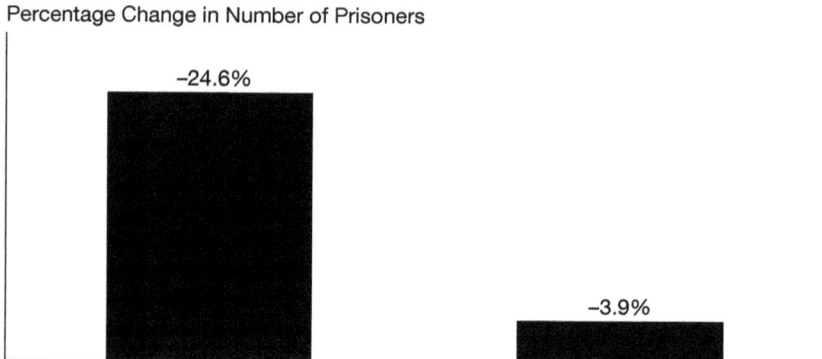

Figure 5.2 Reduction in Prison Population in California and the Other States from 2007 to 2017. *Source*: Bureau of Justice Statistics; Vera Institute of Justice 2018.

experienced a reduction. Most declines in the volume of prisoners or the rate of imprisonment are modest. This pattern seems like modest variations around a new normal in most states, the essential pattern of business as usual outlined in the introduction of this chapter. The substantial drops in California and a few sister states suggest that substantial change is possible. But the statistical profile of more than 80% of American states a decade out from the peak rate of prison use in modern history shows no clear signs that substantial change is on the horizon.

There is one hopeful pattern in the 2007–2017 data. The most significant statistical difference evident in the population trends is not the number of states that report increases (15 of 50) but the relatively small increases reported by larger states. In the 10 years after 2007, only three of the states that increased rates of incarceration reported increases over 6 percent, and these three are small states. By contrast, 24 of the 35 states that reported declining rates of incarceration had declines of over 10% (69%), and many large states, including the three largest states, reported declines of 17% or more.

The remarkable element of this asymmetrical pattern is the small size of any increases after 2007, and while the difference between the small sizes of increases and the larger sizes of decreases is substantial, it is not difficult to interpret. After the huge increases that the generation before 2007 added to prisons, many if not most of all the states were close to the limit of the number of prisoners that they could accommodate at even modest levels of decency. The fact that many state systems were close to their physical (not to mention their financial) capacities probably limited the number of new prisoners these systems were willing to absorb.

The good news conveyed by this clear pattern is that the very large prison populations that characterize most systems in the United States of 2020 may limit the scale of additional increase in state prison populations without major building programs. This limit suggests that the United States has already experienced one major transition in rates of imprisonment, from an acute grown phase in which population expanded at a high rate to a chronic high-imprisonment policy where rates of incarceration stay high but do not relentlessly increase.

Four Lessons from California

The strategies and impacts of the California correctional realignments were the most important prison population policy events of the period from 2007 to 2017. California teaches four important lessons about the opportunities and limits of state-level efforts to reduce the prison population:

1. The singular nature of the California intervention.
2. The need for structural changes to generate quick and substantial results.
3. The necessity of combining measurements of prison and local jail populations to assess the impact of structural reforms on levels of confinement.
4. The large yet limited reductions that can be produced without the aggressive cooperation of local prosecutors and criminal court judges.

A ONE-OFF EVENT

The circumstances that produced California's epic drop in prison population combined a major judicial intervention, requiring a sharp reduction in persons in the custody of California prisons, with an executive branch and legislative "realignment" plan to transfer the jurisdiction of parole failures from the prison system to local government and to shift the facilities used for the custody of some categories of property offenders from state to local institutions. The cases that were merged into *Brown v. Plata* by the time that case was decided the US Supreme Court in 2011 began as separate lawsuits claiming prison crowding amounted to cruel and unusual punishment, and litigation claiming an unconstitutional failure to provide California prison inmates with necessary medical care. A judgment by a three-judge panel under the provisions of the Prison Litigation and Reform Act upheld the inmates' contentions of unconstitutional defects in prison housing and medical care and further found that these defects could not be remedied without significant reductions in the number of prisoners confined in existing facilities. The opinion's requirement of a substantial decrease in prison population in prison conditions litigation was a substantial extension of remedial authority from existing prison conditions cases and was thought to be vulnerable on appeal to the Supreme Court. But the Court affirmed Judge Thelton Henderson's order in *Brown v. Plata* in 2011, and this precipitated a far-reaching plan to reduce California's prison population by shifting to county governments and county jails both the responsibility to hold or release those who violated parole and the authority to determine length in custody for such violations.

The California litigation and order was the only federal court litigation with major impact on state correctional populations in the twenty-first century, and there is no litigation of this scale on the horizon. In that sense, the California case history involves a reform strategy with little prospect of emulation. But the methods California used to reduce prison crowding involve institutions of government and levels of government present in most other states. So the causes of California's need for action are not likely to recur, but the methods used to achieve the reduction are applicable in most other states.

THE USE OF STRUCTURAL SHIFTS IN CUSTODIAL JURISDICTION

To comply with the mandate of *Brown v. Plata*, the state government needed large and swift downward adjustments in prison population. The least painful method of doing this was to shift responsibility for segments of the prison population to other levels of government capable of maintaining persons in secure custodial facilities if they wished to do so. The state government provided cash allowances to the counties as compensation and also gave county governments discretionary authority to determine whether and for how long the parole violators and minor felons in their new jurisdiction would be confined.

A cynic could view this strategy as providing the formal terms of the decarceration that Judge Henderson ordered without requiring any real reduction in the scale of confinement or improvement in conditions of confinement. Exploiting the fact that county facilities were not within the jurisdiction of the court in *Brown v. Plata*, all of realignment could be viewed as more trick than substantial reform. But the history of the program's effects contradicts this pessimistic hypothesis, as an expanded profile will presently show.

THE NEED FOR EXPANDED MEASURES OF SECURE CONFINEMENT

California's shifts in jurisdiction mean that measurements restricted to prison population are inadequate as an assessment of trends in levels of secure confinement. The obvious and correct measure of incarceration at either the state or the national level should be to combine state prisoners and local prisoners, whether serving sentences or awaiting adjudication behind bars.

Figure 5.3 provides data on California trends in both prison and jail confinement by year since 2007.

By separately showing prison population in California, jail population in California, and the two populations combined, we can discern the different patterns over time as well as the litigation's impact on total confinement. Figure 5.3 shows that the major drops in prison population in 2011 and 2012 were associated with increases in jailed inmates in those early years, but that total confinement was declining throughout that period. By 2015, however, the jail numbers were quite close to 2010 levels, so that almost all of the sharp decline in prison population over the period was also a net decline in prison and jail population. To the extent that local government institutions become an important part of efforts to reduce prison populations, trends in both jail and prison volumes will be necessary measures of impact.

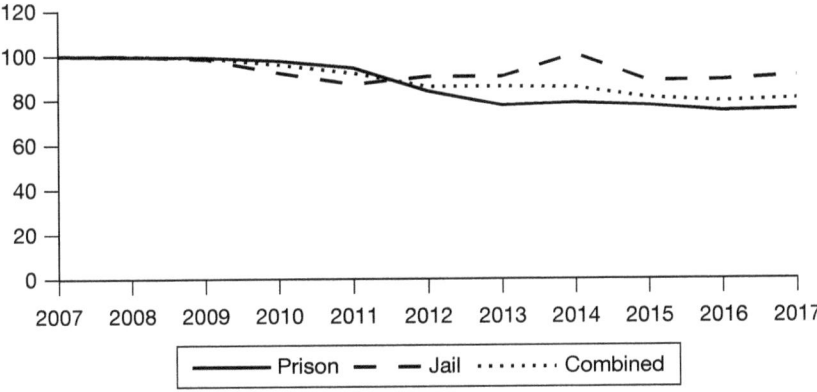

Figure 5.3 Changes in California Prison and Jail Populations from 2007 to 2017. *Source*: Bureau of Justice Statistics.

THE POTENTIAL AND LIMITS OF STATE GOVERNMENT

The reforms launched in California were almost wholly initiatives at the state level to which local levels of government responded. While local governments' response was an important reason why the realignment reduced the total rate of confinement as much as it did, the impetus for population impact was almost exclusively from central state government. What the California experience suggests is that with appropriate financial incentives and delegated powers of discretion to limit confinement, local governments will not frustrate state efforts to reduce total confinement by up to 25%.

But the potential for pushing populations down further is not evident. Prison admissions and total prison populations have both stabilized in California rather than continuing to trend downward.

The habits and incentives of local prosecutors have not changed much in California, and this is an important leading indicator that, even with two important electoral propositions that reduced prison and total confinement, California may be close to a new stability in rates of secure confinement. If so, the scale of California's best-in-the-nation performance still predicts a long-term level of confinement that would retain two-thirds of the increases that happened after 1970, perhaps a transition from "mass incarceration" to "mass incarceration light."

Two Contrasting Patterns after Major Population Reductions

One other issue of importance in projecting the long-term effects of the growth in American penal confinement concerns the impact of dramatic reductions of prisoners in systems that have experienced big drops in population. If some state systems do drop by half or more, will the declines be lasting? Do unused facilities tend to fill up, or do systems adjust to lower levels of confinement? American prisons and jails have no case studies of big drops to test such issues, so other places or other systems are our best hope for useful knowledge.

There have been drops in three analogous systems of total institutional confinement that are of potential value in examining the aftereffects. They show two very different patterns over succeeding decades.

One instance of substantial reduction in institutional populations is in secure confinement of dependent psychiatric, developmentally disabled, and senile persons in state institutions from the 1950s onward. Sharp population declines were followed by closure of institutions, and once the state hospitals closed, they were rarely replaced (Harcourt 2011). While there is concern that the state institutions were not replaced by decent community treatment facilities, the population in such state institutions now is a small fraction of the population in the middle of the twentieth century. Several characteristics of the populations confined and of the social and political changes in postwar America doomed such state institutions. Few of the confined were actively dangerous. Most of them needed supported living environments, not locked doors. Expanded Social Security payments for the elderly provided economic support for lives, often with some assistance, in community settings. And the widespread use of psychiatric drugs created alternatives to locked cages. Whatever the failings of community-based support, the mega-institutions of state mental health confinement are properly dead letters.

A second example of shuttered institutions is state facilities for the protracted confinement of juveniles. Most states had divided institutions of high security for young offenders into short-term detention centers and camps run by county governments (and roughly equivalent to jails) and longer-term "state training schools" for boys and some girls that were, in terms of governance and length of confinement, the equivalent of state prisons. Often, as was the case in California, the state government paid the full costs of these institutions so that something close to the correctional free lunch was operating when county judges considered state institutions for juvenile offenders.

By the mid-1990s, the system of state institutions (the California Youth Authority) had a combined population in excess of 10,000, and the California legislature began a program that was in many ways a precursor of the 2011 realignment but without the forcible intervention of federal courts. The idea was that for most of the young offenders in CYA facilities, prolonged confinement was harmful and unnecessary. The idea was to shift most kids from those long terms to shorter stays in county facilities, either detention centers or camps. The effect of the change was a sharp drop in the population in CYA facilities from 10,000 in 1996 to under 700 in 2016. The average daily population dropped substantially, as seen in Figure 5.4.

The essential character of both the state mental hospital deinstitutionalization and the near disappearance of the California Youth Authority is a structural shift away from the institution's primary functioning for most of the persons who are confined.

A different pattern of institutional history can be seen in the study of the long-term effects of sharp drops in prison populations in the client states of Soviet domination after the collapse of the Soviet Union in 1989. Published studies of prison amnesty programs show that the rate of confinement is usually substantially elevated toward the old rate rather quickly (Zimring and Hawkins 1991, 194–96; Su 2016). But these cases involved the release of prisoners who were not at risk of reconfinement since they had been political prisoners. Table 5.2 shows, for six former Soviet satellites, the short-term impact of the unraveling of Soviet influence (trends from 1985 to 1990) and the reported prison population in 2010, 20 years later. This is an interesting

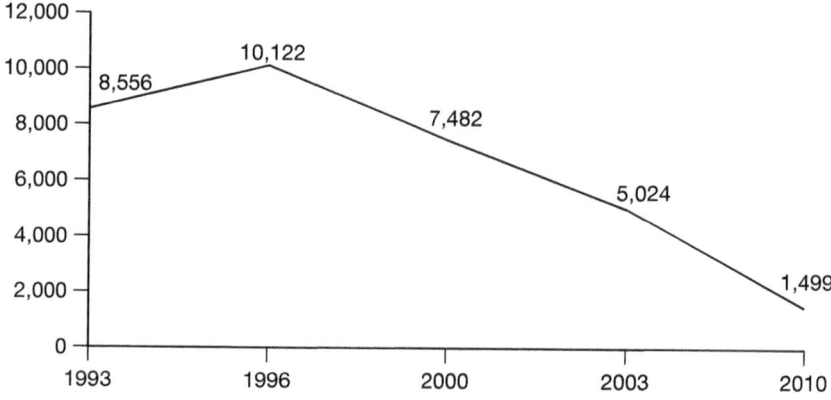

Figure 5.4 Population of California Youth Authority, 1993–2010. *Source*: CDCR; Krisberg et al. 2010.

Table 5.2

Drop in Number of Prisoners 1985–1990 and Imprisonment Rate in 2010, Six Soviet Satellite Nations

	Imprisonment rate 1985	Imprisonment rate 1990	Change	Imprisonment rate 2010	Change from 1990	Change from 1985
Poland	295	132	−55%	210	+59%	−29%
Czech Republic	270	80	−70%	209	+161%	−23%
Slovakia	236	87	−63%	186	+114%	−21%
Romania	260	112	−57%	140	+25%	−46%
Bulgaria	167	123	-26%	119	−3%	−29%
Hungary	218	119	-45%	163	+37%	−25%

Source: World Prison Brief n.d.

subsample of nations because we anticipate that political prisoners will be released between 1985 and 1990 and that there is little likelihood that many of these political offenders will find their way back to prison. So the open question is whether the empty cells will be filled by other sorts of prisoners.

The imprisonment rates reported in these six nations for 1985 were *much* higher than during that era in Western Europe (see Figures 1.1 and 1.2), as we would expect with political offenders included. The decline in rates of imprisonment by 1990 is large—in five of the six nations, the imprisonment rate drops by 45% or more in five years, with a mean decline of 53%. And every prison system reported lower imprisonment rates in 2010 than in

1985. But there is also a clear tendency for imprisonment rates to increase from the low levels achieved in 1990. The reported rate of imprisonment in 2010 is more than 25% higher in 2010 than in 1990 for every nation except Bulgaria. The governments with the biggest drops between 1985 and 1990 also reported the largest increases over the next two decades.

This pattern suggests that space created when one class of inmate is removed from an institution is likely to be used to incarcerate other types of prisoners as long as the institution remains open and its function is still regarded as a legitimate public purpose.

And for all the talk of "punishing smart" and disapproval of mass imprisonment in the rhetoric of current reforms, there has been no fundamental challenge of imprisonment as a vehicle of incapacitation or retributive isolation. So that even the removal of a class of prisoners in what Chapter 6 will call a categorical policy change might free up capacity for other classes of potential prisoners.

What the natural experiment in former Soviet satellite nations shows is some tendency for prison capacity that is created when formerly incarcerated offenders are released to be used to confine other types of offenders. The massive release of political prisoners in Soviet satellite nations was a successful categorical reform, but not all of the correctional capacity that was freed up by this change remained unused after 1990. Might this also happen in the aftermath of the California realignment?

Probably not. The intense overcrowding of California prisons that provoked judicial intervention limited the reduction of prison population to levels that do not create obvious opportunities. And most other states in the federal union also seem to have accommodated expanding prison populations by pushing prisoners into existing capacity rather than building new prisons. Whether judged by measures of operational capacity, rated capacity, or design capacity, most states report prison populations close to their limits (see "State Prison Capacity" 2018). As a practical matter, the legacy of exceeding designed prison capacities suggests that substantial declines in levels of imprisonment will be necessary before available space in state prisons will invite new types of prison commitment. As the next section will show, crowded state prisons will probably limit the expansion of state prisoners in the next two decades. Conditions will have to improve dramatically before excess capacity invites expansion of confined populations. But the long-term tendencies to reuse custodial capacity if institutions remain open has implications for state policy that Chapter 9 will address.

If Current Trends Continue . . .

If California is a one-off federal court intervention unlikely to recur, the national pattern without California included moves close to what I have called a "business as usual" pattern in two respects: no strong downward tendency in the national prison population and no tendency for states to trend in the same direction. Four states—New Jersey, Colorado, New York, and Connecticut—had substantial drops in rates of imprisonment and in admissions that were much more substantial than other large states, apart from California. In these four states the downsizing was attributable to in-state processes and institutions, and they would be better models for what might provoke change in other jurisdictions.

But even if the circumstances that provoked California's need to reduce prison population are not likely to be seen elsewhere, the programs California used to reduce the number of prisoners are attractive and potentially workable in many American states.

One encouraging aspect of trends after 2007 is that the 15 states with growing prison populations in the period report smaller increases than in prior periods and smaller increases than the declines in other states from 2007 to 2017. This moderation in population growth may be a result of limited capacity in existing facilities. And if those restraints continue, they will limit the prospect for further increases in prison population. So things may not get much worse in the coming decades. But how much reduction in population can be expected over the next two decades? The constraints on expansion due to limited remaining capacity will bias a "business as usual" mixture of state increases and decreases in a modestly downward direction because the upward movements will be smaller than the downward movements in other states. But that drift toward slightly smaller levels is far from the end of mass imprisonment.

The one clear positive trend in secure confinement that might generate some basis for optimism is confinement trends for juvenile offenders in the United States. After substantial increases in arrests for violent offenses from 1985 to 1993, rates of youth crime fell dramatically during the middle and late 1990s, the same period when adult arrests dropped. But the rate of secure confinement for juveniles also dropped very substantially in the years after 1999. While imprisonment rates climbed until 2007, juvenile confinement started falling by 2000 and dropped by 55% nationally, from 107,493 in 1999 to 48,043 in 2015 (Office of Juvenile Justice and Delinquency Prevention 2017). This decline was much larger than the single-digit drop in prisoners reported in the second section of this chapter. If trends in juvenile confinement are a "leading indicator" of trends in prison population, the much larger drop in juvenile confinement may signal that more substantial drops in prison population are on the horizon.

But trends over time in both youth crime and confinement are usually simultaneous with adult trends rather than sequential—they tend to rise and fall together. And while local government is the power center for both criminal justice and juvenile justice in the states, there is more power held in local juvenile justice by judges and probation staff (Zimring 2014). So trends in youth incarceration as harbinger of trends in adult confinement would be without significant precedent.

Why the Small Numbers?

A detailed analysis of the first ten years after the imprisonment's high point shows that this transition period is far removed from both the aggregate magnitude of the prison boom and the consistent pattern that characterized the 35-year upward trend for state and federal prisons. But why? There are two features of the first years after the peak that are of importance in explaining the lack of dramatic declines in incarceration. The first key to the modest declines is the absence of systemic or economic pressure to moderate prison and jail numbers. California was the only place where a federal court order generated systemic pressure, and that single state had almost the same decline in the total number prisoners as the 49 other state systems combined. What was missing outside California was a strong motive to downsize. Whatever economic or operational issues most other states confronted were not considered important enough to motivate significant decline. In the vast majority of American states the all-time high in prison population in 2007 was not regarded as a crisis.

In the absence of an operational crisis or a federal court order, the 51 different prison systems that operate in the United States experienced wide diversity in outcome over the next decade, and only a very few produced significant drops in prisoners. In most states, there was no major change in the important powers that county government exercised on prison numbers. So both the allocation of authority and its operational impact on prison admissions were business as usual in 90% of American state penal systems. But business as usual in the United States incorporates all of the practices, attitudes, and expectations of the fivefold expansion in rates of imprisonment since 1970. This is what the title of this book calls the "momentum" of mass incarceration. The exceptional growth has been followed by a relatively stable "new normal" that takes for granted rates of penal confinement that were unknown in developed nations before the last quarter of the twentieth century.

Thus, a major shift away from high rates of imprisonment hasn't begun yet in the United States. And we don't know whether a sustained downturn will take hold at any point in the first half of the twenty-first century. That rather gloomy perspective argues for broadening the objectives for penal reforms. Reductions in the number of prisoners and the length of confinement remain important goals. But reducing the needless deprivations that incarceration exacts also demands attention. Reducing the stigma and unnecessary civil and economic harms of a prison record becomes all the more important when these privations are multiplied by the millions of Americans who will pass through the process.

Part II

STRATEGIES OF SENTENCING REFORM

6

Two Categorical Alternatives to Prisons

THIS CHAPTER AND Chapter 7 address two different but complementary strategies for shifts in criminal justice policy that can reduce rates of imprisonment in federal and state systems. This chapter addresses two of what I shall call *categorical* reform efforts, by which I mean attempts to replace prison sentences with nonimprisonment alternatives for an entire category of offenses or offenders. A categorical reform goes well beyond attempts to reduce the rate of prison sentences per 100 eligible offenders, to shift instead the assumed preferred outcome in an entire class of cases from confinement in prisons to something else. One obvious method of categorical criminal law reform would be decriminalization of behaviors formerly punished as crimes. While decriminalization of all forms of drug possession and use has been a consistent theme in the discussion of drug control policy in recent years (see Zimring and Hawkins 1992, ch. 4), removal of all criminal sanctions for drug possession and use has been widely advocated to date only for "soft" drugs, nonnarcotic psychoactive substances such as marijuana and peyote.

But complete removal from criminal prohibition is only one form of categorical reform strategy. Treatment and educational programs can also become alternatives to incarceration, and perhaps even to criminal prosecution. Medical and treatment programs as criminal justice outcomes in narcotics cases are the first of the two categorical disincarceration strategies discussed in this chapter.

The second categorical shift strategy this chapter surveys is the use of local jails as a preferred venue for a wide variety of violations of supervisory conditions or minor criminal offending. While there is irony in reformers suggesting urban jails as alternatives to prisons, there are good reasons to examine this exchange of institutions as a method of penal reform. A careful analysis of recent experience in California suggests that the creative use of local facilities can reduce total rates of incarceration.

There are structural and organizational reasons to consider what this chapter calls "categorical" reforms separately from the next chapter's focus on the governance of criminal sentencing principles and practices. The main arena for categorical reforms is often exterior to the machinery of criminal sentences and involves, instead, changes in legislative policy. These are often wholesale changes where the attitudes and practices of local judges and prosecutors are not of primary importance. While my analysis of remaining charging and sentencing discretion where the potential for criminal liability of drug-dependent persons for commercial offenses warns us that even sweeping categorical reforms might be frustrated by relabeling criminal charges to recreate potential liability for imprisonment, the most substantial policy changes in truly categorical reforms are exterior to the conventional locations and actors in criminal sentencing.

Strategic Changes in the Drug War?

The moral panic about hard narcotics that launched what has been universally called "the war on drugs" in the mid-1980s generated an intense but one-sided debate about both the nature of the drug problem in the United States and the appropriate emphasis of law and policy to address the problem. On one side of the debate were observers who defined the principle concerns of government policy as "reducing the harmful consequences produced by the consumption of psychoactive substances: problems such as health costs, time off from work, family problems, and a shortened life span" (Zimring and Hawkins 1992, 8). "The public health generalist worries about these consequences whether or not the substances that produce them are legal or illegal." (Zimring and Hawkins 1992, 8) Thus, patterns of morbidity and mortality, rather than the statute book, are the priority for drug policy in this view. Dependency on drugs, whether legal or illegal, is usually regarded as a disease process and successful drug treatment as the central objective of government policy.

By contrast, the "legalist" definition of the drug problem that was forcefully argued by the nation's first "drug czar," William Bennett, was concerned only with illegal drugs as a threat to legal authority of the state. From this perspective, what the public health generalist regarded as the primary concern of policy, the crime and disease generated by some drug use, the legalist dismisses as mere "symptoms": "the drug problem in its essence: drug use itself" (Office of National Drug Control Policy 1989, 8). The primary tactic of the legalist war on drugs was criminal law enforcement and severe punishment. Federal and state prisons were the primary governmental weapons in the domestic drug war that preoccupied American criminal justice from 1985 to 2000.

There are two features of this phase of American drug and criminal justice policy that require sustained attention prior to considering more recent drug policy concerns. The first is the rather limited focus of the dispute in the 1980s and 1990s between public health and legalist advocates. There was substantial disagreement about what tactics should be emphasized but much less disagreement about the size and location of the drug emergency of the 1980s. The drug war debates of the period were about cocaine and to a lesser extent heroin, and the particular emphasis was on crack cocaine, a smokable and inexpensive form of delivering cocaine. The drug emergency of the period was about what the official document of the federal policy told us was "in fact, the most dangerous and quickly addictive drug known to man" (Office of National Drug Control Policy 1989, 3). The distinctive hazards of the crack epidemic were "crack houses" located in inner-city neighborhoods where "crackheads" got high, then committed violent crimes to get money to reignite their swiftly dissipating highs. The long-term costs of this terrifying form of cocaine were thought to include "crack babies" both developmentally damaged and addicted and born to crack-smoking pregnant women.

The widespread agreement that crack cocaine was the central problem in the drug emergency also meant that there was complete overlap between the legal prohibition and the social problem. If crack cocaine was the problem, then 100% of the users were violating criminal laws and 100% of the suppliers of this uniquely dangerous drug were criminals. This completely criminal character of the central problem gave a rhetorical head start to criminal justice countermeasures as the primary focus of governmental efforts at control.

The second important feature of the criminal justice dominance of governmental drug programs during the 1980s and 1990s is that changes in the resources and personnel that were devoted to expanding drug law enforcement and drug prosecution had long-term impacts on arrests, prosecutions, and prison terms for drug crime in federal and state systems. While the growth in prison admissions was highest in the peak years of the acceleration of the drug war, the volume of drug offense prison admissions stayed high for 15 years after the political and public opinion end of the emergency in 1995. The operational consequences of concentrating resources on particular crime issues may persevere long after the heyday of the public opinion and political priority that inspired them.

The Second Drug Panic

If the operational momentum of expansion in criminal justice drug enforcement is long-lasting, why is this chapter anticipating the possibility of a categorical shift away from the hegemony of prosecution and imprisonment in the response to drug use? The ironic cause of the current vulnerability of

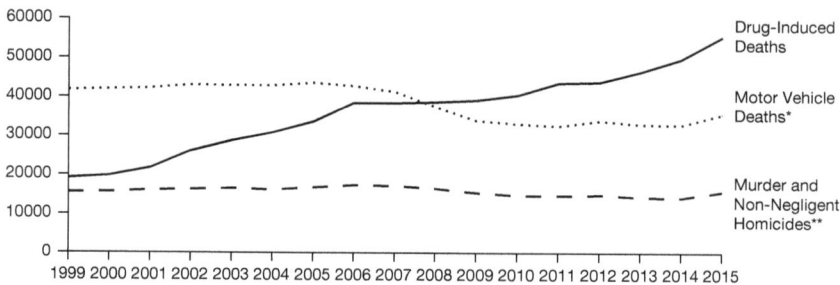

Figure 6.1 Deaths by Three Causes in the United States, 1999–2015.
Source: Federal Bureau of Investigation 2015 (motor vehicle deaths); IIHS 2019 (murder and nonnegligent homicides).

criminal justice as the primary element of governmental drug policy is not any reduction in public concern about hard narcotics as a threat to American life, but exactly the opposite. The United States is now in the middle of a major drug use emergency that in terms of its fatalities and injuries and destructive impacts on workers and the economy has much larger costs than the crack cocaine emergency of the mid-1980s. But this current drug crisis contradicts every stereotype that provoked the criminal justice drug war. Many if not most of the most deadly and addictive drug dependencies have their origin in mainstream pharmaceutical research and production. The race, age, gender, and history of criminal behavior of this generation's drug abusers are mainstream, Middle American, and working and middle class—the polar opposite of stereotypical ghetto-dwelling crackheads of the 1980s. Figure 6.1 compares the volume of overdose deaths reported in the United States with deaths from two other traumatic events, auto accidents and intentional homicides.

The count of persons who have died from drug overdoses in the twenty-first century starts high—with just under 20,000 fatalities in 1999—and then triples in 16 years to more than 63,000 deaths in 2016. The total overdose deaths in 2015 are almost triple the deaths the FBI reported in that year for criminal homicide, and substantially more than traffic deaths. The 63,632 deaths exceed the aggregate death rate from both homicide and traffic combined!

The volume of overdose deaths by 2016 is a major public health emergency by any measure. But the overlap of the drug users dying with the targets of criminal drug enforcement over the period of this growth was quite slight. To begin with, the origin of the opiate dependencies that were the precursors to many of these overdose fatalities were prescription medications such as OxyContin and fentanyl, and the origin of the victim's demand for such drugs was the medical management of pain. But supporting any opioid addiction requires criminal conduct in obtaining

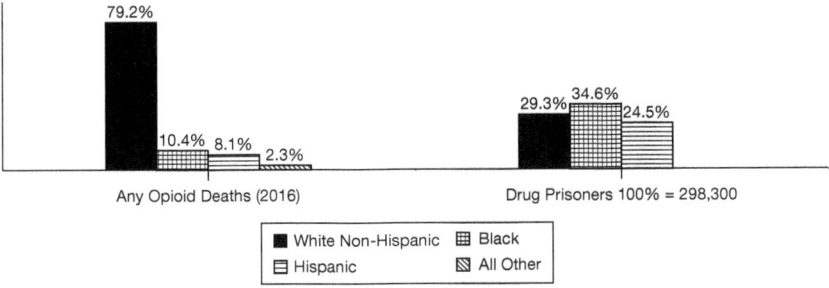

Figure 6.2 The Contrasting Demography of Drug Deaths and Drug Prisoners, 2014 and 2016. *Source*: CDC 2016 (opioid overdose deaths); Bureau of Justice Statistics 2016.

drugs fraudulently. The addicts and overdose casualties of the new opiate epidemic barely overlap with the quarter of a million inmates in prison for drug offenses. The demography of the new public health crisis is overwhelmingly white non-Hispanic, while more than two-thirds of those in prison are black or Hispanic, as shown in Figure 6.2.

The predominance of white non-Hispanic fatalities in the current drug epidemic is so great that both African American and Hispanic rates of overdose deaths are not even equal to their proportion in the general population. Yet two-thirds of the drug prisoner population are the black and Hispanic "usual suspects" for the urban police who are apparently indifferent to opiate sales and fatality. Why is the proportion of African Americans in the prison population three times the proportion of African Americans among drug deaths? Why are the eight out of 10 white non-Hispanic overdose deaths so underrepresented in drug imprisonment?

The age structure of overdose deaths is also a marked contrast with the criminogenic young. Figure 6.3 tells that story.

Overdose deaths of those under age 25 total about one-third the rate in *each* of the three older age decade groups in the figure. There is no published pattern of index crime participation remotely similar to the age profile of these fatalities. Instead, the age distribution much more closely resembles that of middle-aged patients seeking medical treatment for pain.

The geography of drug overdose fatalities is yet another demonstration of its independence from the jurisdiction and competence of criminal justice concentrations. For 2015, the CDC reported that the states with the five highest overdose death rates were West Virginia, New Hampshire, Ohio, Kentucky, and Rhode Island. The state of Utah had a death rate at over 22 that was twice the death rate in California and significantly higher than New York (13.6) (CDC 2016).

Table 6.1 explores one dimension of the current gap between criminal drug law enforcement and the overdose death rate epidemic by comparing

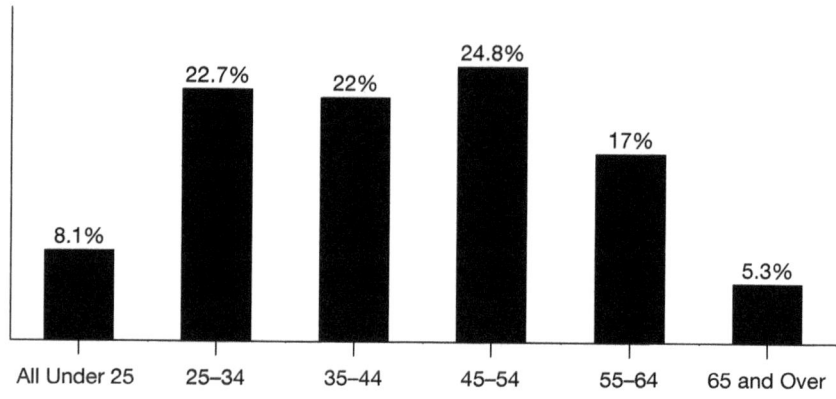

Figure 6.3 Drug Overdose Deaths by Age of Victim, 2015 (%). *Source*: CDC 2016.

Table 6.1
Distance between State Capital and DEA Office Responsible for Federal Enforcement in the State, Three Highest Death Rate States

State	DEA office	Driving distance
West Virginia	Washington, DC	363 miles
New Hampshire	Boston, MA	68 miles
Ohio	Detroit, MI	164 miles

Source: DEA Offices.

the state capital of the three highest death rate states with the location of the regional office of the Drug Enforcement Administration responsible for enforcement in that state.

Each of the three leading death rate states have federal enforcement administration located elsewhere, and the median distance between the DEA office and the state capital of the overdose problem is 164 miles. That's a three-hour drive in Ohio, but there is no indication in the prison statistics that enforcement officers spend much of their time on the interstate. There were 31 states higher in death rate than the state of Washington in 2015 (death rate 14.7 per 100,000), yet the DEA office responsible for Utah (death rate 23.4) is in Seattle, which is 843 miles from Salt Lake City. This seems a demonstration of the geography of irrelevance of criminal enforcement in the deadly current drug crisis.

But what about the trends in drug enforcement and imprisonment for these three opioid epidemic states, since the majority of all imprisonment (even for drugs) is the result of state and local government? For state government, the two most important measures of prison policy in the earlier chapters of this book were the percentage of all persons in prison by type of crime and the percentage of all prison admissions for any recent year by type of crime. The most sensitive of these measures for trends over time is prison admissions data, but the national statistics program of the Bureau of Justice statistics doesn't collect or report this data by state. However, two of the three states of special interest in this analysis reported drug offense volumes in prison admissions for 2000 and 2016. Table 6.2 reports this information for West Virginia, Ohio, and the US total.

In West Virginia, the number of drug offense admissions increases from 13.1% of year 2000 admissions to 22.7% of admissions in 2016, but both relative concentrations of drug offenders in the incoming cohort of prisoners and in the total prison population are less than the national average for 2016. Ohio, by contrast, starts with a higher year 2000 concentration of drug offenders (at 26.5%) but shows no increase in either the volume of drug offense admissions or the percentage of all new prisoners committed for drug offenses. And Ohio's 24.6% share of all new prisoners committed for drug offenses stays below the national average for 2016, the last year available.

New Hampshire provides data only on the percentage of prisoners in custody, as opposed to new admissions who are committed for drug offenses. The national average for this category of drug offenders was reported in Table 2.1 as 15.7% in 2014. For New Hampshire, the percentage of prisoners committed for drug offenses was below the national average in 2000 at 8.9% (207 of 2,323) and increased to just the national average in 2016 at 16.1% (442 of 2,738).

The trends in opioid deaths in these three states are at least an order of magnitude larger than the prison population drug offender trends shown in Table 6.2 and Figure 6.4.

The volume of opioid deaths per 100,000 expands 10-fold in New Hampshire and 20-fold in Ohio and West Virginia, a spectacular expansion that produces no strong evidence of impact in the average to below-average concentration of drug offenders in state prisons in the three epidemic states.

Table 6.2

Drug Offense Prison Admissions for 2000 and 2016, West Virginia, Ohio, and US Total

	West Virginia	*Ohio*	*United States*
2000	13.1% (204/1,557)	26.5% (6,302/23,780)	33.8% (178,418/528,245)
2016	22.7% (814/3,584)	24.6% 5,609/22,792)	25% (125,613/504,128)

Sources: West Virginia Department of Military Affairs and Public Safety 2017; Bureau of Justice Statistics 2016 and n.d. (national data for the year 2000); Ohio Department of Corrections 2000.

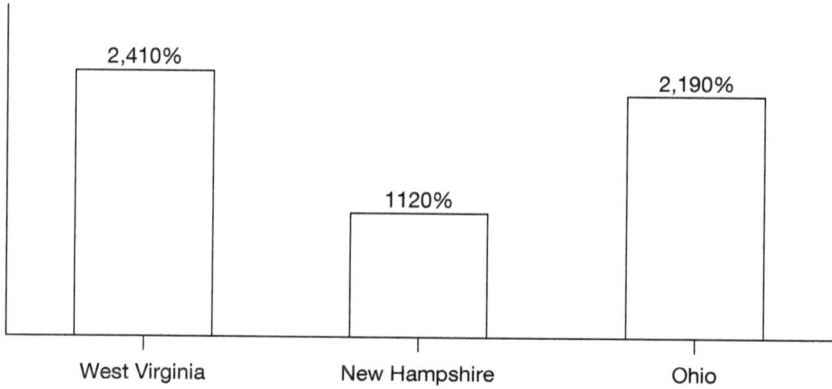

Figure 6.4 Growth in Death Rates from Drug Overdose by Opioid per 100,000, 1999–2016. *Source*: Kaiser Family Foundation 2018.

Under these circumstances, it is probably unfair to conclude that drug police and prosecutors have failed in their mission to reduce the lethal hazards of opiate overdose. They couldn't suppress the supply of legitimate medications. They have no competence in the medical treatment or appropriate drug content in the types of withdrawal that would involve the participation of persons at risk of overdose. The only major avoidable error of the criminal drug enforcement leadership has been its failure to loudly proclaim its irrelevance to effective harm reduction programs to counter the current epidemic. The criminal law is no more equipped to effectively treat the current overdose crisis than it is to cure Ebola. But why then have we invested the great majority of public resources in governmental programs that are irrelevant to our most serious current drug problems?

The Path to a Categorical Shift

Very little beyond formal withdrawal of criminal enforcement would be required before the de facto decriminalization of addicted pain patients in favor of state-sponsored withdrawal and treatment programs could be achieved. There might be reservations among drug enforcement officers and prosecutors about charging opioid abusers who violate other criminal laws to obtain contraband pain medicine. And this is a not unimportant tug of war, because almost all drug-dependent offenders will be potentially chargeable with other drug offenses—small sales, conspiracy to divert or obtain drugs with co-offenders, and the like. But the formal withdrawal of the DEA and local drug authorities from the responsibility for overdose fatalities would probably be a painless first step in a general de-emphasis of imprisonment as a drug policy.

The only alternative to explicitly abandoning the use of imprisonment as a policy priority for drug-dependent former pain patients would be a radical *increase* in the flow of new drug prisoners into federal and state prisons. The number of drug-dependent and drug-using pain treatment veterans must be well over a million (see NAS 2017, 2). And while many policy changes have been put proposed during the overdose crisis, there has been zero evident enthusiasm for incarceration of this population at risk. So the only alternative to rejecting a new and massive cohort of middle-aged, white drug war prisoners would be to acknowledge that treatments are the only just governmental priority. In this regard, what amounts to a substantial step toward decriminalization would actually be a less radical shift in policy for this group than a conventional criminal law crackdown.

The official endorsement of treatment rather than incarceration as a primary strategy for the army of opiate-dependent former pain patients will not substantially reduce the quarter of a million drug prisoners, but it should doom the primacy of prison for a very large fraction of those black and Hispanic inmates currently incarcerated for drug offenses. A substantial majority of persons locked up for drug crime in the United States have histories of drug abuse and probable drug dependency. The 2015 National Academy of Sciences panel on opioid overdoses was fully aware of the overlap between drug dependency and prison and jail populations, reporting that "more than 53% of state prison and local jail inmates meet diagnostic criteria of the *Diagnostic and Statistical Manual of Mental Health Providers* 4th ed. for drug abuse or dependence" (NAS 2017, 324). That 53% estimate in 2015 comes very close to one million inmates in prison and jail in the United States. As I will later show, the panel reporting this stunning finding did not address the issue of what should be done to address this epidemic behind bars, but it at least admitted the magnitude of the problem. Many of the drugs abused by the incarcerated are identical to those used by the opiate-dependent former pain patients, because heroin is a frequent substitute for opiate pain medications and pain drugs like fentanyl are a frequent (and very dangerous) addition to street drugs. There is also a substantial totally illicit supply of synthetics.

So the etiology and substances of abuse of the medical use addicts and the African American and Hispanic drug abuse populations are similar if not identical. The only differences between those imprisoned as offenders and those treated as victims are race, age, and geography. Even for a nation with more than its share of racial double standards, the obvious injustice of reserving prisons and jails for racial minorities should put at risk the preference for imprisoning inner-city residents dependent on illegal street drugs and in the path of urban drug police. If a shift to drug treatment included drug abusers with liability for sale and distribution offenses linked to their own drug habits, well over 100,000 current federal and state prisoners could be removed from prison.

The Asymmetrical National Academy Report

The National Academy of Sciences panel on opioid overdoses as a public policy problem was both a landmark in consideration of public policy toward drugs of abuse and an indication of the powerful persistence of inconsistent policies toward the new opioid users and the usual suspects that have preoccupied the agencies of criminal justice for the past 50 years. The panel report reports that two million Americans have an opioid-use disorder (NAS 2017, 2) and that half of 2014 opioid users self-reported illegal means of obtaining drugs (2017, 224) and 500,000 persons reported purchases from drug dealers (2017, 224).

The legal and health systems strategies the panel endorses for opioid abuse are the full range of public health approaches, including making antidotes available, regulatory and public health assessments of pain countermeasures, and drug treatment. There is in this report zero emphasis on the use of criminal prohibitions or incarceration as important tools in reducing the terrible toll from opioid overdose. In this very important respect, the 2017 panel report is an explicit and complete rejection of the national drug control strategy document of William Bennett (Office of National Drug Control Policy 1989). Where the 1989 policy rejected any public health strategies as addressing "mere symptoms" and emphasized only punishment as prevention, the 2017 panel adopts only public health strategies rather than criminal law or punishment. This is a revolutionary shift in public policy in a single generation. Why then do I call this report "asymmetrical" in its analysis and significance for policy in a book on mass incarceration?

I say this because this embrace of public health and rejection of punitive drug policy is a silent revolution that does not raise explicit criticisms of punitive drug policies and nowhere suggests that adopting the panel's priorities to the broader range of drug abuse should change drug control policies for the big city and largely minority populations who represent up to half of all prisoners according to the panel's report. The existing system of criminal enforcement and punishment is not considered in this report, and changes in a huge and (according to the panel's analysis) inappropriate government policy are nowhere mentioned. The large and expensive current casualty list of the American war on drugs is missing from the document that has clearly rejected its central assumptions.

Revolution or Evolution?

Might the United States already be in process of a transformation from legalist drug policy to an era of nonpunitive harm reduction? Optimistic observers can point to encouraging recent developments, including declines in drug crime prison admissions, the rapidly accelerating shift from plenary marijuana prohibition to legitimation of medical marijuana in half of all states, and regulatory regimes of recreational marijuana in an increasing number of states. The drug war rhetoric of the mid-1980s is now regarded as overkill by a cross section of informed opinion, and the role of drug punishments in the excessive imprisonment of racial minorities is widely acknowledged (see Alexander 2011; Forman 2017). Won't the continuation of these trends in public opinion and soft drug toleration lead naturally to declines in criminal law severity for street drug offenders?

Probably not. Drug crime prison admissions are down from the stratospheric heights of the early years of the new century but are still an order of magnitude higher than the levels that characterized the early 1980s. The volume of inmates of state and federal prisons committed for drug offenses remains clustered not far from historic highs.

The impact of marijuana decriminalization is easy to overstate because the number of persons in prison for marijuana use has never been large and because criminal charges related to marijuana sales and regulatory infractions may still be substantial. The most compelling analogy for the marijuana transition would be the impact of the end of alcohol prohibition on jail and prison usage in the 1930s, and the volume of offenders committed to federal prisons after repeal because of violation of taxing and other alcohol regulation violations was substantial. The only hope that marijuana trends might lead to smaller prison populations would be if the example of marijuana policies created momentum toward decriminalization of hard drugs like cocaine and opium, and there are no indications that this type of contagion is on the horizon in the United States.

Even the extraordinary dissonance between the Middle American opiate epidemic and the inner city street-to-prison pipeline has so far not yet brought together these two parallel universes of American drug policy. It appears that the criminal justice institutions that continue to fill the prisons remain insulated from any widespread consciousness of the double standard that is the predominant characteristic of contemporary hard drug policy. Until the current double standard becomes the central focus of concern about drugs in state capitals and the District of Columbia, the separate criminal justice drug track will probably continue to function independently, an astonishing case study of immunity based only on racially segregated personnel and institutions and a policy of "separate but equal" in the drug control context that is just as racially discriminatory and just as unprincipled as in the notorious double standard of Jim Crow public education. The primary campaign to liberate drug-dependent minority drug offenders from prison has yet to start.

Back to the Future? From Prisons to Jails

A local facility to confine persons accused or convicted of crime is most likely the very first and most ancient method of governmental penal confinement. When dungeons evolved into jails is probably a difficult and uncertain matter, but it was certainly long before anything resembling what we now call prisons (Morris and Rothman 1995, ch. 10). Harry Barnes and Negley Teeters assert that jails in England date back to the reign of Henry II in the twelfth century (1946, 490). So there is irony in any suggestion that local jails may be an important correctional innovation in the current circumstances of American criminal justice.

In part, as I argued in Chapter 3, the identification of the local jail as an "alternative to imprisonment" is a function of felt retributive necessity. The problem with identifying totally noncustodial regimes of supervision as acceptable "alternatives to prison" is that having to see a probation officer or even wearing an electronic monitor is not a severe enough deprivation of liberty or status to represent a credible equivalent to the discomfort that prosecutors and perhaps citizens demand for convicted criminal offenders. In this sense, what makes time in jail a credible alternative to imprisonment is that persons in jail don't want to be there. But what makes sending people to jail rather than prison into a correctional reform worth serious consideration?

The three potential virtues of jail as a reform alternative to prison are location, duration, and flexibility. Jails are located in the cities and towns where persons who commit crimes live and work. Prisons are distant from such communities and difficult for families to reach to visit and to maintain relationships with the prisoner. But the advantages of local settings go well beyond connections to an offender's friends and family. Jails are located in the same communities that most of their occupants grew up in and where they will be living when released. For the majority of those in custody, there are links to probation and job-training agencies they have had prior relationships with, and they will also have future service needs that should be linked to these prior contacts. All other things being equal, continuity in contacts and service relationships is less disorienting for the client and often for the service agents who value and learn from prior experience with their clients.

Even during periods of uninterrupted secure confinement, being locked up in one's community of residence is less disorienting than transplantation to an unknown environment. And then when a transition from institution to community placement takes place, a known community setting and links to service institutions that know the offender and that he knows are also an important advantage. A local jail also has relationships with court correctional supervisors and service providers who will serve and supervise the inmate when released. There is often also continuity of funding and of fiscal interest when both custodial and postcustodial service agencies are funded by the same units of government.

A second major advantage of jails over prisons is the much shorter duration of both the average and maximum term of confinement. Putting aside the open-ended periods spent awaiting a disposition in court, the definitive difference between jails and prisons in the United States is length of sentence for sentenced offenders. While prisons also readmit former inmates returned for violation of parole conditions, the general rule for the border between jail and prison for sentenced prisoners is one year as the minimum prison threshold and shorter effective sentences to be served in jail. Shorter stays are an obvious advantage from the prisoner's perspective because the loss of liberty is shorter, and that shorter exile minimizes the gaps in the interrupted relationships and engagements with community institutions. Shorter stays also minimize the negative impact of things that jails may lack in programming and medical and educational support for their residents. Three- and six-month terms of confinement are also much less likely to render the confined person completely incapable of functioning in a less totally institutional environment.

The final major advantage of local community-based and shorter-term jail confinement is flexibility in program, in security classification, and in the mix of community involvement and physical custody. The location of jails and the habituation of jails to short stays can link to a variety of different programs where confinement is short and intermittent and community resources create opportunities for work, drug treatment, or essentially nonincarcerative programs that use short stays in local facilities as a backup to punish nondangerous failures of supervision (see, e.g., Kleiman 2009). Such flexible programs can use much lower levels of confinement as disciplinary backups yet avoid being considered the toothless probationary programs that local prosecutors disdain.

State prisons, by contrast, are distant from community resources, isolated, and embrace total institutional ambiance for any programs that take place within their walls.

The contemporary jail is far from an ideal correctional setting, notwithstanding its substantial attractions. The physical facilities are often antiquated, frequently atrocious. The sheriffs and assistants responsible for governance of jail facilities are often both punitive and corrupt. Given the long and undistinguished history of jailing, there is what journalists used to call a "man bites dog" character to advocating local jails as instruments of penal reform. In substantial part, the effective use of jail facilities will depend on both administrative reforms and physical upgrades of what Hans W. Mattick called "the Cloacal Region of American Corrections" (quoted in Hawkins and Zimring 1984, 321).

The rest of this chapter briefly outlines two considerations of how jail-based reforms might be designed and implemented to reduce state prison populations. The next section uses the experience of California legislators and correctional planners as an object lesson about methods of instituting diversion to local jails and some potential problems in their implementation. The final section considers the portability of California-style diversions to local authorities under nonemergency conditions in other states.

If and when local jails replace prisons as places of confinement, those in jail can spend much less time locked up, and the periods they are detained can be combined with programs and links to community institutions. So there is a potential for a double advantage—less incarceration and a more constructive and less disorganizing period of confinement.

Diversion to Jail in California: Lessons and Limits

The major role of diversion of inmates from prisons to jail jurisdiction in California as part of that state's "realignment" in 2011 and subsequent reforms may have been in large part an accident of the limited jurisdiction of the federal court order that precipitated California's need to reduce prison population and improve crowding and medical care in the prison system. While the federal court had extensive power over the conditions of the state's prisons in *Brown v. Plata*, the jails were not the subject of the litigation or under the judge's supervisory control. So local facilities could provide alternatives to facilities in the state prison system with far less initial scrutiny (see Simon 2014). But California had also historically used local options, if not jails directly, as substitutes for prison confinement for adults (on probation subsidies see Lehrman 1975) and for juveniles (see my discussion of the CYA reforms in Chapter 5).

The resort to local government and local jails created an opportunity for constructive reforms that could serve as models for other jurisdictions. The program started with realignment and continued with two state ballot propositions that voters approved in 2014 and 2016, which introduced diversion from state to local responsibility with no fewer than five strategic features that should inform other states' efforts to substitute jail programs and local options for state prison terms:

1. Emphasis on categorical exclusions rather than discretionary options for local officials
2. Fiscal incentives to encourage local cooperation and goodwill
3. Flexible requirements for actual time served that encouraged substantial reduction in total duration of incarceration
4. No requirements of facility expansion
5. Sequential rather than a single comprehensive reallocation to local facilities

Each element in the California program made a substantial contribution to the cumulative effectiveness of the five-year result—a substantial reduction in California prison population with little or no apparent net increase in the aggregate rate of confined population in California's jails.

The Categorical Imperative

The distinction between shifting policy for an entire class of subjects from one jurisdiction to another versus encouraging the same persons and levels of government to choose nonprison alternatives when making sentencing decisions is sufficiently important to motivate the treatment of the two methods in separate chapters of this book. In the case of the California realignment, one important risk of maintaining power in county officials and local actors to choose prison or jail was the fact that local governments don't pay for prison use. There is also some incentive for local officials to ship their problem cases to distant locations and institutions. When the entire class of parole violators is shifted to county responsibility, only criminal prosecutions for new and serious changes can alter the jurisdictional responsibility of the county.

A similar distinction between categorical and local discretionary choice informed the substitution of only misdemeanor treatment in Proposition 47 for offenses that used to be called "wobblers" in California because prosecutors could choose to charge them either as felonies or misdemeanors. Of course even most categorical attempts to shift responsibility from prisons to counties and their institutional facilities leave some discretionary power in local actors—new felony charges to avoid county responsibility for parole failure and ramping up criminal charges beyond the offenses downgraded by Proposition 47. But the costs of these extraordinary efforts are not trivial, and the message carried by categorical reforms about the state government's intent is clear.

Fiscal Incentives

There are two rather different methods available to state governments to neutralize the problematic "free lunch" character to local governments of sending local offenders to state prisons, the carrot and the stick. The fiscal equivalent of the stick is to charge local governments fees when they commit offenders to state facilities so that prison is no longer a free good to those with sentencing power. But a long tradition of state fiscal responsibility makes any large-scale effort to shift to a county payment requirement for sending prisoners would be politically difficult. The only successful state fiscal charges against counties were made in the legislative plan in the juvenile system to phase out the state's expensive and long-stay California Youth Authority staring in 1996, where county responsibility for juveniles was already quite substantial. For realignment in the prison system, the state chose to use modest and unconditional grants to counties, ranging from $400 million in the first year of the program to about $1 billion in the third year (Bird and Hays 2012, 13).

The funding to county governments was, given the scale of their increased responsibility, not trivial but also modest. No county could take its funding and build large new jails with it, but the money was also given without conditions, and the counties were free to make their own judgments about whether and for what length of time their new parole failure charges would be required to be in custody. A billion dollars in unconditional funds was regarded as good news by most county governments since they were to determine when and how to spend the funds.

So there was a fiscal incentive to accept the new program but no clear reason to expand total jail facilities or even total inmate custodial counts to earn or to justify the funding. One could argue that that level of unconditional support may have produced less total confinement in the counties or statewide than higher levels of state funding would have produced.

Flexibility of Policy

The counties that inherited responsibility for dealing with parole failures were neither required nor encouraged to lock up such persons, nor for any specified term. This grant of discretionary power to county government generated two important side benefits, one to the state and a second to the county. What the state has done is free itself from responsibility if those sent back to the counties reoffend or otherwise generate visible trouble. What the counties gain is that they also are not formally accountable for how they govern parole failures. Precise data on how many parole failures are incarcerated in county facilities and for how long need not be reported, and general profiles of the number of persons in jail need not show whether confined parole failures have been jailed in space formerly used for short-sentence county offenders or whether there is instead a county preference for new offenses to be the preferred use of scarce jail space. Observers report a wide variety of patterns of total jail confinement (see Loftstrom and Raphael 2015) in different counties. And because of the county-level autonomy to decide details of parole failure policy, the state is freed of any responsibility to account for or report the impact of its policy on confinement patterns.

A final characteristic of the California program that helped reduce total confinement levels in the state was the lack of any requirement or expectation of constructing new facilities. The funds provided to county government were for programs rather than the bricks and mortar of expanding physical facilities. There was thus no incentive to the counties to expand institutional capacity or, for that matter, to expand the number of persons locked up in existing facilities.

And while the absence of an expectation or requirement of locking up parole failures now governed by the counties can be characterized as the state staying neutral on confinement policy, there is in reality a tilt in the financial consequences of the new state funds. The out-of-pocket costs of incarceration are much higher per prisoner than is supervision in the community. With no required custody or additional funding linked to confinement, there are more substantial financial rewards to the counties in minimizing levels of confinement.

The final strategic principle that minimized the resistance of local governments to larger correctional caseloads and smaller levels of subsidized confinement was the decision to introduce several different reforms sequentially rather than all at once. The realignment responsibility for parole violators came in 2011. The additional responsibility for a substantial number of persons who had to stay in county custody because Proposition 47 had eliminated the power to prosecute them as felons was not added to the caseload of the counties until 2014. And the additional increased authority to return life-term prisoners via parole release was not added to the new scene until November 2016 brought passage of Proposition 57. So each new increment of penal reform could be integrated into county expectations and practice before additional changes were put forward.

Missing Pieces for a New Category

The six years of increased use of county facilities in California are by no means a completed model of how jails can be used as instruments of successful categorical criminal justice reform. Some of the California legislation is misguided—as when the current law would permit long sentences to be served in county jails. If there is a serious intention to tolerate four- or five-year terms of confinement in the vast majority of jail facilities in California (or any other state), the lack of appropriate space, programs, and physical facilities in county jails would make the practice objectionable. Indeed, the lack of fit between current facilities and long periods of sustained confinement suggests that the sophisticated California planners meant the possibility of that long a jail sentence as a bluff. A five-year term of secure confinement in a local jail for a property crime may have been designed as a theoretical sentence that no conscientious judge, prosecutor, or sheriff would approve. The problem, however, with such policy bluffs is that sometimes a local actor may call the bluff!

A second shortcoming that many local governmental actors would identify in the current California prison-to-jail program is the lack of adequate funding for local governments to carry their responsibilities, but this is a tricky issue. Putting too much state money into local jails and correctional facilities might encourage the expansion of jails.

If more funding is to be made available to local institutions, the best way to invest it is to promote programs of mixed custody and service that could also divert felons to community corrections, and programs of community treatment like Project Hope, which use brief jailings as a sanction. Halfway houses that combine night custody with work release or drug treatment or both for persons convicted of serious street crimes are also promising.

The antiquated dungeons that serve as county jails in many American cities can serve as the launching pad for creative community-based programs that mix custody with community life. But the more successful such programs become, the more they should be detached from their antiquated launching pads.

A successful transition from distant prisons to urban residential facilities linked to community institutions can start in our current urban jails, but should never aim to stay in those spartan institutional origins.

7

Restructuring the Governance of Imprisonment

THE INSTITUTIONS OF criminal justice in the United States serve a wide variety of different purposes, both symbolic and operational. One purpose of all criminal punishments is to denounce and stigmatize the culpable offender. And this need to reinforce the condemnation of the criminal behavior may in much criminal law theory require penal confinement, as when, in the terms of the Model Penal Code analysis, any lesser sentence than imprisonment would unduly "depreciate the seriousness of [the] offense" (American Law Institute 1963, Sec. 7.01(1)(c)). A wide variety of penal sanctions may also contribute to crime control by either incapacitating a confined or otherwise restrained potential recidivist or by reinforcing the credibility of the threat of punishment to other potential offenders. Other purposes of penal sanctions can include the generation of income to government or restitution to victims from monetary sanctions, and potential public safety benefits from compulsory therapy or restriction of privileges. There are also, as discussed in Chapter 3, two types of symbolic value that the imposition of harsh punishments can provide: as a measure of adversarial success for prosecutors and police that tells them they are the winning side and as a reassurance to crime victims that the system values their interests more highly than of criminal offenders (Zimring, Hawkins, and Kamin 2001, 223). With so many competing purposes and with important counterweights to punishment such as public cost and excessive severity, every choice of punishment is a compromise—a mix of different types and levels of purposes of punishment. The notion that a single level of punishment can be an optimum for all the purposes and limits relevant to punishment is an obvious absurdity. Instead, a mix of different purposes and limits produces an outcome that probably shouldn't and cannot represent the ideal punishment for a single purpose.

There are two important consequences that should follow from recognizing the plural and imperfect calculus of penal justice. The first is that different decision-makers can come to different conclusions on appropriate kinds and amounts of punishment. And the second is that different types of institutions will have different priorities in making punishment decisions.

With respect to imprisonment, the branches of government and levels of government that have both interests and special competence in setting conditions of imprisonment and terms of imprisonment include local criminal justice systems, the branches of state government that administer and pay for prisons and administrators, and professionals who supervise and treat offenders.

The fallacy of singular punishment decisions under these circumstances, the notion that there is a single time, place, and institutional actor who should be given the power to set all terms of punishment, is problematic, as the recent history of American criminal justice demonstrates. When sentencing reform advocates attacked parole board power to determine when indeterminate penal terms should result in release from prison, they often assumed that deferring to point of decision-making about release until late in a prison term could only be justified if data on whether a prisoner had been rehabilitated was valid and properly used (Messinger and Johnson 1978). So when the rehabilitative basis for determining prison release was rejected, most of the power to determine how long an offender would serve in prison was shifted much closer to the time of criminal conviction and to the locality of the crime's commission and the criminal trial. The trial courts that became the main arena for determinate sentences were close in time and place to the crime and thus more focused on the role of a prison term or its absence as the symbolic currency of denunciation.

And the attempt to constrain local prosecutors and judges by specifying a fixed term for offenses based on previous average sentences was not effective for a variety of reasons. Prosecutors can and did charge multiple counts of the main offense and also add the aggravating circumstances (e.g., gun use or prior record) the legislation permitted. The initial fixed terms were often elevated by later legislative action. And the "fixed terms" used in legislation such as California's 1977 determinate sentencing system were only for those who were sentenced to prison in prior periods, often a minority of those convicted. So expanding the proportion of each type of conviction that resulted in a prison term was not regulated or restrained (Zimring 1983, 112).

The effort to generate early fixed terms often pushed power to local officials who were not concerned by cost and were preoccupied with retributive and adversarial concerns.

When prison terms of any substantial length are a punishment choice, any single time for determining the sentence is probably wrong, and close proximity to the time of conviction and the adversarial system compounds the problem.

The Uses of Mythology

Many of the single-standard proposals for criminal punishments that emerged in the reform dialogue of the 1970s are best viewed as innocent mistakes made in good faith (see, e.g., Von Hirsch et al. 1975 and Twentieth Century Fund Task Force 1976). But the more recent state laws marketed under the label of "truth in sentencing" were cynical attempts to use typically inflated nominal sentences issued at trial in states with traditions of parole or administrative reduction as if these were a gold standard of the appropriate actual term to be served. The strategic aim was simply to increase prison terms during an era—the 1990s—when public attitudes were particularly angry. This was also the decade when imprisonment levels seemingly defied criminological gravity, because sharp declines in serious crime volume were associated with continuous and substantial growth in prison population. In many ways, the persistence of prison growth in the decade after 1995 was the most stunning evidence yet of the capacity of political pressure and the priorities of local actors to maintain penal expansion that was not connected to increase in either crime or drug use.

Is There a Perfect Punishment Decision-Maker?

In the 51 different criminal justice legal structures in the United States—50 different state systems and the federal criminal justice system—a wide variety of different institutions share power in determining types and terms of sanctions. Figure 7.1 provides a brief description of how these institutional actors differ in terms of the level of government where they operate, the primary focus of their decisions, their concern about the costs of imprisonment and jail, and when in the history of the crime and its punishment decisions are usually made.

Figure 7.1 profiles current institutions that participate in determining criminal punishments on four dimensions that influence the type and severity of punishments imposed on convicted felons. The critical dimensions for these institutions include the level of government where the agency is located (state versus local), the focus of institutional decisions (individual cases or system distribution of sanctions), the concern of institutions about the public costs of punishment (none, some, or substantial), and the timing

A. Levels of Government

<u>State</u>
Sentencing Commission
Parole Board
Prison Administration

<u>Local</u>
Criminal Courts
Prosecutors
Judges

B. Focus of Decision

<u>Individual Case</u>
Criminal Courts
Parole Board

<u>Systemic Policy</u>
Sentencing Commission
Legislature

C. Concern about Costs of Confinement

<u>None</u>
Criminal Courts for Prison
Prosecutors

<u>Some</u>
Criminal Courts for County Jails
Parole Boards for Prison

<u>Substantial</u>
Sentencing Commission
Legislature
State Executive
Prison Administration

D. Timing of Decisions

<u>Close to Crime and Trial</u>
Criminal Courts
Sentencing Commission

<u>Later in Prison Terms</u>
Parole Board
Prison Administrators
Executive Clemency

Figure 7.1 State and Local Institutions Determining Imprisonment.

of decisions about prison release (close to the time of the offense and trial versus later in the course of substantial prison terms).

Every institution used in punishment decisions has its own priorities and biases. Criminal courts are local and close in time and space to the communities where crimes were committed. The local and close-in-time tends to put more emphasis on both punishment terms that communicate denunciation and sanctions that are sufficiently severe so that prosecutors feel their adversarial advocacy has been recognized and rewarded. In almost all criminal court settings, the local nature of criminal courts biases outcomes toward higher levels of penal severity, a larger proportion of prison sentences, and a tendency toward longer sentences.

Local criminal courts also focus on individual cases and individual punishment without paying much attention to what Figure 7.1 calls the systemic impact of individual sentences to prison on the scale of imprisonment. And because there are often no cost consequences to prison sentences on local governments, the local criminal courts often have no direct incentive to worry about the public costs of long prison sentences.

There are, however, some circumstances where local power has been associated with lower levels of custodial confinement and punitive bite, but not in criminal courts. When California's statewide system of juvenile institutions—the venerable California Youth Authority—was radically downsized beginning in the mid-1990s in favor of county-level institutions and the power of county juvenile court judges and correctional administrators to determine a juvenile's length of stay, the net effect of larger local control was a reduction in the number of young offenders confined on any given day and a substantial reduction in the average length of incarceration (Krisberg et al. 2010). But at least three important aspects of this California story separate it from the normal biases of local control. First, the juvenile justice system invests juvenile court judges, probation staff, and local correctional administrators with much more power than is found in criminal justice systems, and prosecutors therefore have much less power in juvenile courts. Second, the predominant ideology in juvenile justice favors short or no secure confinement and returning young offenders to community settings. And the final distinction of the California reforms was a set of financial incentives that generated costs for excessive use of the state facilities and provided funds for counties that the counties could keep without expanding custodial facilities or usage.

There are two further aspects of local punishment decisions in the criminal justice system that bias outcomes toward state prisons—the timing of trials and penalty setting close to when and where the crime occurred and the traditional lack of concern within county governments about the costs of imprisonment that are paid by other levels of government.

The final characteristic of sentencing power in local criminal courts has both advantages and disadvantages for restraint on use of prison—the focus on individual rather than systemic perspective. Local criminal courts make decisions one person at a time, and that individual focus can inject some notice of the individual offender's interests as a human being into the sentencing process. On the other hand, the complete lack of any systemic perspective when local courts sentence when combined with lack of concern about costs means that imprisonment may not be regarded as a scarce resource. This may not be balanced by focus on the individual interests in the offender when mechanical processes like plea bargaining remove from judges and prosecutors any real awareness of the human individual at the receiving end of a punishment decision.

Parole boards have only limited jurisdiction for setting prison release at the back end of prison sentences, so that only felons who serve prison sentences come within their powers. For persons sent to prison, however, they can correct two of the biases that are problems with sentences generated by criminal courts, the lack of concern about costs that happens because local government doesn't pay for prisons (see Gartner, Doob, and Zimring 2011) and the preoccupation with condemnation and adversarial effectiveness that are byproducts of the relatively early timing of sentencing decisions by criminal court. In theory, the parole decision is focused on individual prisoners rather than systemic concerns, so that issues like crowding, correcting disparities in the sentences served by persons guilty of the same crime, or staying within state correctional budgets should not be major influences on parole board behavior, but there are periods in documented history when systemic concerns create broad policy shifts in parole release. Gartner, Doob, and Zimring (2011) show a deliberate use of parole release to reduce California's prison population by more than 20%. So while the formal jurisdiction of parole boards is to make release decisions and supervise life in community settings in individual cases, systemic criteria and policy goals are not unknown.

But the limiting of jurisdiction to cases that result in prison terms is a very severe limit on the capacity of parole authorities to discover or correct disparities between those sent to prison and those spared imprisonment. Even in eras of extraordinary penal severity, most criminal justice systems will send less than half the defendants they convict of crimes to state prisons.

A state administrative body called a *sentencing commission* has a much broader jurisdictional reach and a more substantial capacity to discover sentencing disparities. A sentencing commission is a special agency, usually located in the executive branch of state government, that constructs standards for typical punishments that judges in local government are expected to impose when particular combinations of current offense and criminal record come before the court. These typical expected sanction statements are called "guidelines" and may in some systems be a reviewable basis for appeal if a sentencing judge fails to sentence a defendant within guidelines (American Law Institute 2018). But the typical sentencing commission does not have authority to adjust individual prison terms.

The statewide sentencing commission is a creature of state government that is expected to use systemic policy considerations in formulating policy and is usually expected to take issues such as prison costs and crowding into account when formulating guidelines. Like judges and prosecutors, the sentencing commission enters its guideline expectations early in the history of particular criminal cases. But unlike sentencing judges, the guideline for a sentence is not focused on individual offenders but on where particular classes of offenders fit in a hierarchy of criminal harms deserving punishment. A sentencing commission either must argue for imprisoning or excluding from imprisonment very large blocks of criminal offenders or must leave substantial discretion to individual judges and prosecutors to decide between prison and community supervision in individual cases. The use of firm rules for large blocks of offenses and offenders may invite overpunishment and puts enormous weight on a sentencing commission's moral intelligence. Delegation of wide discretion to individual judges and prosecutors risks disparity and arbitrary choices between prison and community supervision.

One further disadvantage for sentencing commissions is their temporal location early in any sentencing process that may produce long prison sentences. The sentencing commission is thus removed from individuals serving long prison sentences both by the lack of individual focus in the way it frames its rules and by the timing of the rules it issues—before the fact of sentencing even when the offender may serve 15 or 30 years in prison and decades removed from the standards that set his term.

Three Wrongs Make a Right?

This review of institutions and principles has served notice on my answer to this rhetorical question. Given the multiple goals of criminal punishment and differential perspectives of existing institutions, any attempt to vest total power to determine punishment in a single institution or a single point in time generates substantial errors of justice. And the primary focus of many reform efforts in the states on local sentencing of judges and prosecutors systematically led to overpunishment by eliminating the perspectives and cost-consciousness of statewide decision-makers. It was, in this sense, a prescription for mass incarceration.

And any single institutional shift to counterbalance the biases of criminal court sentences—parole boards or traditional sentencing commissions—is not sufficient. Parole can adjust excessive prison terms in their late stages but can't address the inequities generated by decisions to imprison or not imprison at the front end. Sentencing commissions can play important roles in guarding the "in versus out" decisions made by criminal courts to protect against unnecessary imprisonment as an adversarial reward to prosecutors or a symbolic reassurance to crime victims. But unless the general rules of sentencing commissions lead into selective discretion by individual judges, the products of sentencing commissions will have to choose between overpunishing or underpunishing in administering in-out guidelines.

The most appropriate mix of sentencing powers that address the legacy of overimprisonment employs statewide sentencing commissions, individual sentencing judges and prosecutors with substantial in-out decision discretion, and parole boards to correct the excessive length of prison terms that serve primarily symbolic purposes when criminal courts and legislative structures produced them decades earlier.

Sentencing adjustments need to simultaneously pursue systemic goals of reducing imprisonment and individual goals of penal justice. Obviously, the coordinating of local sentencing authorities with commission-issued guidelines and parole board individual sentencing reductions is a task of substantial complexity. To restate the rhetorical slogan in the introduction to this section: "Three wrongs can make a right but only if they are integrated very carefully." And the tools for careful reform must be more useful than verbal formulas. The next section is my attempt to use the statistical findings on prison admissions trends outlined in Chapter 2 to identify strategic priorities for each segment of the tripartite legal framework for sentencing reforms.

There is one final and important power that some branch of state government must exercise, and that is to determine how many prison beds a state should maintain. The issue of prison capacity is a critical issue of penal policy, but it is not an issue of a criminal sentence for an individual offender. It is instead a precondition that individual sentencing decisions and even sentencing guides must accommodate. If this power is given to a sentencing commission, it is a dramatic expansion of the commission's authority. An alternative arrangement would be for another state executive branch agency to make decisions about the bedspace in the prison system and for the state's sentencing commission to observe those limits when determining sentencing guidelines.

Without fixed limits on the scale of imprisonment in state government, the administration of criminal justice operates in anarchy. Each individual criminal sentence is issued without regard to its impact on the institutions of confinement and supervision. The aggregate supply of penal resources can only be determined when all individual sentences are added up. The local actors who make these decisions have no reason to regard prison spaces as a scarce resource. In a very real sense, no agency of government at any level has made a principled decision on the size of the government's penal responses and the costs that should be incurred.

Data-Driven Reform Priorities

How much change in prison use would eliminate half the extra prisoners added since the 1970s? Just as prison admissions were the principal cause of the rapid expansion of total prison population, the reduction in prison admissions must be the major effort of sentencing reform, and the strategic center of shifting prison admissions is the sentencing commission and a sharp restructuring of sentencing guidelines. Figure 7.2 profiles the annual national volume of prison admissions for two years during the prison expansion, the level of admissions during 2015, and finally, a plausible target level of prison admissions to hold a prison and jail population at or under 1,100,000 by 2050 and the prison population per 100,000 at or under 300 per 100,000 for the United States.

The three historical admission totals from recent history are significant indications of the appropriate target for maintaining a million-inmate nation. The 1990 number 461,000 happened with the prison population already at 300 per 100,000 and on its way up to 411 by 1995. So that 460,000 admissions per year would pretty clearly push prison growth up and away

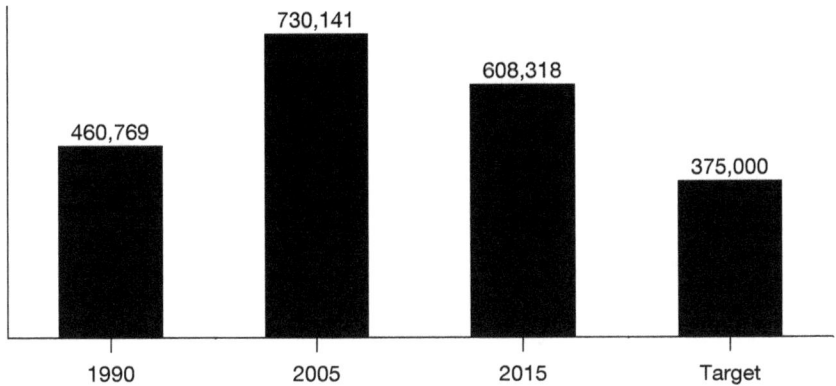

Figure 7.2 Prison Admissions in 1990, 2005, and 2015 and Target.
Source: 1990, 2005, and 2015 are from the Bureau of Justice Statistics, "Prisoners in the United States" for those three years; the "target" estimate is mine.

from a stable 300 per 100,000. The 608,000 admission total for 2015 is the best measure of the status quo in prison admissions so that number is where state agencies commissions trying to facilitate declines would have to begin to cut to drive down admissions. My best guess at the number of admissions that could maintain a stable prison population of 300 per 100,000 would be about 375,000 per year in a total US civilian population close to its current levels. The margin of error in estimates of a steady prison population of 300 per 100,000 is very large—stability at that level has never happened in the recent past (or at any other time in American history).

There are two indications that reducing prison admissions to 375,000 would be a very difficult target to achieve. First, it has been more than a quarter-century since there was any year so few admissions. The 1990 level of prison admissions was already more than 85,000 greater than Figure 7.2's target for stability at 300 per 100,000. Even more daunting is the gap between 2015 US penal policy (at 608,000) and the target level of admissions (375,000). The 233,000-person drop in prison admissions from 2015 is almost exactly twice as many *additional* declines from future policy as the total drop by 2015 in the decade since the all-time high in admissions in 2005. How could this be done?

Chapter 6 suggested some broad policy shifts that would help. The first and most substantial drop in prison admissions would come from policies that explicitly divert drug offenders with current or recent histories of hard-drug abuse into community treatment programs. The impact that this would have on the more than 200,000 drug offenders admitted to prisons each year would depend on how the guideline for eligibility dealt with the effect of either a "possession for sale" (usually a presumption based on amount possessed) or drug sales charge. Neither quantities larger than those indicating daily use of drugs nor petty retail sales (often the means to fund personal use) should undermine the assumption that the drug-related crime was an outgrowth of the defendant's drug dependency. Drug enforcement personnel and prosecutors often argue that these types of possession and retail sales make the offenses too severe to merit community treatment. But a guideline that includes petty sellers and potential sales quantity of drugs if the defendant manifests a need for treatment would divert perhaps 100,000 of the more than 200,000 drug cases into community treatment and might reduce drug-related admissions by 70,000 or 80,000 per year. Some of the failures in community treatment from this group might reappear as prison admissions after failure, so the net reduction in prison admissions would be less than the initial number diverted.

A second large group of attractive candidates for exclusion from prison are candidates at the margin between short prison stays and shorter jail time or community probation. The massive increase in prison admission for virtually every offense group that was documented in Figure 3.1 includes large numbers of persons with a second or third conviction for auto theft, burglary, or non-life-threatening assault as well as the great mass of drug offenders just discussed.

But a guideline to avoid prison in marginal cases here is preaching only forbearance rather than treatment; the alternative to prison custody might be either shorter stays in jail or often simply giving a low-severity offender one more chance than has been characteristic of felony prosecution during the massive increase in imprisonment commitments. Each state sentencing commission that undertakes this type of guideline would have to study its own sentencing history and then draft examples of both the old and new cut lines, and some cooperation from local prosecutors and judges would substantially assist in the successful administration of this kind of effort. If there is resistance to this sort of effort, feedback from the sentencing commission to local courts and prosecutors with statistical targets for reduced prison terms as well as substantive guidelines might prove necessary.

Even then, criminal court judges and prosecutors are reluctant to examine statistical targets as part of sentencing decision-making, at least traditionally. Would statistical prison commitment targets help? It would be more than a mild irony if the same levels of data-processing sophistication that have generated my suspicion that the prosecutor management systems helped launch the surge in prison admissions might now play a role in reducing prison admissions to less stratospheric levels.

Is there a data-based method available to identify the impact of policy changes on prison admissions? One way to estimate how much room might be available for reducing the volume of persons sent to prison from various offense categories is to examine the extent to which specific crime categories expanded over the years after 1970. Figure 7.3 provides a rough measure of the growth in prison use by showing the percentage increase between the 1970 volume of prison commitments for each of seven nondrug

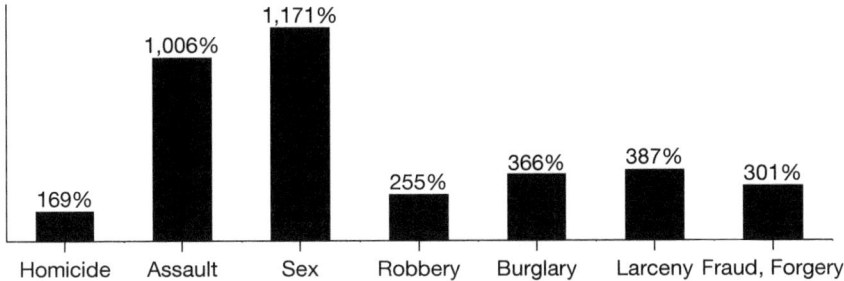

Figure 7.3 Percentage Growth in Prison Admissions, 1970 to 2006, Seven Crime Categories. *Source*: Bureau of Justice Statistics, "Prisoners in the United States," 1970 and 2006 (data produced from Figure 3.1).

crime categories. The volume of arrests for the three most prison-prone offenses (homicide, rape, and robbery) actually declined by 12.2% from 1970 to 2005, while the volume of arrests for the three less prison-prone offenses profiled in Chapter 2 went up 42%. The net effect of this set of arrest volume changes is probably to expect about a 15% increase in total prison admissions independent of policy changes, although the unknown impact of the growth in assault arrests generates a large margin of error for what should happen in a constant policy environment.

What happened in the national totals over the 35 years is reported as percentage increases in prison admissions by crime type in Figure 7.3.

Because the growth rates reported in Figure 7.3 are of prison admissions rather than the number of offenders in prison at any given time, the growth is in commitments to prison independent of the length of prison sentences, so this is the most appropriate indication of the offense-specific elasticity on the way up in prison growth and also presumably the potential reduction from changing policy directed at moderating prison population. One major offense category—drugs—is not profiled in Figure 7.3, but its expansion from 10,000 to more than 200,000 would have shown a 26-fold increase, yet another strong indication that drugs provide a major opportunity for very substantial decreases in new prisoners, perhaps as many as half of the extra 230,000 prison decreases that will be necessary to meet the target of an eventual million-inmate United States. But where will the other half of reduced commitments be found?

If Figure 7.3's history of admission growth is a good measure of potential declines as well, the major opportunities are distributed differently than much of the rhetoric about reductions in imprisonment has suggested. The rhetorical case for reducing prisoners emphasizes, in addition to ending the war on drugs, the use of nonimprisonment dispositions for nonviolent offenses. Violence and the wide variety of crimes with sexual behaviors and motives are rarely mentioned.

But examining the offenses where the changes in prison policy created mass incarceration produces sharply different conclusions. To be sure, the growth in nonviolent crimes has been extraordinary—more than tripling for theft and for fraud and forgery. The usually nonviolent crime of burglary also sent four times as many convicted offenders to prison in 2005 as in 1970. So there is plenty of room for moderating imprisonment policy for these offenses to reduce prison numbers.

But the growth rate in imprisonment for crimes of assault was more than twice as great as any of the property or other pure violence crimes, a volume of increased prison commitments that is more than 10 times the volume of assault imprisonments during 1970. And the vast majority of that epic growth was the result of changing policy. The rate of homicide in the United States was higher in 1970 than in 2005 and the volume of citizens killed was pretty close to even with the population expansion (16,692 versus 16,000). So the volume of life-threatening assaults—best measured by variations in the volume of deaths—was also within 5% of the total for 1970, yet the increase in prison sentences for nonfatal assaults was up by just over 1,000%. But what sort of nonprison sentence might best suit the range of behaviors in criminal assault? The answer is certainly not fines, because the government is rarely a directly interested party.

Investigating the reason why the assault category resulted in so few imprisonments in 1970 (only 3,000) provides important indications of appropriate nonprison sanctions. The distinguishing characteristic of most criminal assaults is the fact that victims and offenders usually know each other and often also live in the same communities. These are the community and social overlaps that make both personal restitution programs and restorative justice interventions seem positive and promising without diminishing the seriousness of the injury or the offense. And for domestic violence, the creation of shelters and programs to support separation and separate households can probably provide as much or more recurrence prevention as nonsustained incarceration.

As was mentioned in Chapter 3's analysis of changing levels of prison admissions, the sex offense category included in 2005 some offenses that were not part of imprisonment statistical records—such as child pornography—and other offenses where rates of incarceration have increased substantially, such as child molestation. That said, the 12-fold increase in prison admissions makes careful policy analysis of the different types of crimes and offenders in this category an important undertaking.

And the prison admission statistics also provide important guidance on the very different patterns for different offenses in the sex category. Forcible rape is a traditionally serious crime with high rates of imprisonment (and also long prison sentences). It is also the subtype of sex crime with the smallest growth rate in prison population. Two typically nonviolent but otherwise quite dissimilar sex offenses are child molesting and child pornography. Child molestation is nonviolent but predatory hands-on sexual abuse of minors, most often young children. The age difference between offender and victim makes the offense criminal independent of any element of physical force. Child abuse concerns and prosecutions have increased substantially since the 1980s, but there is little reason to believe that the actual rate of victimization has increased since the 1990s, and some studies, using family reports of incidents of victimization, have suggested that the rate of sexual abuse of children has declined (Finkelhor and Jones 2004). With very low rates of reporting to authorities a chronic condition until late in the twentieth century, a dramatic expansion of reporting and prosecution and punishment is not unlikely in recent decades.

There is also a sharp difference between the imagined and the actual character of child molestation that may be of importance in fashioning alternative, non-incarcerative punishment for child molesters. The prototype of the child molester the public most fears is a predatory stranger happening across a potential victim who is not someone he knows. The great majority of adults reported to have molested children are family members or acquaintances of either the adult custodians of the child or of the child (US Department of Health and Human Services 2018). The prototypical offender in the public mind is a pedophile on the prowl for juvenile victims and not otherwise sexually active or involved. The actual child abusers do not conform to that pattern. The prototypical child molester is thought to be a multiple offender with an almost inevitably high likelihood of repetitive acts of child predation. Actual recidivism rates of hands-on child abuse are rather low.

The high rates of friend and family relationship provides some potential for these offenses, like assault crimes, to respond to restorative justice interventions and not infrequently even family therapy. And the lack of explicit sexual pathology and modest levels of recidivism also may indicate community supervision in many circumstances where victim families are supportive.

A final category of sex offense with growth in the rate of imprisonment is the production, distribution, or possession of child pornography. Federal and state enforcement efforts in child pornography cases have generated very large increases in prison admission and often also very long prison sentences. Possession and peer-to-peer emailing of child pornography is in no direct way a further physical harm to the subject of the pornographic film or video. Yet it can produce prison sentences in the federal system longer than those for drug sales (Zimring and Harcourt 2014, 715). With so little additional harm to the child victim from possession and small scale distribution, the severe punishment imposed seems a product of assuming that the defendant is also at high risk of hands-on child molestation and other predatory criminality with child victims. The data on such risks are of poor scientific quality and do not provide strong evidence of strong predatory histories or future risk. The possession and peer-to-peer sharing of child pornography seems a currently overpunished category of crime where long penal confinement should be drastically reduced.

Parole or Prison Administrative Release

The exclusively prospective focus of most sentencing commissions leaves substantial problems associated with individual cases and particularly with lengthy prison terms. Reducing disparity in prison sentences and releasing offenders who have been punished enough are important functions far removed from the traditional rationale of parole in the rehabilitative rhetoric of midcentury correctional policy. There are three serious problems associated with long prison terms that require substantial power to alter individual penal terms or conditions of confinement: sentencing disparity, changed circumstances, and the low productivity of penal confinement of older offenders serving long terms.

There are ample opportunities for prosecutorial and judicial decisions to produce widely different prison terms for offenders with similar criminal backgrounds and current offenses. Even though the traditional objection to parole discretion to release was framed around its potential to generate disparity, the removal of any review of long prison terms generates its own substantial problems of similar crimes generating very different terms of penal confinement. Because the exclusively prison-based jurisdiction of parole boards excludes most punishment decisions, the power and jurisdiction of sentencing commissions is much more substantial than any prison-based system, but the two sets of different types of authority might fit nicely together into a comprehensive system of disparity assessment.

A second problem with sentencing reviews that begin and end at the front end of terms of confinement is that the circumstances of persons serving long sentences change dramatically over the decades that are the frequent temporal currency of the most severe American prison sentences. Prisoners get older and much less physically and sexually aggressive in ways that reduce dangerousness independent of traditional concepts of rehabilitation. Older prisoners get sick or weak or otherwise dependent. Prisoners acquire skills and priorities widely different from their earlier lives. And the anger and need for condemnation that required long penal terms as a symbolic underscoring of the community's loss and anger have abated in most cases. Only the most superficial theories of penal desert would require that terms of required confinement cannot change as time passes.

If the potential injustice of not allowing changed circumstances to alter prison terms provides one justification for adjustment of long prison sentences, so too does the waste of penal confinement on low-priority threats to public safety. The fine irony of lengthy prison terms is that the cost of incarceration reaches its peak just as its productivity for public security diminishes toward zero.

While the powers and functions of sentencing review late in prison terms are of importance, the ideology and claimed competence of those who are responsible for such decisions are less pressing issues. The more practical and administrative the orientation of a prison release authority, the better. The less tied prison release is to elected political officials, the better. And there is no reason in the practical politics of the adjustment of long penal terms to require any finding that the original prison term was excessive or that the prisoner has "paid his price" for the criminal harm he inflicted. It is more important to remove such reviews from the zero-sum assumptions that frequently motivate long prison terms than to claim that the authority to authorize releases is a relitigation of penal desert.

The Strategic Focus of Penal Legislation

At the root of mass imprisonment is a failure to impose an appropriate strategic focus of legislation in the administration of penal confinement. One problem was the concentration of punishment power in levels of government that had no financial stake in minimizing the cost of a penal system. A second problem was the unprincipled claim that early and locally based penal terms had a priority claim to just punishment.

The appropriate role of a state legislature and federal Congress in criminal punishment is strategic rather than comprehensive. What Morris and Hawkins called an "administrative law of crime" (1977, 15–16) evolved in the generation after 1970 to reinforce most of the vectors that produced explosive growth in prisons. What is required in most state government now is a shift not in the form of sentencing governance but rather in its accountability and perspective. What is needed is not a rejection of the administrative law of crime but rather its radical improvement.

The conceptually easy part of this legislative agenda is taking out the trash—removing the distortions deliberately inflicted by gambits like truth in sentencing, mandatory minimum sentencing regimes like three strikes, and firearms enhancements like 10–20–30 in California. The life without possibility of parole criminal sentence makes no operational sense in a decently functioning government and it is a terrible risk of excess even in governments that can't be trusted with discretion to release (Zimring and Johnson 2012).

More complicated will be aligning the authority to choose between carceral and noncarceral sentences and designing financial incentives for local governments that minimize carceral costs. There are two ways to align financial incentives and the powers to punish. The states can reward county reductions in commitment, or they can punish county over use of state prisons. Rewards were used in the California prison realignment with evident success. And fiscal punishments for sending nonserious juvenile offenders to the California Youth Authority also seem to have been successful (Krisberg et al. 2010). The choice of emphasis may depend more on the relative health of state government finances than on judgments about the relative effects of incentives versus disincentives on the behavior of local governments.

A further complication relates to which level of government should be encouraged to maintain confinement capacity or to reduce it. The California realignment was an overdetermined case history in this regard because only the prison system was covered in the federal court order that necessitated the downsizing of prison confinement.

When governments are free to choose between local and state penal facilities, there is often a trade-off between location and habitability when comparing the consequences of a choice of target for downsizing. Local jails are usually much closer to the communities where inmates are confined, but as the last chapter emphasized, the physical facilities and availability of programs and some work opportunities inside the walls may be better in prisons.

Two Additional Legislative Concerns

There are two further issues that could be the subject of federal and state legislation that to date have not been an element of legislative policy: the scale of imprisonment and conditions of confinement. The California realignment created a de facto prison population target for state policy but without the population target becoming an explicit goal in the realignment legislation. But why not attempt numerical goals of prison population as an explicit aspect of a state's punishment policy? And certainly a preference for community-based institutions and for work and work-training programs could become a part of the legal framework of criminal justice without changing the focus of legislation from strategic to tactical.

Toward a Fully Administrative Law of Imprisonment?

The sentencing commission in its Minnesota structure is closer to being an administrative agency of sentencing than any other current institution. It is at the appropriate level of government—the state level, where prisons are paid for and administered. It is the appropriate branch of state government for an administrative agency—the executive branch (though some commissions are designed as hybrids of the executive and judicial branch). In the case of the federal sentencing commission, there were two reasons for it to embrace judicial members and power and call it an "article three" judicial agency—as a sop to federal trial judges who were losing autonomous sentencing power and as an endorsement of the view of the sentencing commission's first architect, Judge Marvin Frankel, who imagined that the determination of guidelines for sentences could best be viewed as a collective variety of the jurisprudence of criminal sentencing. Notwithstanding their debt to Judge Frankel, the sentencing guidelines produced by the sentencing commission bear no resemblance to any sort of jurisprudence, but rather adopted the structure and affection for quantitative aspects of offenses and offenders that could be tied into sentences in a pattern similar to the much-resented federal parole guideline grids.

The less "judicialized" Minnesota Sentencing Commission is closer to an executive branch administrative agency and has a better reputation than the federal commission (see Parent 1988 for a description). But this version of a sentencing commission lacks three types of power that would create even stronger influence on sentencing choices in state systems:

1. Power over individual cases including prison release
2. Authority to distribute financial incentives to local government in patterns similar to the payments to counties in the California realignment program discussed in Chapter 5
3. Explicit authority to review patterns of local criminal justice outcomes

INDIVIDUAL OFFENDER PRISON RELEASE

The guidelines issued by sentencing commissions are both prospective and collective. In the federal sentencing guideline system, the design was to have guidelines instead of a parole release authority, although there was no logical inconsistency in these two procedures coexisting. To date, there are no sentencing commissions that also administer prison release determinations in individual cases, although, here again, there is no reason why individual review late in a long sentence is inconsistent with also creating prospective sentencing guidelines. To the extent that in-prison behavior (discipline, program completion, substance abuse organizations, etc.) is a relevant standard, traditional parole boards or prison administrators might have the comparative advantage over sentencing commissions, but concerns with disparity and with re-evaluation of appropriate sentence length for individual offenses as offenders age in prison seem clearly to be a comparative advantage for a Minnesota-style sentencing commission, as is prison crowding. Health conditions, senility, and personal needs inconsistent with prison confinement are best identified by prison administrators, but their dispositional consequences could be best determined by either parole or commission personnel.

FINANCIAL INCENTIVES FOR LOCAL GOVERNMENT COMPLIANCE WITH MINIMIZING COMMITMENT

No sentencing commission has direct control over money that could be used to reward compliance with either reducing confinement in state institutions or using local institutions of custody or supervision as substitutes for programs of state confinement. There are precedents for trying to create fiscal rewards for local drug treatments (see, e.g., California's Proposition 36 in 2000) or local control for shifted populations in the later California realignment (see the third section in Chapter 5), but states have not yet issued sentencing commissions a checkbook to administer such rewards. Should they?

If the appropriate model of an expanded sentencing commission is as a state administrative agency, financial rewards and punishment might be powerful and appropriate tools. Obviously, no executive branch of a state government can either print its own money or generate its own system of enforceable financial sanctions. So legislative authorization is required, and legislation that authorizes financial assistance to local governments is much easier to generate than the authorization of financial penalties.

If it is assumed that fiscal rewards are appropriate instruments for reducing state prison populations, there remains the issue of what office or function in the state executive branch is best suited to administer aid programs designed to reduce local use of state prisons. The three alternative places in state executive government are (1) the executive office of the governor, (2) the sentencing commission, or (3) some other branch of the state executive. The executive office of the governor has two areas of related expertise—detailed knowledge of the totality of the state budget and deep knowledge of the specifics of local governments. What the governor's office probably doesn't have is (1) much time to devote to this small part of the massive financial reality of state governance and (2) detailed knowledge of correctional caseloads as well as the likely consequences of different incentive systems. This job requires an expert on prisons and jails. Is there another office in state government with detailed knowledge of criminal sentencing and correctional caseloads? The two possibilities are the state department of justice or office of attorney general or the state department of corrections. The department of corrections knows a great deal about prisons and about prisoners but very little about local governments or about the costs and character of local sanctions and treatment programs. The state attorney general or department of justice might know more about local politics but will start with no knowledge of incarceration costs and alternatives unless it has already administered an aid program to local governments.

If a sentencing commission has been seriously involved in calculating the prison and jail consequences of various programs and has studied trends in use of both state and local facilities over time, it would seem the best prepared to design and administer state financial assistance to local governments cooperating in reduction in prison numbers and levels of aggregate state and local secure confinement.

How much fiscal assistance should be available? To the extent that local governments have to spend to absorb and program offenders they had not been responsible for, a good rule of thumb would be to provide counties with at least twice as much state money as the state government believes they should spend on the new local responsibilities. If the California realignment is any guide, even this will still save the state substantial funds from what would have been spent for extra prisoners.

INTERGOVERNMENTAL AUTHORITY

The key issue in creating a large role for state sentencing commissions is the competition for sentencing power between local criminal justice actors and institutions and the central state government. For the work of a sentencing commission in generating and enforcing guidelines, the formal contest is between the commission and the local judges who issue sentences. But the real power in local sentencing is prosecutors and plea bargaining. The appropriate channel for adjudication of whether a sentence fits or permissibly deviates from guidelines is a review of the individual sentence by a state court of appeals. That is a long, slow, and one-at-a-time retail review process in which one of the real parties to the dispute (the prosecutor) is not identified as a primary contestant. It never works well in the United States.

The natural way to expand a commission's powers and focus on the real parties of interest is state legislation, but the most significant incentive for prosecutorial compliance is the presence of a fiscal incentive for county governments and the credible prospect of its withdrawal.

In the long term, and at a deeper level, the issue is weakening the motivation as well as the power for prosecutors to choose sanctions. The long-term objective of sentencing law and practice to reduce massive overincarceration should attempt to weaken the proclivity of prosecuting attorneys to regard severe punishment as a measure of their success in the adversary process. This is an issue of legal power and financial incentive but also an issue of the hearts and minds of local prosecutors throughout the United States. This chapter has considered some modification of prosecutorial and local judicial powers. The next chapter will consider whether prosecutorial attitudes might also change.

The Uncertain Pace of Change

This chapter has considered changes in the state systems that regulate criminal sentences and imprisonment that should reduce the scale of imprisonment. Citizens concerned about the current numbers of prisoners in the

United States will assume there is a need for substantial reforms in the governance of punishment in state and federal systems. But there is in fact no sense of emergency about criminal sentencing in the United States and little reason to suppose that legislative reforms in criminal sentencing systems will be either swift or substantial in the next few years.

The inertial characteristics of criminal justice governance in the United States should not be underestimated. The federal system means that there are 51 different governments with distinct legal systems of punishment. Some will change, but many others will not. Some changes will facilitate larger levels of control by central authorities, but other systems may reinforce local controls. The quarter-century after 1970 that created the imprisonment boom was a relatively rare period when policy in all 51 governments in the federal system changed radically in the same direction. The multiple centers of government policy produce different directions of policy in most eras, and this is a natural restraint on the pace of change in the national aggregate.

There are two other current conditions that tend to slow down the pace of governmental change—vested interests and the absence of any strong sense of crisis or emergency in criminal sentencing and criminal justice. The obvious incentive for local officials who now hold power in criminal sentencing is to expend efforts to retain their powers. And local judges and prosecutors have substantial political influence to use in attempting to retain their powers. The usual counterweight to the power of vested interests when legislative change succeeds is a sense of emergency or crisis that motivates reformers to spend time and effort responding to a significant problem. But there is no acute sense of emergency in evidence in either the federal or state criminal justice systems. Crowded and expensive prison systems are a problem in the United States, but they are a chronic problem rather than presenting as a crisis that must be resolved for the system to function. Close to 2 million persons in prisons and jails is a stable condition of American life in the twenty-first century. The governments and social systems in the United States may have already developed a capacity to tolerate that level of confinement.

8

Prosecutorial Power and Adversarial Focus

THERE IS A curious contrast between the levels of governments and the governmental agencies that were the principal focus in the chapters that discussed how prison populations exploded in the United States after 1972 and the first two chapters in this book's analysis of methods of reducing prison populations. The level of government that was dominant in increasing rates of prison admissions was local government, with county prosecutors and judges as the primary agents of change. And yet it was state legislation and state-level sentencing guidelines that preoccupied Chapters 6 and 7. Why is that? Since the powers of local government were the main ingredients of the explosive increases in imprisonment, why shouldn't efforts to change local prosecutorial preferences and policies be the most important starting points for reform efforts? If the hearts and minds of county prosecutors were the change agency on the way up the penal staircase, why isn't changing the hearts and minds of local prosecutors the central arena for reforms?

One reason why the agencies and concerns discussed in Chapters 6 and 7 are important keys to imprisonment rates is the distinction between prosecutorial preferences and prosecutorial powers. One important method of altering prosecutorial discretionary power to put people in prison is to create a series of what Chapter 6 called categorical exclusions from using imprisonment as a primary sanction—drug-dependent offenders and parole violators and property offenders being important examples. Another method of sharply reducing rates of imprisonment for specific offences is creating sentencing guidelines with firm preferences for programs with local custodial or noncustodial content. And changing the economic incentives that made confinement in state prisons free of cost for county government makes prosecutorial preferences less attractive to judges, mayors, and local legislative and budgetary authorities. All of these strategies can reduce rates of imprisonment by changing the power of prosecutors without major shifts in the hearts and minds of local prosecutors.

But wouldn't the deconstruction of mass incarceration work better and faster if local prosecutors become less attached to seeing levels of imprisonment as evidence of their professional accomplishment in the adversary system? The obvious answer to this question is yes. Changes in prosecutorial perspective would generate swifter reductions in the volume of prison admissions and the number of confined prisoners and generate much less contention in coordinating criminal punishments and their aftermath in the criminal justice system. But how might this be done? And what sorts of changes in prosecutorial attitude are realistic goals?

The Myth of Adversarial Justice

In the televised world of Perry Mason, every criminal case rushes to climax in an adversarial criminal trial (complete with jury). This was never close to the reality of American criminal justice and will never be in the future. The vast majority of criminal charges that lead to convictions are the result of negotiations between prosecutors and defense attorneys that produce guilty pleas by the defendant and some agreement between the lawyers on the punishment that the prosecutor will recommend to the sentencing judge, a recommendation that is frequently accepted by a judge who has not been involved in the dispositive negotiations.

If the evidence of defendant's culpability is strong, the most important tug-of-war between prosecutor and defense attorney will typically be about the type and duration of punishment. The reason defense lawyers prefer noncustodial sentences and try to minimize the duration of any term of secure confinement in prison or jail is because that is the strong preference of their clients. But why might prosecutors wish to put criminal defendants in prison, and why might they prefer longer terms to shorter terms? And why might this type of preference of prosecutors be so much more important in the United States than in many other fully developed nations?

There are three linked factors that shape a prosecutor's influence on sentences of penal confinement and on its duration: the preferences of prosecutors for types and terms of punishment, the importance of punishment types and terms to prosecutors, and the power of prosecutors relative to others in the system. The shorthand labels for these three dimensions are the *preferences* of prosecutors for punishment, the *priority* of punishment to prosecutors as opposed to other objectives in a case, and the *power* to influence punishment choices.

Most prosecuting attorneys in the United States prefer severe rather than lenient punishments for most criminal defendants. They think many offenders deserve severe penalties, not just those they prosecute. That is one reason why they choose to pursue careers as prosecutors. Prosecutors tend to believe offenders both deserve punishment and that sanctions like jail and prison reduce crime volumes by incapacitation. But just as these attitudes about offenders deserving punishment and requiring incapacitation might set American prosecutors apart from other American lawyers, these characteristic prosecutorial attitudes will also likely be shared with prosecutors in most other nations, certainly including Japan, the United Kingdom, Canada, Australia and South Korea (see, e.g., Johnson 2002 for Japan). Further, these characteristic prosecutorial attitudes have been a consistent distinguishing feature of criminal prosecutors in the United States for a long time, yet punishment levels were relatively stable prior to 1970. And criminal prosecutors in France and Argentina and South Korea are also much more likely than other citizens in these nations to believe that criminal punishments are appropriate and effective. That's why they became prosecutors and those are also the attitudes of most of the other prosecutors they work with. Yet rates of imprisonment are not either extremely high nor increasing at a rapid rate in most nations where prosecutorial preferences are similar to those we encounter in Columbus, Ohio or Seattle, Washington. So the common general bias of prosecutors in favor of punishment is nowhere a sufficient condition for sharp increases in rates of imprisonment.

Then perhaps what explains the American penal explosion is changes in prosecutorial power over case disposition in the period since 1970. In part, the notion that there has been a recent expansion in prosecutorial power is plausible, with rising citizen concern about crime giving prosecutors more political power in state and federal legislative bodies to draft new laws and pass them. The high salience periods for citizen crime concerns were the first half of the 1970s and then the late 1980s and early 1990s. And certainly the early 1990s was a period of sharply punitive changes in state laws (Zimring, Hawkins, and Kamin 2001, ch. 9) and federal crime legislation (Windesham 1998). But there are many nations that have extremely powerful prosecutors, such as Japan (Johnson 2002) and South Korea without levels of imprisonment that are extraordinary.

The explosive growth in US imprisonment was associated with one attitudinal characteristic of local prosecutors that is distinguishable from prosecutors simply preferring high levels of punishment. American prosecutors in recent decades have cared about what punishments were imposed in the cases they administered and they have often cared deeply. This dimension of prosecutorial attitude, what I have called the prosecutor's priorities for punishment as an element of case outcome, is a critical part of the software of modern prosecutors in the United States that both distinguishes the most recent era from earlier times and sets American prosecutors apart from other prosecutors even in adversarial systems.

Of the two features of prosecutorial attitudes, the preference for substantial punishment and the deep importance given to punishment outcomes, the general support for severe punishment is a long-standing and almost universal characteristic of prosecuting attorneys and most police. It goes with the territory of criminal law enforcement careers, inevitably in adversarial legal regimes but quite frequently also in inquisitorial systems. Most prosecutors would resist efforts to question the professional legitimacy of their having pro-punishment orientations, and not without reason. In an important sense, asking a prosecutor to suppress his personal preference for severe criminal penalties seems like asking a leopard to change its spots. If these nearly universal prosecutorial attitudes are sincerely believed, there may be nothing inappropriate or unprofessional in these views. And prosecutors are firmly on the right wing on matters of penal policy in a large number of nations where the actual distribution of penal sanctions is not extremely harsh. If prosecutorial law-and-order sentiments caused mass incarceration, it would be an international epidemic rather than a phenomenon that is largely confined to the penal systems in the United States.

But converting prosecutors in the United States from hardline sentiments may be unnecessary as well as difficult. As long as dominating the actual selection of punishments is not a major priority of prosecutors, the lawyers who represent the state's interests can retain their personal affection for hardline policies without imposing these preferences on criminal sentences. In this view, it was the importance that district attorneys attached to obtaining harsh punishments in cases they handled rather than the hardline sentiments that generated the upward trajectory in imprisonment in the United States. The motives for this were discussed in Chapter 3. A successful attempt to soften the insistence of prosecutors on prison sentences might best be framed as delegating more power to judges, to sentencing commissions, or to correctional authorities to choose the type of sanction in individual cases.

A Tale of Two Nations

This chapter will review the limited evidence now available about punishment priority as a contributing cause of high rates of imprisonment and then discuss methods of changing these attitudes. The focus on prosecutorial attitudes will begin by referring to the emerging attention legal scholars are devoting to comparisons of prosecution in different national systems and then discuss the attitudes and impacts of prosecutors in two neighboring nations with adversarial criminal justice systems—Canada and the United States. After that short and speculative comparison, the next section of the chapter will contrast "bottom up" versus "top down" strategies for reducing the punitive priorities of American prosecutors. The concluding analysis in this chapter addresses the question of whether prosecutors should be assigned the primary blame for the penal explosion after 1970 or whether other branches of government are also at fault.

We are just beginning to accumulate the empirically based comparative study of criminal prosecutors in modern nations. Detailed comparative studies of criminal justice are an important source of information about the different types of governance of criminal justice systems as well as the common problems they face (see Langer and Sklansky 2017). The reason for this brief comparative exercise is more specific—the search for clues about why local prosecutors drove an unprecedented expansion in prisoners in the United States.

The international comparison I'm using is between Canada and the United States during the 35 years after 1970. There are three reasons Canada is an important case comparison with the United States in the era after 1970. The first important foundation for comparing Canada and the United States is the substantial similarities between the two countries in both crime trends and criminal justice systems. Both nations have criminal justice systems that are based on English law and are adversarial systems in which prosecutors represent the government's punitive interests. Both nations are also federal systems in which most criminal cases and most prosecutors are part of the provincial or state systems. These two neighboring nations also had rather similar trends in crime over time in the half-century after 1960, although Canada's homicide rates are much lower than those in the United States. Over the period after 1961, homicide rates in the two nations went up, then down, almost in lock step (Zimring 2007, 132, Figure 5.23) and both nations had very similar crime declines in the 1990s (Zimring 2007, 107–34). Figure 8.1 shows yearly homicide trends, starting each nation at 100 for its 1961 rate of homicides.

But the second important reason why the comparison between prosecutors in the two nations is of potential value is the sharp contrast in

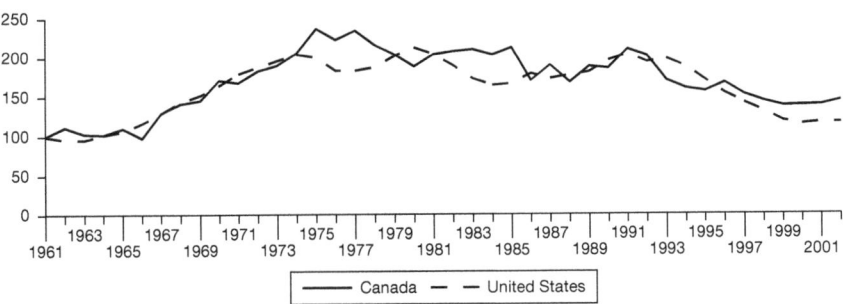

Figure 8.1 Homicide Trends, United States and Canada after 1961.
Note: Canada, 1961: 1.28 = 100. United States, 1961: 4.8 per 100,000 = 100.
Source: Reprinted from Zimring 2007, 132, Figure 5.23.

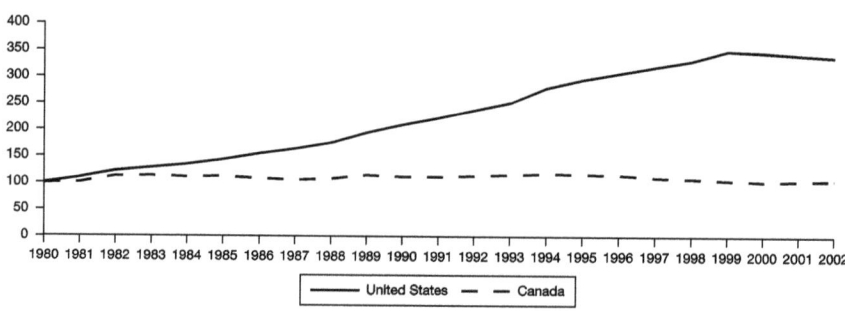

Figure 8.2 Trends in Imprisonment Rates, United States and Canada, 1980–2002.
Note: 1980 = 100. *Source*: Zimring 2007, Figure 5.17.

imprisonment trends that resulted from these similar crime trends in both nations in the 1980s and 1990s. Figure 8.2, also taken from an earlier study of the two countries, shows the contrast in imprisonment trends over the 22 years after 1980.

The figure normalizes the base rates of imprisonment in both Canada and the United States at 100 for 1980 to focus on the changes over time. Over the 20 years after 1980, the rate of imprisonment increased a total of 4% in Canada, while it tripled in the United States. With similar crime trends, there obviously had to have been substantial differences in how the two systems reacted to crime. This makes the comparison between prosecutors in the two systems a potentially rich source of clues about the causes of difference in imprisonment outcomes.

The third advantage of a comparison with Canada is good information on the system of selecting and promoting Canadian prosecutors and one remarkable study of prosecutorial attitudes toward criminal sentences. The two structural differences between local prosecutors in the United States and the Crown attorneys who prosecute criminal cases in Canadian provinces are (1) provincial rather than local control of the selection of prosecutors who are responsible for criminal prosecution in local courts and (2) much less involvement of prosecutors in electoral politics at any level. All staff attorneys involved in local offices are selected by the provincial ministry of justice. The chief officer of each provincial ministry in Canada must stand for democratic election in one parliamentary district in a province but is then appointed to the cabinet position of minister of justice by the premier of the province. This shift from local to statewide governance and the more remote linkage of the lawyers who work in Crown counsel offices to democratic elections create a much stronger self-concept of the prosecuting attorney as a civil service job tied to the interests and concerns of government as a whole rather than to the people and concerns of a particular community.

In 1985, the Canadian Sentencing Commission conducted a survey of prosecutors and defense attorneys across Canada. The commission asked two related questions about their views of criminal punishments: the quality of justice in the courts before which they appeared, and the quality of justice in courts across Canada. Figure 8.3 shows the national pattern for answers to both questions.

Since these lawyers know the questions are being asked by a government agency, any bias in the answers would probably inflate the proportion who would answer "about right" to tell the agency what they think it wants to hear.

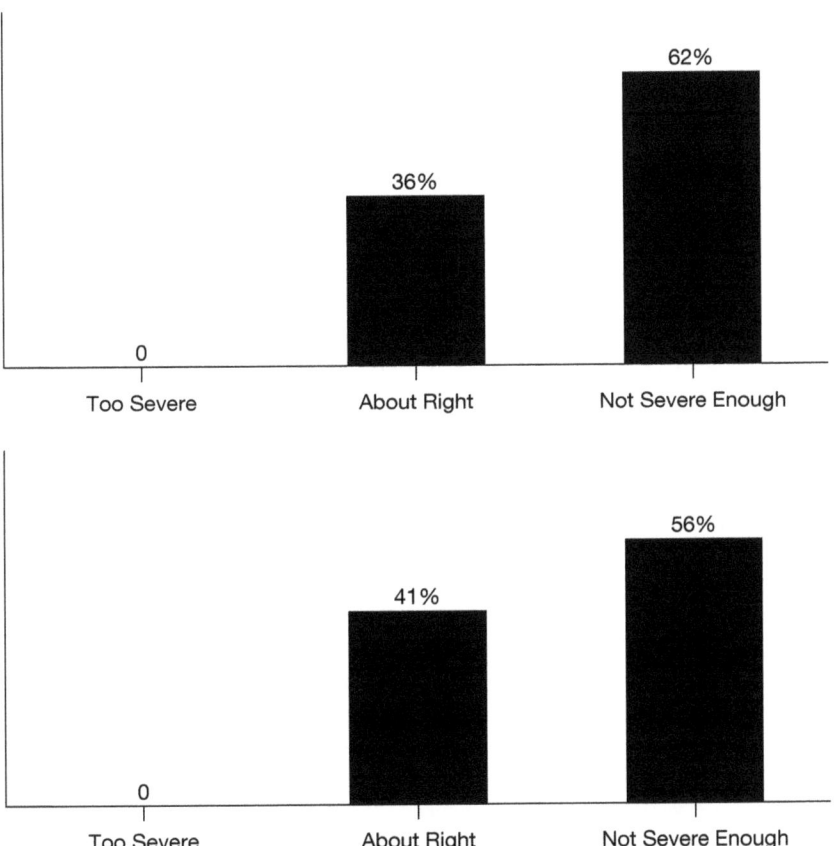

Figure 8.3 Responses by Crown Attorneys to Question on Severity of Sentences. *Note*: The questions asked were "In general, would you say that the sentences handed down by the courts before which you appear are . . ." (N = 352) and "In general, would you say that sentences handed by courts across Canada are . . ." (N = 329). *Source*: Landau 1988.

But only 36% of the Crown attorneys think the punishments in their courts are about right, while 62% of the prosecutors think the punishments are "not severe enough." This complaint about where these lawyers practice (62% "not severe enough") is slightly more pronounced than the same lawyers guessing about Canadian national patterns as a general matter. But in both questions, the pattern of answers shows what I have been calling a "hard line" bias—a clear majority of Crown attorneys think the courts are too lenient with criminal defendants, and not a single Crown attorney of the more than 300 asked thought punishments were too severe either in their courts or in the nation. The severity tilt is overwhelming (62% to 0%) but there is no way of estimating the size of the gap between what happens and what prosecutors think should happen. There is also no way of comparing these Canadian results with the views of local prosecutors in the United States since no such survey has ever been reported in the United States.

But this disagreement in sentiment measured in 1985 did not create any serious tensions despite the fact that Canadian rates of imprisonment declined in the years after 1985. One plausible reason why the sentiments of Canadian Crown counsel are not an evident problem for Canadian sentencing trends is that Canadian prosecutors are not deeply concerned about levels of punishment, and might not see penal outcomes after conviction as a direct reflection of their professional achievement in representing the state's interests. In part, this is a reflection of more limited power in the system, but it also probably reflects an attitude of being part of a governmental system where judges and administrators should have power. I suspect that a Crown attorney would not regard being in total control of criminal sentencing as a professional aspiration.

The lessons to be learned from examining the attitudes and impacts of prosecutors in Canada are mildly encouraging for American reformers. There is evidence that prosecutors in adversarial systems can adjust to sentencing outcomes that are far more lenient than the pattern in American state and local government and less severe also than the personal preferences they report. But some of the circumstances that produce this toleration will be hard to duplicate south of the border. While Canadian local prosecutors are linked to elected government officials in Canada, they are appointed by provincial officials rather than elected local prosecuting attorneys. The ministry of justice is not exclusively devoted to criminal prosecution but covers a wide variety of legal concerns and legal services.[1] This gives the minister of justice both a wider variety of objectives and interests and a much more administrative perspective than a political actor elected solely to prosecute criminal offenders. And the provincial rather than local governmental structure also puts the minister of justice further away from reactions to a

---

[1] See Ontario Ministry of the Attorney General, www.attorneygeneral.jus.gov.on.ca.

criminal offense in a specific community and closer to levels of government where administrative perspectives are quite common. The minister of justice is further removed from the local police chief and closer to those who administer courts and prisons.

But there is no plausible strategy available to transplant the currently local offices of district attorneys in the United States to the state level of government. How, then, can the analysis of this comparison be used to facilitate reform in circumstances where prosecution of crime will remain a function of local government?

One promising tactic is to shift some power to determine punishment from prosecutors to other agencies of government. As was mentioned in Chapter 7, one important aspect of sentencing commissions that have been introduced in American state government is that they shift power from county to state levels of government for elements of criminal sentencing policy that are subject to sentencing guidelines. This is also one effect of expansions of parole authority to release state prisoners. Thus, careful designs of sentencing reforms can shift power from local to state government even where prosecutorial powers remain a local governmental function.

Bottom-Up versus Top-Down Reforms within Prosecutorial Offices

The extent to which the attitudes and behavioral choices of prosecutors can change over the coming decades will have a major influence on how extensive a drop in commitments to prison will be possible and how quickly it can happen. This short analysis discusses two related issues about strategies of changing prosecutorial behavior: what must be changed and how can reformers best promote the most strategically important alterations in prosecutorial behavior.

The Lester Maddox Theory of Prosecutorial Reform

Lester Maddox was a reactionary segregationist whose resistance to desegregating public accommodations resulted in his election as governor of Georgia in the 1960s. The deplorable conditions in Georgia's prisons were provoking protests and lawsuits that Governor Maddox opposed. What brings this sad chapter of American history into the present discussion was Lester Maddox's response to the prison protests: "What our prisons need," he said, "is a better class of prisoner" (McPhersson 1984).

What I am calling the Lester Maddox theory of prosecution reform is reform strategies that seek to change the attitudes and punitive preferences of the men and women who are the front-line troops of criminal prosecution in the United States. The central priority in this approach is changing the hearts and minds of working prosecutors. The argument for a focus on the attitudes of practitioners emphasizes the tremendous amount of discretionary power that individual prosecutors possess. The second chapter in this book showed one obvious impact of this discretionary power by noting that the US prison population more than doubled in the 15 years after 1973 without any major legislative changes in most state governments. If the wrong kind of discretion can double prison population, why can't the right kind of decentralized discretion cut prison populations in half? And why shouldn't reform effort focus on fostering that kind of attitude change?

Changing the hearts and minds of prosecutors one at a time is what can be called a "bottom up" reform strategy of reform, a combination of a legal ethics curriculum and a course in empirical criminology to create what would be, from the reformers' perspective, a better class of prosecutor in thousands of county criminal courts in the United States.

But bottom-up strategies of attitude change are probably both unnecessary and inefficient. It is much easier to alter power relations and incentives in criminal case dispositions than to change hearts and minds, and this is best achieved by changes in legislation and administration. Within the office of the local prosecutor, there are the same administrative and budgetary officials one finds throughout modern governments. The county prosecutor is an administrative officer as much as a legal officer, and his or her office requires a budget that is governed by officials in other parts of county and state government. If counties face financial costs when prison commitment rates go up, these consequences will be brought to the attention of the district attorney by legislators and budgetary officials in county government who face these financial consequences.

The chief prosecutor in county government is also an administrative officer who creates standards and incentives governing the performance of the individuals and groups in his or her agency who generate case dispositions. If prison sentences are treated as a scarce resource instead of a free good in the evaluation of line prosecutors by their supervisors, this can quickly influence the types of negotiated plea agreements and thus the rate of prison admissions.

The political economy of top-down reform for local prosecution is a simple two-step process. Step 1 is changing the rules and incentives that local governments face as a consequence of their use of state imprisonment. Once local governments face these consequences, local prosecutors can expect that their success or failure on managing the case outcomes produced by their staffs will be reflected in future budgets and in their ability to gain other powers and concessions in the give and take of local government.

And a motivated chief prosecutor is a powerful administrator. Criminal convictions will remain an important measure of prosecutorial success, but prison sentences might no longer be regarded as an unqualified good once they carry costs. The same prosecutorial management systems that may have helped launch the imprisonment boom in the 1970s may also be useful in bringing mass imprisonment under control, if appropriate rules and incentives are invoked.

Just as Canadian prosecutors have learned to live with penal outcomes that are less severe than they would prefer in the cases they litigate, so too can assistant district attorneys in Syracuse and Chicago and San Diego, if the incentives for promotion and professional recognition can be appropriately adjusted. The power to generate appropriate incentives and evaluate individual performances is the responsibility of administrative leadership. And the strategic importance of this power may have implications for the moral obligations of top-level prosecutors, an issue I will revisit in the next section.

Blame It on the Prosecutors?

Most of the explosive growth in rates of imprisonment and jailing in the generation after 1970 was produced in state and local government, and the most prominent moving parts in the process that increased incarceration were felony convictions and prison admissions engineered by plea-bargaining local prosecutors. For those who regard mass incarceration as a failure of democratic government, is it appropriate to assign most of the fault to the prosecutors who were the proximate cause of the prison boom?

There are two reasons why it might be wrong to single out prosecutorial aggressiveness also as the moral failure responsible for the imprisonment catastrophe: the very different responsibilities of different branches of government that participated in the prison boom and the important role at many levels of government of culpable failure to act that exacerbated the scale and the squalor of the great American lockup.

In adversarial systems of criminal justice, public prosecutors are supposed to emphasize the guilt of those they rightfully accuse of crime and the importance of punishment in the achievement of retributive and utilitarian objectives. Just like the Crown counselors surveyed in the Canadian study reported in Figure 8.3, prosecutors in the United States are much more likely to support strict punishments than other lawyers or the average citizen. That's why they wanted to become prosecutors. Other officials and other legal institutions are supposed to counteract the hard-line sentiments of prosecutors to bring balance to the system—trial and appellate judges, public defenders, probation staff, prison administrators, and state governors.

Why blame only prosecutors for acting just as we expect prosecutors to act when so many other actors and institutions failed to control a growth process that was out of control?

One analogy that emphasizes the relationship between expected behavior and moral fault concerns the predatory behavior of coyotes when sheep ranchers leave their herds unprotected by security fences. The farmers want to argue that only the coyotes are at fault since if they had not attacked the herd, none of their flock would have perished. But the moral fault in this account is more complicated than the issue of cause-in-fact. The coyotes in my story were behaving just like coyotes always behave when sheep are freely available, and this could not have come as a surprise to the sheep ranchers. Fences were expensive but available. Who was most at fault?

The parable of the coyotes and the sheep ranchers involves a second contrast of substantial importance to considering the moral fault for mass incarceration, what I wish to call the distinction between active and passive modes of morally problematic behavior. A rather primitive argument the ranchers might use to deflect the blame for the loss of their animals is that they have done nothing wrong because they have done nothing. But most moral systems are willing to condemn knowledge that harm will result if the actor fails to perform a preventive act when that knowledge is combined with a duty to act and the capacity of action to prevent harm. And four decades of epic prison crowding in the United States was the result of an epidemic of culpable inactivity in state government and in prison administration.

The most dramatic success story in control of prison population in recent years was Chapter 5's report of the realignment of California prison jurisdiction that eventually also involved changes in penal law and parole eligibility. But all these governmental actions came only after a federal court ordered the state government to sharply reduce the number of inmates confined in California's prisons. Prior to Judge Henderson's order in *Brown v. Plata*, the photographic evidence of fantastic crowding of beds into public spaces in prisons had not inspired any meaningful reform efforts as the situation worsened. The federal court's finding of outrageous crowding and substantial increases of inmate deaths as a result of inadequate medical attention were substantially ignored by three California governors and an army of correctional administrators (Simon 2014, chs. 4 and 5). While local prosecutors and judges continued to send thousands of prisoners a year into the California prison system, the correctional and executive branches of California state government knowingly tolerated conditions of neglect and crowding that even a relatively conservative US Supreme Court found beyond the pale of civilized penal confinement (Simon 2014, ch. 6).

And the morally repugnant record of executive branch inactivity was probably closer to a common standard of executive state government in most states than the creative emergency remedies that animated realignment in California when the US Supreme Court rejected California's appeal in 2011.

* * * * *

None of this, to be sure, absolves local prosecutors of fault in the American imprisonment epidemic. What it suggests, instead, is that a balanced analysis of the moral responsibility for mass imprisonment should implicate a wide array of public officials in many branches of state and local government. Governors and state correctional officials had better information on the character and the consequences of mass incarceration. Prosecutors had more power to influence the inflow of prisoners but less information about the systems they were feeding.

Just as I have argued that the best strategy for reform in local prosecution is a "top down" program in which chief prosecutors alter the incentives and methods of evaluating staff. I believe that the more substantial measure of blame for the current circumstances of local prosecution also should be assigned to top administrators, and for the same reason. The moral failures in state and local prosecution are, in large measure, management failures. For decades, the prosecutor has been in charge of what Norval Morris and Gordon Hawkins called an administrative law of crime, negotiating penalties and guilty pleas and managing large numbers of cases through pipelines that are only incidental in their judicial content. But they have all too often ignored the administrative character of their work and failed to develop sophisticated strategies for managing criminal penalty allocations. My major complaint about chief prosecutors in the current era is not that they are organizational managers but rather that they are not good managers who can administer levels of penal confinement as scarce public resources that should be carefully distributed to serve public safety without excessive offender suffering. A truly sophisticated administrative law of crime can lead to a parsimonious and humane penal system. Excessive punishment is evidence, among other things, of bad management.

Afterword

Explaining the Limited Estimates of Decarceration

MANY WHO HAVE read through the prior eight chapters of this analysis may be troubled by two puzzling aspects of the book. The first is a procedural eccentricity in the presentation of my thinking. The most sustained discussion of future trends in American prison and jail populations was presented in Chapter 5, at the end the analysis of the historical patterns in the first half of the book. But that analysis came before the detailed outline of different methods of reducing prison and jail numbers. Chapter 6 analyzed excluding traditional categories of prison-eligible offenses from potential imprisonment. Chapter 7 outlined important changes in the governance of criminal justice, and Chapter 8 considered changes in the power and incentives that characterize current local prosecutors. Why shouldn't the type of analysis put forward in a chapter titled "What Happens Next?" have been postponed until strategies for reducing imprisonment have been discussed in greater detail?

The substantive puzzle about Chapter 5's analysis relates to the modest potential declines that the chapter projected for the coming decades. The California realignment story involved a 25% drop in incarceration over a five-year period, yet the chapter concluded that the inflated current national prison and jail population was likely to decline by perhaps a third in three decades' time. Why couldn't a nation that accommodates such swift and extraordinary prison population growth also produce much more dramatic declines? The wholehearted endorsement of categorical exclusion of the drug dependent from prison and shift of presumptive custodial sentences from prisons to short-term commitment to county facilities could go a long way toward cutting prison populations by almost half in many systems.

But the reason that Chapter 5's analysis was based on the experience of federal and state systems rather than the potential of new strategies to decarcerate is that the real test of decarceration strategies will be in the decentralized decision-making of 51 different criminal justice systems with thousands of local prosecutors and police agencies and little in the way of incentives from the national government to motivate unity of action.

Ten years after an all-time high in prison commitments and total imprisonment, the median imprisonment trend of the 49 states not under a federal statewide population limit was a less than 10% decline. One important reason for limited decline is that there was, in most states, very little change from all-time high levels of incarceration.

The strategies and tactics profiled in Chapters 6, 7, and 8 could produce substantial decreases in incarceration if most states adopted them and committed resources to pursuit of decarceration. But the only experience-based estimates of the near future suggest diversity between and within state governments and levels of incarceration much closer to the peak rates of 2007 than to either the American experience in the 1970s or the current levels of incarceration in any other developed nation on the planet.

And if that is the likely American future, it will be necessary to make serious improvements in both the conditions in which Americans are confined and the consequences of a confinement on the political rights, economic opportunities, and social standing of the formerly confined. One million prisoners in 2030 are 10 million former prisoners in 2040, and 30 million children and families of former prisoners. Add to that the 500,000 to 700,000 in jail or other community confinement at any given time and the additional volume of the formerly jailed.

Strategies of reducing confinement are of course of critical importance. But so are programs of harm reduction in the conditions of penal confinement and the elimination of needless and excessive collateral disabilities to those who have survived active incarceration. The less likely a major and sustained reduction in confinement becomes in the coming decades, the more important it becomes to reform the conditions and consequences of American incarceration.

Part III

POLICY PROBLEMS FOR A MILLION-CELL FUTURE

9

Strategy and Tactics for Building Institutions

THIS IS NOT a chapter on the purposes, operations, or limits of prisons in modern governments, but instead a selective discussion of strategic choices about building penal institutions in the United States of 2020 to 2050. The prisons and jails in the United States are deficient in a large number of ways, including grossly inadequate programs and educational content, punitive and excessive levels of security and isolation, inadequate connection to other social institutions, deficient work opportunities, and inadequate medical care. But I will not attempt to build a comprehensive list of priority reforms for institutions of custodial confinement in this chapter. Instead, I want to focus on issues that state and federal systems are likely to encounter when large periods of expansion are followed by stability at historically high levels of prison and jail populations. How have the lessons of recent history and the range of current correctional policies among American states changed our understanding about how to respond when currently available prisons and jails get crowded? If particular states decide to expand confinement capacity, should the emphasis be placed on local custodial facilities or on state prisons? If state prison populations decline substantially, should this produce smaller populations in the same number of facilities ("thinning out") or an emphasis on closing institutions? What methods are helpful in making midrange and long-range forecasts about future needs for prisons and jails?

I address these sorts of issues in two stages. The first section of the chapter isolates two lessons that should have been learned in the tumultuous half-century of criminal justice policy since 1970. Then the next three sections of the chapter try to apply the wisdom of recent experience to issues about the scale, location, and function of institutions of confinement in the midterm policy future of American crime and punishment.

Two Lessons from Recent Experience

The first chapter of this book, profiling the single generation of huge growth in imprisonment in the United States, is titled, "An American Surprise," and it is likely that no professional group in America was more surprised by the advent of mass incarceration that the professional staff of American prisons and prison administration. One irony of the era in which prison populations exploded was that it was also the period during which criminal justice planning as an activity and as a profession became an institutional part of national and state government. The 1970s witnessed the growth of the Law Enforcement Assistance Administration and, with its financial support, state law enforcement planning agencies (Feeley and Sarat 1980; Cronin, Cronin, and Milakovich 1981). The ambition of criminal justice planning was to bring information and evaluation into the process of state and local governance of criminal justice. Yet the first of the lessons to be learned in this introductory section was the misleading failure of an important effort at criminal justice planning, the forecasting (usually by state agencies) of future correctional institutional populations.

The Mythological Science of Correctional Forecasting

One reason correctional forecasting was all but nonexistent prior to the 1970s was the absence of interest in variations in prison population in academic research and the absence of formal planning agencies in states, where more than 90% of prisoners were confined. When planning agencies came to the states in the 1970s, correctional forecasts arrived as well, but with limited focus and little methodological rigor. As Zimring and Hawkins told the story in 1991:

> The history of correctional forecasting . . . never mingled with academic social science or formal theoretical experiences. Correctional forecasting grew from the culture of correctional administration and criminal justice planning. Its practitioners were part of the closed loop that links state and local government, state legislatures, public planning agencies and consultants. (1991, 62)

The fact that those who developed and executed correctional forecasts worked in and for the governmental entities that operated the prisons makes the central methodological flaw in standard forecasts an unforgivable high-magnitude mistake, an assumption that Zimring and Hawkins identified as central to the forecasting enterprise:

> The correctional planners commonly viewed prison population as though it were a natural phenomenon like rainfall totally beyond the control of policy agencies. "We take what the courts send us" was the response of a New England state to a request for information about their projection methods. (Zimring and Hawkins 1991, 62)

But the correctional forecaster as weather forecaster is a self-serving fiction that deliberately misrepresents the nature of governmental power in imprisonment policy. When state agencies suggest that the variations in prison terms and populations are a natural process, they suggest that imprisonment is beyond the control of government. The weather forecaster cannot control the weather, but the state and local governments that control criminal justice policy can create and can change correctional outcomes. Imprisonment is a proprietary enterprise of a state government that possesses a wide variety of methods to produce outcomes. The weather forecast image is an attempt to avoid responsibility for outcomes well within the powers of government.

This same fantasy that government is a passive observer in the processes that determine prison populations creates the fictional assumption that it is necessary to choose between prison crowding and prison construction when too many prisoners have been pushed into too few residential prison facilities, as with the epic overcrowding in California litigated in *Brown v. Plata*.

One clear demonstration of the self-imposed limits of policy planning in state government comes from California's prisons, which produced the judicial order discussed in Chapter 5 and then produced substantial declines in population. The massive overcrowding of California's prisons was neither sudden nor surprising. The Department of Corrections reported 160,655 persons confined in California's institutions and camps in 2000, the vast majority in institutions. That was 190% of the population the facilities had been built to house (California Department of Corrections 2001, Table 1). By 2006, the overcrowding had become worse, with 172,598 persons confined and the institutions holding 201% of design capacity. But a new reform governor, Arnold Schwarzenegger, had been elected, and legislation had proposed and passed to reorganize the state's adult and juvenile correctional functions into a single comprehensive California Department of Corrections and Rehabilitation (CDCR 2007).

The first report of this new agency provides an interesting contrast with the realignment program put in place after the intervention of federal court orders. It was titled *Successes and Challenges: The CDCR Story* and placed immediate emphasis on the crisis levels of overcrowding:

The Division of Adult Institutions has met the overcrowding challenge head-on, looking for both short-term and long-term solutions in an innovated manner. For the short-term, out-of-state and community-based beds have been the only reasonable options. For the long-term, construction of new facilities and expansion of rehabilitative programs and partnerships with various community-based organization is key to providing a high level of public safety. (CDCR 2007)

There is no overlap between the short-term and long-term programs to combat overcrowding, and no mention of any of the major changes that reduced prison populations during realignment because the only methods to combat overcrowding considered in the new department's plan are short-term expansion of carceral capacity (the out-of-state and local "beds") and long-term expansion ("construction of new facilities"). Those are the only options in the worldview of the governor and his department of corrections to confront the overcrowding in facilities that a very few years later was quickly reduced by a series of structural changes.

The contrast between the Schwarzenegger worldview and the strategic approach of the California realignment was not a one-off event. The assumption in this report that animated the governor's method to meet "the overcrowding challenge head-on" was that changes in the volume of persons confined or the terms of their confinement could not be considered. But why was that? The reorganization plan involved the same cooperating branches of state government—a popular executive and the department of corrections—and the capacity to obtain legislative cooperation. Yet the Schwarzenegger strategy couldn't solve a crowding problem until new prisons were added.

The operating assumption in most states and the federal system during the 1980s, 1990s, and the first years of the twentieth century was that significant alterations of the policies that produced the prison population explosion were neither operationally feasible nor politically prudent. That is one reason why there were no significant interruptions in the swift increases in imprisonment nationally and why there was no major state divergence from the threefold and fourfold nationwide increases in rates of prison confinement. And the assumption almost everywhere that variations in major confinement policies were not feasible is one reason why the forced change in California was the most dramatic reduction in the nine years after the 2007 peak.

The Noncrisis in Correctional Administration

In the aftermath of California's successful realignment, however, it is difficult to regard the failure of central state governments to assume more power as just a failure of imagination rather than a failure of will. Inaction when there is no crisis carries no substantial political risks for a governor and a legislature without a visible failure in administering the prison systems. Large populations in prisons and jails has become the new normal in the American states. The dynamic growth in incarceration has created a stable, large population of prisoners, expensive but predictable. The transition that we have been experiencing in the first two decades of the twenty-first century is from explosive growth to stability of inflated levels of incarceration, a transition from an acute to a chronic problem with little pressure to reform. It was no accident that almost half the net reduction in American prisoners after 2007 came as the result of an aggressive judicial intervention from outside the ecology of American state and local government in a single state.

The problem in 2020 is not that we do not know how to reduce prison populations, but rather that government actors lack incentives to reduce incarceration.

The Dilemmas of Correctional Construction

Why should an analysis of prison and jail policies include a discussion of building institutions of confinement? The 400% increase in the US rate of imprisonment required a massive expansion of the physical plant for confinement. With levels of incarceration a decade past their peak, should questions of further construction programs be irrelevant to reformers concerned with parsimony and decency in the secure confinement of criminal offenders? Are there reasons to build new prisons and jails? Would construction simply add to the already massive scale of American incarceration?

The current environment for discussion of correctional construction is a perplexing mix of good reasons to build new penal facilities and substantial dangers that new construction will add prisoners to an already problematic mass.

The reasons for new facilities include crowding in many state systems and a misfit between needs and the kinds of facilities on hand (remote when the needs are local, and high security when the needs are for lower security). The level of crowding in US state systems is still substantial. While states can shift their definitions of "operational capacity," a recent survey had 16 states self-reporting that their prison populations equaled or exceeded their operating capacity, and 22 states reported that inmate counts were higher than the maximum number the prisons were designed to accommodate, with six of those 22 states at least 50% over population the facilities were designed to house.

The pattern is reported in Figure 9.1.

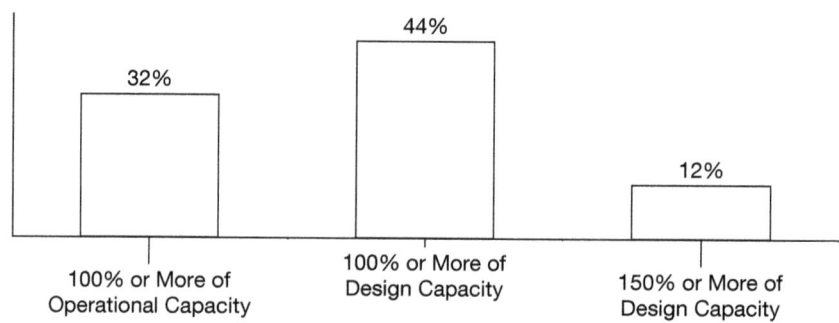

Figure 9.1 State Prison Systems Report of Crowding, 2013 (2014). *Source*: "State Prison Capacity" 2013; Bureau of Justice Statistics.

The simple arithmetic of population distributions shows why a decade of slow aggregate decline can leave so much overcrowding. Recall that almost half of all reduction in prisoners in state systems came in California (see Chapter 5) and that 16 states reported more prisoners in 2016 than in 2007. Further, for many of the states that experienced some decline after 2007, it was quite modest. For the 49 states other than California, there were only 38,601 fewer prisoners at the end of 2016 than at the end of 2007. So many of the states with prison crowding in 2007 have remained crowded. What was an acute problem in a number of systems has now evolved into a chronic problem.

And the absolute shortage of institutional capacity is only the beginning of the problem, because a lot of the institutional capacity we have isn't a good fit with the institutional capacity we need. There are two major types of misfit between current prison capacity and institutional needs—location and level of security. State prisons are case studies in the geography of exile, far removed from the urban areas where those sent to prison lived prior to commitment and where thy will return after release. This isolates the prisoners from family and interested community members and separates the offender from employers, local educational institutions, community treatment programs, and religious and community leaders who may be helpful upon release. There may be some operational savings from isolated locations, but there are no programmatic advantages or significant security benefits. The remote location of prisons provides steady employment for citizens of economically depressed areas and nothing else of significant public benefit. When prisoners are housed near the communities where their clients will return after release, connections with community programs and employment can be established and sought out (see Chapter 6). There is therefore a surplus of remote and isolated institutions of penal confinement and a shortage in the community settings where prisoners can benefit from community contacts and transitional opportunities.

The second misfit is the concentration of prisons at the high end of the security spectrum. Most prison systems in America have many too many institutions of high or maximum security and also invest in expensive and debilitating institutions of hypermaximum security with designed solitary confinement (Reiter 2016; Diagard, Sullivan, and Vanko 2018; ACLU 2014; Austin and McGinnis 2004). Isolation and paranoid security are too much of a bad thing both for prisoners and for correctional systems, which grossly overpay for unnecessary security.

The point of the problematic fit between the type and location of the institutions a state needs and the type it operates is that the wrong kind of prison cannot be a productive element in a rational prison system even if it provides an appropriate number of beds.

The Saga of the Tamms Supermax Prison

For those who believe that in an era of correctional crowding all prison bedspace is essentially interchangeable, the more than 10-year career to the Tamms Supermax prison in Illinois is a cautionary tale. Illinois at the end of 2013 was one of the six most overcrowded prison systems in the United States, with a population greater than 150% of both its operating and design capacity (152% and 173%, respectively, in December 2013) ("State Prison Capacity" 2013). Yet a year prior to December 2013, the state had closed its newest major prison, the "supermax" Tamms facility that had been designed to isolate 500 hyper-dangerous offenders. Because of its intense manpower requirement for security staff, it had an operating cost per prisoner three times the variable cost per prisoner in the system's standard prisons (Reiter 2017, 19–20), which themselves were probably more secure than required. Tamms kept a population half its designed capacity only by keeping inmates longer than the facility was supposed to observe as a limit (Reiter 2017, 19).

Can we estimate with precision the total shortage of appropriate housing capacity once inappropriate facilities are excluded from the stock of penal housing? The criteria for making this kind of judgment are not well developed, and extreme and obviously expensive situations like the expensive Tamms disaster are relatively rare. The higher one's standard of location and habitability, the larger the gap in correctional capacity that the right kind of new facility should be built to remedy. As soon as minimum standards of location and humanity are introduced, the shortage of space becomes guesswork with a high margin of error. But even excluding only the most remote and obsolete of America's state prisons would require creating new space for more than 150,000 persons. Should we start building?

Field of Dreams?

The problem with building new prison space is the danger that the new beds will soon fill with new prisoners. The slogan we could borrow from the fantasy film about a baseball field in a rural area is "If you build it, they will come." In its pure form, if every new correctional bed generated an additional prisoner to fill it, then no level of prison construction would ever reduce crowding.

A rigorous empirical assessment of the degree to which prison construction is a cause of increases in imprisonment is a difficult if not impossible task. To begin with, after 1970 the prison population was growing as never before all over the United States. Bedspaces introduced over the same period would correlate with prisoners to fill them. And comparing states that build with those that don't doesn't isolate new construction as a cause of new prisoner growth because states facing larger than average population growth will be more likely to invest in construction expenditures, in which case growth in imprisonment is the cause of new construction rather than vice versa. In theory, testing for differential growth in prisoners after new construction produces new operating institutions could help to unravel the causal sequence, but use of jails and delay of judicial commitments to prison because of correctional crowding may also confuse construction as an effect of growing demand with construction as a cause of larger prison populations.

Five Issues for State and Local Policy on Institutions

The cross-currents that permeate discussions of policy concerning the physical plants of American penal confinement make selection of policy difficult and generalizations across the range of different levels of government and types of institutions problematic. With 50 different state governments and thousands of localities, there are limited opportunities for rational "one size fits all" rules and constraints for capital expenditures. We have too many places of confinement in the United States, and many of them are inappropriate in location and security. But any effort to improve the physical facilities for confinement will attract public investment only if it expands the holding capacity of the target institutions. So the hard choice for aging and remote institutions will often be between expanding numbers or tolerating substandard conditions.

This section isolates five policy issues that will be a necessary part of policy analysis in state and local governments over the coming decades:

1. To build or not to build?
2. Priorities for institutional improvement in aging and obsolete remote prisons

3. Choosing between closing and thinning out prisons when prison populations fall
4. Diversifying the functions and levels of security of local confinement facilities
5. Deciding appropriate roles for private enterprise in correctional programs

TO BUILD OR NOT TO BUILD?

The existing stock of penal facilities is unfit both for its existing population and for its likely population over the next three decades. They are badly located, old, more secure than necessary, and in many instances overcrowded. But the price of investing in more modern facilities is almost always the expansion of capacity. One can wish for a regime in which facilities could be built without net expansion, but capital investments of that scale are more than difficult to accomplish without some added space to incarcerate. And reformers should keep this trade-off in mind rather than imagine that they can deliver big-ticket public investments without creating more space to incarcerate.

Should this inevitable danger lead to a flat no-building policy in the near future? Something close to a nationwide no-build prison policy might be maintained without extreme crowding in most if not all states. The rapid drop in prison numbers without much new state or local bedspace in California is evidence of this potential when genuine reductions in secure confinement happen. But whether the same net reductions are achievable without federal court scrutiny is unknown. And prison conditions in California are now better but still bad (Anderson 2017). Is that the best reform advocates can hope for?

Not quite. A path to improve conditions of confinement might better serve improvement of institutional life without much or any net increase in secure confinement spaces if it combines a per se prohibition of traditional remote state prisons with permission to build and—with some limits—expand a range of local bedspaces from highly secure in traditional jails to semisecure and nonsecure facilities for work release, halfway out and halfway in dormitory facilities, and dedicated residential substance abuse treatment space.

Every penal system in the United States has too much long-term, high-security, remote-location prison space. Some states have *much* too much traditional prison space, but no state has a genuine shortage of space for offenders who really need the measure of control now provided in that environment. Between a quarter and a half of the persons now imprisoned in high security don't need to be in that setting under any rational standards (see Diagard, Sullivan, and Vanko 2018; Austin and McGinnis 2004). People are sent to prison because that has become the standard form of confinement for felons. So a federal or state zero-construction policy would not frustrate the real need for that specific type of confinement.

Then why not close many of the institutions that currently confine 1.3 million persons? The capital investment in a prison system will keep most of its facilities functioning as long as the alternative to maintaining that scale of obsolete remote facilities requires major capital investment. The Tamms hypersecurity closure mentioned earlier in the chapter was the contrary exception that proves the rule. Tamms had two important drawbacks for an era in which prison space needs are measured in big states in the tens of thousands. It was small—built for a maximum of 500—and expensive to operate. The 250 or so persons confined in Tamms could be shifted into larger facilities. So closing it could be, in the artful phase of a British wit, a combination of high moral principle and modest pecuniary economy. By contrast, closing Stateville or Joliet in Illinois or Jackson in Michigan or any of California's more than 30 men's prisons, given the current prison population levels of those states, would require a major capital expenditure somewhere.

But the fact that remote and oversecure institutions can persist as long as total confinement populations remain sufficiently high that replacing them requires large capital costs should alert reformers to how long term can be the costs of creating new penal institutions. What we build next year could last out the twenty-first century.

We now know better than to accept the metrological mythology of projecting "needed" prison space from population trends or court statistics. We will need as many remote high-security dungeons as we have on hand, but only because replacing them will have high capital costs. We will, however, find other alternatives when we have to. So a moratorium on traditional remote prison construction could be a sound long-term investment.

But there are no compelling reasons to prohibit the construction of many kinds of residential spaces in the communities where sentenced offenders reside. Local jails and lockups confine hundreds of thousands of persons either pending adjudication of criminal charges or serving short sentences for a wide array of crimes. Some of the local physical facilities in which people are jailed are even older, less functional, and more needlessly secure than the prison facilities that were the subject of my lamentations in earlier paragraphs (see Schwirtz 2017; Elmahrek 2017; Davey 2008; Mattick and Aikman 1969). But three aspects of local residential settings recommend them over prisons for offenders: their closeness to the families and community resources that connect to the lives of those in jail, the shorter duration of almost all jail sentences, and the availability of community program contacts and postconfinement opportunities that can connect a resident of a local facility to a future in the community. Because the duration of confinement is usually shorter by far in local facilities, fewer beds can also accommodate a greater number of offenders.

One of the many reasons why so much confinement space has been concentrated in remote and high-security mode of the traditional prison is the same accident of differential fiscal incentives that produces the "correctional free lunch" for local governments when they decide to send offenders to state prison—the state government pays all of the costs, not only of operating prisons, but also of building them. And state departments of corrections rarely pay the full cost of constructing residential penal facilities in metropolitan locations. While state governments often provide some support for constructing and operating jails, it is county governments that often must pay a substantial proportion of the construction and operational costs for facilities that are the administrative responsibility of local governments (Vera 2015).

But prohibiting the construction of new remote high-security prisons could alter the usual financial consequences of building and operating local facilities for both state and local governments, in one of two ways. Once only local locations could be built, state government might build facilities that are funded and administered as part of the state system. Or state governments might increase the level of its financial contribution to building and operating facilities that counties and perhaps even cities administered. Either strategy would reduce the traditional reluctance of local governments to absorb most of the cost of local facilities. If the jurisdictional limits between state and local institutions remain at the usual one-year sentence boundary, then local control, with state subsidies increasing, would lead to lower total costs and minimize sentence lengths for administrative convenience rather than penological need.

While remote state medium and maximum security prisons tend to have large sizes and designs that sacrifice aesthetics to security, a wide range of different types and sizes of local facilities might be constructed in the near future. The one-size-fits-all maximum security men's jail is often as bad or worse than state prisons (see Mattick and Aikman 1969). Huge local institutions might minimize the objections of local residents to smaller facilities not located next door to criminal courts in governmental ghettos. A single huge jail is, however, much more secure than many local prisoners need and for that reason is more expensive to operate. Halfway-in and halfway-out programs work better in smaller sizes, and residential drug and alcohol treatment programs might better combine offenders and nonoffenders in common residential treatment settings. Violations of restrictions on movement or substance use could then produce short stays in regular city jail in the pattern of programs like Project Hope, discussed in Chapter 6.

Many of the problematic trade-offs I have mentioned when discussing upgrading prisons will probably also haunt efforts to upgrade large jails without substantial expansion of their capacity. Perhaps federal assistance programs that provide funds only for nonexpansion upgrades could make a difference in the planning process, but there is in the current circumstances of federal Justice Department administration and federal criminal justice assistance programs no early indicators of this type of targeted assistance to upgrade the physical and programmatic circumstances of confinement.

HARM REDUCTION IN REMOTE MEGAPRISONS

Most of the more than 2 million Americans now locked up are in the remote, security-obsessed, poorly programmed, and large penal institutions that are the stereotyped paradigm of American imprisonment. Many of the prisons now functioning were built prior to the James Cagney and Edward G. Robinson films of the 1930s that communicated that prison stereotype to much of the world. But the oldest of American megaprisons are by no means the worst institutions when compared to the hypermaximum security institutions such as Tamms in Illinois and Pelican Bay in California. Deprivation rather than crowding is the primary characteristic of the supermax, with solitary confinement a feature of the design: indoor isolation for 23 hours a day, seven days a week and near-total lack of human contact face to face. Keramet Reiter titled her history and profile of Pelican Bay *23/7* because the isolation by design was the heart of the penal regime. When such conditions are imposed without limit or necessity, the governments that allow them fall below minimum standards of civilized decency.

Less isolating but dilapidated facilities combine crowding with boredom and lack of programming. Boredom and purposeless days become the rule rather than the exception.

Even if reformers halt construction of remote high-security prisons, such facilities as now exist will be the institutional home for the majority of American prisoners in 2040 and 2050. How can these ready-made gulags be improved? There are a number of the problems of the current version of medium- and maximum-security imprisonment that can be significantly improved *if* either the courts or the administrators of the prison wish to improve them. These involve reductions in unnecessary and punishing conditions of confinement, limiting unnecessary security restrictions and gratuitous restrictions on contact within prisons and on communication outside prisons.

The recent reduction in hypersecurity at Pelican Bay is a textbook case of low-cost human rights reform. Professor Reiter detailed both the technology and the economic cost of ending the 23/7 regime she had profiled: "They opened the cell doors." There are also insignificant capital or operational costs to relaxing restrictions on inmate communication with the outside world by telephone or digital means. The extortionate overcharging for telephone communication in prison and jails does generate revenue for those systems that permit it, but cannot be justified as a responsible public policy in modern government. To the extent that downward adjustments in security-related prohibitions of contact and out-of-cell movement increase the rate of disciplinary infractions, that may generate additional cost in maintaining disciplinary controls. But the enforcement of precautionary restrictions in a maximum security environment is probably much more expensive than modest expansions in disciplinary responses to inmates' misuse of privileges. So many aspects of what generates unnecessary suffering in the remote high-security prison system are simple fixes without budgetary impact.

But the problematic geography of American imprisonment is a significant disadvantage without an obvious remedy. The isolation from family and friends will be a chronic defect of the existing stock of prison space for the very long future during which those facilities function.

And many of the indirect costs of remote location further impoverish prisoners and the experience of imprisonment in remote settings. One issue with finding good doctors and medical facilities in many prison settings is the distance from metropolitan areas with extensive medical infrastructure and diversity of specialized practice. Major metropolitan areas have a density of educational institutions and community outreach organizations that can create programs inside prison walls. San Quentin may be the single oldest traditional prison in the vast California system, but it is also the best located, easy to reach from most of the San Francisco metropolitan area. The diversity of educational and outreach programs at San Quentin is a telling contrast with most of California's more distant major prisons, because every advantage San Quentin displays is an obvious example of how remote locations remove the inmates of remote penal outposts from the manifest advantages of metropolitan proximity.

THIN OUT INSTITUTIONAL NUMBERS OR CLOSE PRISONS WHEN POPULATIONS DECLINE?

While there were only modest aggregate declines after 2007, there were double-digit declines outside California, in New York, New Jersey, and Connecticut, and there are other states that report prison populations 20% or more below their operating capacity ("State Prison Capacity" 2013; Bureau of Justice Statistics 2013). But after the huge run-up in prisoners prior to 2007, it is foolhardy to assume that any state that reports a large decline in prisoners has more space than it needs. The leading example of this is California, where a reduction in the system of tens of thousands of persons combined did not generate any surplus capacity.

But the other large- and medium-sized systems that reported drops of 10% or more in Chapter 5's analysis are typical of a pattern that should be more common in the most probable future of state prison populations. States with major metropolitan areas but stable or declining populations include much of the Northeast and Midwest. New York, New Jersey, and Connecticut have already experienced significant declines. Major Midwestern states may soon follow.

There are two contrasting strategies that states usually consider when responding to an excess capacity in state prisons—closing institutions or "thinning out" institutional populations to avoid closures. The primary advantage to state government in closing institutions is cost savings. The primary disadvantages of closing institutions are the disruption of jobs and labor relations with staff as well as ending economic support of the communities in economic decline, which are the usual location of remote prisons.

Are there also important consequences for future levels of imprisonment in the choice between closing institutions and maintaining all of them? There may be, because thinning out institutional populations maintains a larger number of potential additional prison beds that can be swiftly readied for use at minimum cost. And because the prison staff and communities benefiting from the jobs at these prisons are aware of the danger of closure, the thinning out of prison numbers also recruits staff and local political actors as advocates for expanding imprisonment. The data in Chapter 5 for the former Soviet satellite nations seemed to show the eventual increase in nonpolitical prisoners to fill many spaces in national prisons that had been emptied of political prisoners. Removing the institutions is a less tempting invitation to reincarcerate than operating institutions that are conspicuously below capacity. Finality in the life of penal institutions removes an easy path to expansion.

Which Prisons to Close?

There are two contrasting strategies in selecting institutions to close that have surfaced after the 2007 peak. New York State, which has closed a total of 14 penal institutions, has focused on smaller facilities, and these have all been institutions with lower security ratings. "Thus far, only minimum and medium security facilities have been closed; none were maximum security" (Zoukis 2017). The selection process for closure in New Jersey targeted the most controversial of the facilities in the state's penal expansion, the notorious Riverfront facility in Camden, New Jersey. While Riverfront was one of the few state prisons in a metropolitan area, its conspicuous presence in an urban waterfront area was considered deeply insulting to the troubled city of Camden (Steele 2017; Miller 2010). And its closure did reduce high-security space. As a general rule, closing prisons that never should have opened is probably sound policy.

The focus on small and lower-security institutions as targets for closure is not an easy issue to analyze from the perspective of its implications for downsizing imprisonment . Against the emphasis on smaller and less secure institutions is the fact that the larger and higher-security institutions are also in oversupply. Putting aside the impact of highly selective decarceration programs, the cells that should be closed are the high-security variety. But it may be a mistake to ignore the selective efforts of intentional decarceration efforts. If the efforts to reduce prison populations are rational, they will focus on the lower-risk offenders who shouldn't be in state prisons, and those lower-risk offenders are probably concentrated in the low-risk facilities.

For that reason, penal administrators can argue that the smaller and lower-security closures fit the profile of the prisoners they are removing from the system. The extent to which this can be empirically demonstrated is unknown. And the timing of institutional population declines, which precede institutions being closed, makes it difficult to identify the type of offender for whom reduced admissions or increased releases have created extra space.

But there are two more basic problems with the profiles of offenders in any particular security classification. In the first place, the classification of offenders into categories of future risk in prison environments is far from an exact science. The prediction of dangerousness is difficult in all but extreme cases and is even more problematic under circumstances where offenders are under physical restraint. It must be remembered that the physical constraints of prisons produce lower homicide offense rates among the dangerous men we confine than is reported for all adult males in the general population. The Bureau of Justice Statistics (2005) reports homicide rates of three per 100,000 for jails and four per 100,000 for prisons in 2000–2002, under half the rate for unconfined males and far less than half for adult males). So environmental controls reduce risks in secure confinement. The second problem is assuming that risks an inmate presents at one time persist over long periods of time.

All other things being equal, the better argument is that the type of facility to be closed should be selected on considerations not closely connected to how reductions in rates of confinement might affect the security classification of the prison population that remains.

There are, however, other features that probably favor smaller institutions as candidates for closure, including the capacity to make decisions with more modest inmate numbers and with smaller impact on prison system employment. And the choice between closing institutions and thinning out but retaining existing facilities is much more important than the criteria for closure.

When notorious institutions are a serious issue, Tamms in Illinois and Riverfront in New Jersey, the selection process is easy and of importance system-wide. When there are no obviously dysfunctional institutions at risk for closure, the choice of what to close is not a critical issue.

Diversifying Local Correctional Facilities

Most of the secure confinement spaces in American local settings are grim, barebones cells, often crowded, rarely connected to many recreational or programmatic opportunities and often not closely connected to supportive institutions and professions in the surrounding communities. If American jails and lockups were advertised by real estate hucksters in search of good news, the slogan would have to be "The Three Most Important Elements in Real Estate are Location, Location, Location."

Time spent in jail in the United States is punishment, but it is not exile. The confined person is not far separated from family and those who wish to support him or her. To a limited extent, physical improvements in existing jail facilities can make them tolerable for short stays. But the challenge then becomes how to create a wide diversity of service and residential programs in local settings.

One set of new programs can be designed as primarily nonresidential, using nonconfinement methods of monitoring participants as long as participants remain crime-free and drug-free but providing some in-program or short jail stays for disciplinary responses to significant misbehavior. This is suitable for halfway-in treatment programs for drug-dependent persons serving custodial sentences for other criminal offenses in drug treatment, and for persons in programs for either probation failure or modesty problematic failure during parole.

A second set of programs might best be designed with semisecure residential facilities. Work release and halfway-out facilities that serve as a transition from prison will probably require communal residential settings that are best physically separated from central large jail structures.

Apart from difficult issues of where the money for new facilities can be found and which level of government (federal, state, or local) should participate in funding local facilities designed to reduce the burden on state prisons, there are two inevitable problems that a major program of diversifying local facilities will encounter—finding appropriate locations that don't produce hostility from their new neighbors and avoiding or at least minimizing the "net widening" potential of new programs to expand the number of persons subject to intensive monitoring and restrictions.

The dilemma of building local places for offenders to reside or congregate for programs of treatment is this: putting offenders close to community resources and functioning social and educational systems is a positive benefit for the offenders and a frightening prospect for the other residents, who will be in close proximity to criminal offenders and drug addicts. The exile of prisons to distant nonmetropolitan areas was, among other things, the ultimate "Not In My Backyard" solution because penal confinement could be segregated into areas where governmental functions were segregated from most residential communities.

The probable sites for smaller residential and nonresidential local correctional programs will be in parts of cities and towns dedicated to major public and private activities—hospitals, factories, and equipment storage. Many of these areas will be close to older residential zones with concentrations of poverty and social disorganization.

There is also an inevitable tendency for attractive programs that serve as alternatives to incarceration in remote prisons to also expand the total number of offenders that are placed under restrictive legal controls after criminal conviction. The important question is not whether this net-widening effect will occur (it will), but its extent. The larger the enthusiasm for work release or drug treatment programs, the more sustained will be the pressure to spread the good works of the new corrections to all who need it. Recognizing that such programs are most effective when they reduce the harms of more punitive alternatives might curb the enthusiasm to drastically expand their reach.

By far the most important and problematic net-widening influence on nontraditional intermediate controls is making the offender pay fees when he or she is required to subscribe to controls like electronic monitoring. If the government is paying the price of a monitoring program, it may only impose the program when there is evidence of a strong public benefit—either reduction in confinement costs or increases in crimes avoided or both. But when the *offender* pays for the monitoring, the program becomes yet another free lunch for the local criminal justice system, and the volume of imposed electronic monitoring systems expands. So allowing fee shifting subsidizes the enterprise of electronic monitoring and reduces the discipline that paying for monitoring imposes on the scope of governmental monitoring and controls.

The Impact of Bail Reform

A large part of the high-security population of local jails in the United States consists of persons who are awaiting criminal trials but cannot secure pretrial release through money bail or other mechanisms. The prejudicial effects of pretrial confinement are well documented, and efforts to reduce pretrial incarceration are a continuing priority. A frontal assault on money bail as a prejudicial burden on the poor is a prominent part of many current reform efforts. If such efforts succeed, the major impact of reductions in the number of pretrial detentions and on their length would be concentrated in local jails. Real success in pretrial detention reform efforts could produce reductions in jail population in the tens of thousands.

Should any such capacity be used instead to house offenders now confined in remote state prisons? High-security jails are often barebones facilities without programs and services and are much more suited to short-term than to long-term confinement. And many jail facilities are better suited to high levels of security. So the physical plant of many jails would not be easy to convert to halfway houses or other minimum-security programs. But the superior location and proximity to outside programs of most urban jails would still recommend the transfer of prisoners into the spaces in local facilities that bail reform might generate.

THE ROLE FOR NONGOVERNMENTAL MANAGEMENT
OF CUSTODIAL FACILITIES

The prison expansion in the United States was so large that private, for-profit management of prisons, grew from nonexistent in the typical management of state and federal prisons to managing a small share of the total prison population (8% in 2017), creating a business opportunity that has generated at least two billion-dollar corporations, CareCivic and GEO.

A major debate has emerged about both the level of care and security provided by private managers and the appropriateness of delegating to private actors life-and-death power in total institutions. What is the comparative advantage of private sector management of prisons? Lower personnel and fringe-benefit costs is the most popular theory of private advantage. Whether such profit incentive operations operate more efficiently could only be determined if reliable measures of security, food quality, recreational opportunity, and rehabilitative services were available to compare prison content and effects. There is the further question of whether the lobbying skills of private prison management firms might expand the demand for prison as a sanction and for longer sentences.

The empirical evidence on most of these issues is quite weak, and any conclusions that analysts might come to on the current effects of private management also depend on the nature of the regulatory and fiscal incentives that governments currently impose on private firms. It is only if we conclude that private firms by virtue of their incentive to expand are inherently corruptive of the governmental capacity to regulate that profit-maximizing firms might have an uncorrectable negative impact on prison policy. And even if that distortion is found, there is a corresponding incentive for powerful state correctional unions to lobby, in the pattern of California's notorious Correctional Peace Officers (Page 2011).

The debate about the role of private for-profit corporations in prisons is an important one, but the issues I want to discuss here are broader than private prisons in two important respects. The nongovernmental entities that can serve as alternatives to government administrations are not just for-profit firms, including nonprofit organizations with histories of delivering therapeutic and custodial services to dependent persons. The custodial settings that will be most expanded under the policies suggested in Part I of this analysis will not be prisons and will be located in urban areas and at smaller scales. Whatever comparative advantages private firms managing large facilities in nonmetropolitan areas have may not carry over to halfway-in or halfway-out houses. The most extensive experience that the large-scale enterprises have had near cities has been for the federal government because the Bureau of Prisons didn't operate halfway houses and also because private firms operate detention facilities for large numbers of persons in immigration detention facilities.

Should the private sector, for profit or nonprofit, be prohibited from actively managing institutions that impose secure confinement as a government punishment? As a matter of principle, this is a close and important question. It is unlikely that federal courts will find the delegation of secure confinement to private contractors to be a violation of the Constitution, so private prisons can operate where they are allowed. But should state and local governments adopt their own restrictions on delegating such power to nongovernmental actors? Such a prohibition would probably be limited to custodial controls only, and even then might allow providers who must provide security when treatment is administered, as in secure settings for mental health patients in crisis.

What Impact of Reform Legislation and Local Policy for Institutions?

In one respect the previous two sections of this chapter have repeated the assumption criticized in the first section of this chapter: assuming no changes in legislation and prosecutorial policy when discussing the needs for institutions in the coming decades. What if there are major legislative changes in criminal penalties? What if the powers of prosecutors or their incentives for sending persons to prison shift? Assuming no changes in these policies removes the major powers of governments from the variables to be considered—like meteorologists predicting the weather.

The problem with 50 different state systems is that only general trends can be predicted and that even this level of analysis is difficult decades out from the point of prediction. For any given state, the safest bet in the midrange future is no major change. For those states that do experience changes, the general direction of shifts in sentencing governance will be in the direction of what Chapter 7 called sentencing commissions and for that reason will shift more power from local governments, prosecutors, and judges to the statewide commission's guidelines. This can be expected to reduce somewhat the number of new admissions to prison and the length of terms for those sent to prison. It may also increase the use of both custodial and noncustodial local facilities and programs. The extent to which a shift of power to sentencing commissions and a more aggressive use of power by a commission will change the number and length of prison commitments will vary from minimal to modest, with my notion of "modest" in the range of 10%–15%, and the direction of the shift would be downward.

What would be the impact of trends of this magnitude in this direction over a decade or more? Assume 10 states participate in this shift toward administrative controls and that five of the 10 do so with "modest" impact. Those five states would reduce admissions by 10% to 15%, which would reduce total 50-state prison admissions by 1% to 1.5%. Adding five more minimal impact states produces a 10-state contribution of 2% downward national shift from the 10-state subsample. The impact of that 2% decline on the 50-state total depends of course on what is happening to admissions and total population in the other 40 states.

What about explicit attempts to reduce prison commitments by creating fiscal charges to high-commitment counties or economic rewards to counties that lower commitments? The direction of this type of intervention would be similar to the sentencing commission moves discussed earlier, but the magnitude of the impact of cash incentives would probably be larger. The tendency of the shift to increase the use of custodial and noncustodial local facilities will be more pronounced if fiscal incentives are used both because the number of prison commitments avoided will be larger and because the financial resources available to the counties will be larger. For a state seriously involved in incentives to reduce commitments in this pattern, a reduction in new commitments in the range of 20%–30% of total prison commitments could be achievable if the incentives to counties are sufficient. So the single-state impact of this type of move would be substantial, but the aggregate 50-state impact of this tactic would be small if only one or two states are likely to adopt the policy. So the critical issue for impact is whether a substantial number of states would voluntarily engineer a fiscal incentive program of magnitude. The first decade after the peak rate of imprisonment did not witness any major voluntary programs of this kind.

What about other major policy changes that might influence incarceration? One possibility in this respect, the categorical shift of drug-dependent defendants discussed in Chapter 6, will not be rehearsed again here. But a second major change, the attack against money bail conditions as a method of incarcerating those who lack funds to secure release, would, if successful, free up substantial resources in local custodial institutions for other uses. So the direct impact of releasing the poor from pretrial confinement would be a large number of empty cells in local jails and a reduction in total confinement. What of the secondary impacts?

There are two plausible secondary or indirect impacts of reductions in pretrial detention for poor felony defendants, one secondary impact decreasing further use of jails and prisons and one impact tending to increase jail and prison use.

The secondary impact that reduces both jail and prison use is the increased leverage of the poor but now out-of-custody defendant. The data suggest that lower levels of conviction, better plea-bargaining terms, and shorter custodial punishment terms are associated with not being in predisposition custody, and if these advantages accrue to the now-released poor, they should reduce the proportion of guilty dispositions, and the length of postconviction sentences in both jails and prisons (for felony charges). And this kind of impact could be substantial.

The secondary impact that adds prison or jail time is the removal of time credited for time served while awaiting adjudication. To the extent that the time credits for pretrial detention are not wholly neutralized by higher nominal sentences that came from plea negotiations or trial convictions while in custody, these discounts are removed when no pretrial detention has been part of the process. This should increase prison terms and shift toward prison the mix of prison and jail custody. However, to the extent that this species of sentence credit is fictional, and to the extent that it is outweighed by the superior leverage of the noncustodial defendant, the substantial decrease in pretrial jail use comes with no additional utilization of prison space.

There is an additional issue of what sociologists call the potential latent impact of creating empty jail cells that removing poor defendants from pretrial detention might generate. This empty holding capacity might be used to jail rather than imprison offenders at the margin between a longer jail term and a modest prison sentence. This pattern of use would not increase total incarceration and would thus preserve the net savings from the lower pretrial detention levels. It might add some further reduction in custodial confinement because jail terms tend to be shorter than the prison terms they replace. A second possibility for the use of available jail space is expanding the number of offenders at the margin between custodial and noncustodial sentences who receive custodial jail sentencing. The criminological term for this type of expansion is "net widening," and its effect would be to diminish the net reduction in incarceration that the primary bail reform generated by the additional new periods of confinement for those convicted offenders who used to avoid secure confinement.

There are so many things not known about possible bail reforms—how many states might adopt reforms, how extensive the impact might be, the magnitude of indirect effects—that it does not seem prudent to project any specific changes in levels of incarceration from such efforts. If significant bail reform becomes important in many states, that will reduce levels of local and total incarceration and will do so by removing an unjust disadvantage of poverty. It will thus be a double benefit, but the magnitude of its impact can't be projected.

10

The Epidemic of Penal Disabilities

WHILE IMPRISONMENT IS the most extreme form of punishment imposed on criminal offenders in the United States for most serious offenses, the disabilities and prejudices imposed on criminal offenders and on those who depend on or care about them are far more numerous, more broadly distributed across offenders, longer in duration, and broader in social impact than the impact of confinement on the prisoners. This chapter will document how the penal explosion after 1970 drastically expanded the mass of persons punished as felons as well as the millions who care about and depend upon persons convicted of felonies. Because the disabilities and prejudices in law and practice are sustained for long periods after the legal label is affixed, the cumulative impact of the expanding scope of punishment has built over time and has not yet reached its probable peak rate. The elevated cost of collateral consequences and the elevated bite of these handicaps on the disadvantaged are very much a consequence of the penal expansion that was launched in the 1970s, and any attempt to control the damage of penal overreach must spend effort and resources on the long-term costs of penal classifications. So the issues discussed in this concluding chapter are intimately connected to any comprehensive effort to control the damage of mass incarceration.

The epidemic of penal disabilities documented in this chapter was caused by the same dynamic that created the growth in prison numbers. Both processes were generated by the same agents—local prosecutors—and for the same apparent motive—as a measure of their adversarial effectiveness. Just as obtaining a prison term became one way that prosecutors could measure their effectiveness in an adversarial system that runs on pleas rather than trials, so too can a felony conviction by plea seem like a more substantial prosecutorial achievement that a plea to a mere misdemeanor. Indeed, the substantial increase in imprisonment risks in the United States after 1975 becomes an important incentive for defendants to plead guilty to felonies to avoid or minimize imprisonment. And the harms added to convictions by penal disability can continue for a longer period and involve larger populations. The expansion of felony convictions and their related disabilities now threatens tens of millions of Americans. The pathological excess of penal disabilities and overincarceration in the United States are fraternal if not identical twins.

But while the causes of the past generation's epidemic of penal disabilities and of its incarceration explosion are closely linked, the most appropriate methods to reform these problems are different. The tens of thousands of current disabilities need to be cataloged and evaluated, an enormous task for a national commission. Only then can state and federal governments have a road map for the repeals and modifications that justice requires.

This chapter is organized under four headings. The first section provides a guide to the variety of different legal, social, and economic disadvantages associated with criminal conviction and punishment as well as the legal and economic hardships imposed on those dependent on and related to felons. The second section shows the cumulative impact of 40 years of criminal justice expansions on the social impact of collateral disadvantages. The third section discusses the mixture of punitive motives and preventive pretenses that provide justification for long-term collateral disabilities. The fourth and concluding section argues for "zero-based budgeting" as a strategy for wholesale legal reform of the prejudicial obstacle course of legal restrictions on former felons.

A Litany of Impediments

The criminal conviction and criminal sentence to prison, jail, a fine, or a period of probation is only the beginning of the legal, social, and economic consequences that can restrict convicted offenders and all those who live with, depend on, or care about them.

For the offender, there are a wide variety of legal prohibitions and restrictions that I will call *legal disabilities* of various durations with different rationales that are imposed by different levels of government. Prisoners and those on felony parole typically cannot vote, either for the duration of confinement or parole or, in some jurisdictions, forever, if they have been convicted of a felony (Brennan Center 2018b). Persons convicted of felony drug crimes cannot live in federally funded public housing (Love, Roberts, and Klingele 2016; Tran-Leung 2015). Persons convicted of particular types of felony crime are restricted in terms of where they can live (sex offenders) and from the practice of particular work (securities fraud) (Love, Roberts, and Klingele 2016). Legal disabilities are, for the most part, created by state law pursuant to the powers of that level of government to define and punish crimes, but there are a wide variety of federal laws not only providing consequences for violation of federal law but also for certain classes of state law violators and also minimum standards for state registration and public notification of the residence of convicted sex offenders. There is also legislation forbidding certain drug offenders from housing and welfare programs (Tran-Leung 2015; Aussenberg et al. 2016). There are literally thousands of different restrictions and prohibitions distributed throughout 50 states, special provisions of federal law and special regulations in county and municipal government. When criminal records are available for employers and other public and private institutions to inspect, they also become a basis for economic and social disadvantages—unemployment, low wages, difficulty obtaining housing and schooling, and social stigma, all of which are the consequence of the governmental record (Jacobs 2015). These are consequences of legal disability produced when notice of the conviction prejudices the economic and social standing of the convicted offender. So these are *secondary impacts* to the convicted offender that generate substantial and long-term harms.

The prejudicial impact of any legal disability extends to children and adults who are related to convicted offenders and either dependent them economically or socially and who are prejudiced by the low social and economic standing of the offender even though they did not violate criminal laws or even know crimes were being committed. One English study reported that each prisoner in custody had a mean total of 1.3 dependent children (Murray et al. 2009; Smith 2014). Many adults convicted of serious crimes will have adult partners in legal and de facto domestic relationships who will be at risk. All convicted offenders have families of birth who care about them. All of these related persons suffer economic and social harm that is vicarious in the important sense that the child, the domestic partner, and the grandmother of a person convicted of a felony did nothing unlawful. These are the *vicarious victims* of the consequences imposed on criminal offenders.

There are two quantitative issues of importance to policy in considering the appropriate reforms for disability policies and their secondary and vicarious victims. The first important dimension in assessing harms is to count the sheer number of vicarious victims. More prisoners' children get injured by the consequences of legal disabilities than do offenders if that 1.3 to 1 British ratio is representative of current American conditions. Add to the usually dependent children the number of domestic partners of convicted offenders and of caring blood relatives and it seems likely that the total number of persons prejudiced by the legal and related economic and social harm of a serious criminal conviction is at least twice the number of actually convicted offenders. And many of the "vicarious" harms that children and intimates suffer are substantial. If convicted offenders don't have work, they don't provide their children economic support. If convicted drug felons cannot qualify for federal housing programs, their families can gain access to the subsidized housing only if they don't live with a parent. So the population that suffers direct harm from the disabilities and stigma of convicted offenders is much larger than the primary targets of the disabilities, twice or three times as many persons at risk than we estimate when counting criminal court convictions.

The second clear conclusion from these quantitative estimates is that the majority of persons who suffer from the consequences of collateral penal disabilities are not at any personal fault. The forced choice of partners and relations in long-term associations with the targets of legal disabilities is between separation from the primary target of disabilities and sharing the economic and social costs of collateral punishment. For children, that forced choice will be made by other adults.

There may be striking differences between the formal powers that states possess to punish criminal and the practical impact of legal disabilities to disrupt family relationships. It is probable that the Eighth Amendment prohibition of excessive punishment would forbid the termination of parental status to a convicted and released criminal offender absent clear harm from that status to children. Yet sanctions such as the public housing prohibition may indirectly achieve exactly the forced separation that would not be permitted as a deliberate punishment. If the only housing available excludes a parent, the child suffers.

There is another respect in which the informal costs produced by collateral legal disabilities differ from the formal terms of the disability. The term of a formal disability can be limited to any term the enabling legislation provides—two years, five years, or forever. But the secondary economic and social prejudices will last as long as there is a public record of criminal conviction and that usually means the secondary damages last forever.

The Scale of Penal Disabilities

How many types of legal disabilities are found in the United States? The range of disabilities imposed by various governmental entities on persons with felony records is vast. Joan Petersilia, in her masterful 2003 study *When Prisoners Come Home*, identifies no fewer than eight separate categories of legal restrictions and requirements for convicted felons: voting restrictions; publicly available criminal records; employment barriers and workplace restrictions; formal restrictions on jobs, bonding, and licensing; housing restrictions; restrictions on welfare and food-stamps eligibility; restrictions on parenting rights and special registration; and public notification requirements for sex offenders (Petersilia 2003).

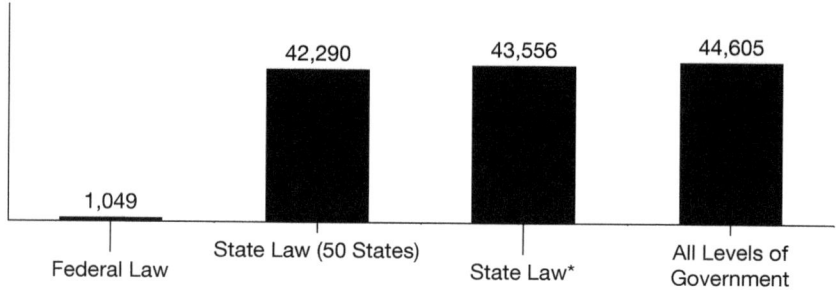

Figure 10.1 Current Restrictions on Persons with Criminal Conviction Records by Level of Government, United States. *Note*: Includes Puerto Rico, District of Columbia, Virgin Islands. *Source*: Justice Center 2019.

Within each of these categories of restriction, there is enormous and frequently arbitrary state-to state-variation:

> In California, for example, parolees are legally barred from working in the professions of law, real estate, medicine, nursing, physical therapy and education. In Colorado, the jobs of dentist, engineer, nurse, pharmacist, physician and real estate agent are closed to convicted felons. All states restrict former offenders from employment as barbers (even though many prisons provide training in barbering), beauticians and nurses. (Petersilia 2003, 113)

The volume and the variety of legal disabilities in American law are nothing short of staggering and present unique problems for strategies of reform.

Figure 10.1 is based on a computer search of legislative provisions that was reported by the Council of State Governments in 2018.

The national government has just under 1,049 separate statutory provisions imposing disabilities on persons with criminal convictions. The statutes of the 50 states add another 42,290 restrictions. When provisions applied in Puerto Ricco, the District of Columbia, and the Virgin Islands are added in, the count of state laws and their equivalent grows to just under 44,000 and the grand total of federal and state restrictions is 44,605.

Table 10.1 provides some data on the variety of different subjects that are regulated by state and federal legislation on penal disabilities. The focus of this table is not the percentage breakdown by subject of penal disabilities but rather the sheer number of laws governing each subject that are part of the legal landscape that persons with criminal convictions must negotiate.

For eight of the nine different regulatory subjects, the laws governing disabilities number in the thousands. More than 3,000 laws cover some aspect of registration, public notification, and residence restrictions for some criminal record categories, while thousands of laws limit employment, government benefits, and political and civic participation.

Table 10.1
Select Federal and State Restrictions by Subject Matter

	State	Federal	Total
Employment	19,008	358	19,366
Political and civic participation	3,900	49	3,949
Government benefits, loans, and grants	967	76	1,043
Housing	1,007	19	1,026
Education	1,273	5	1,278
Family/domestic rights	1,595	10	1,605
Firearms	1,337	12	1,349
Motor vehicle licenses	1,747	9	1,756
Registration, notification, and residency restrictions	2,334	25	2,359

Source: Justice Center 2018.

The volume and variety of penal disabilities in American states not only present substantial problems to persons who become the target of such restrictions but also present strategic difficulties for persons who wish to reform this domain of 44,000 statutes. How should reformers organize a search through this thicket? What areas of regulation should receive priority: Education? Housing? Registration schemes? Should the effort to review this extraordinary collection of regulations be the responsibility of the national government, or should it proceed state by state? I will return to these questions in the fourth and final section of this chapter.

Some collateral consequences can be attached to any law violations should this be the intent of the legislature, but the most general and most severe restrictions in the United States are attached to convictions of felony offences. This formal boundary has resulted in a vast expansion of the direct and vicarious victims because of the huge expansion of felony convictions in the critical generation after 1970 in the United States. As the following section will show, while the impact of legal disabilities on former offenders and on their relations has always been problematic, the size of the total population suffering these harms and the total social cost of these policies in the United States has expanded tremendously with each decade in the last generation and has continued to expand even after the total prison population reached its peak rate in 2007.

The Expanding Population of Direct and Vicarious Victims

But why are the legal disabilities and vicarious damages imposed on persons with criminal records and their families a topic that demands a separate chapter in a book about the penal expansion in the United States and its legacy for the mid-century destiny of American legal and social policy? The reason is that the expansion of criminal convictions has multiplied the millions subject to such harms over the period since 1970. The simple arithmetic of the severity of a social problem would multiply the harm suffered by affected victims times the number of such victims affected and the duration of whatever harm they suffer. Adjustments might be made to draw particular attention to harms suffered by persons who are particularly vulnerable because they already live in high-risk circumstances.

By these criteria, the direct, secondary, and vicarious victim damages of legal disabilities for persons with criminal records has always been a significant social problem striking hardest in populations of low income and opportunity. But the penal explosion after 1970 made a serious problem many times worse in terms of the population being punished by disabilities and the economic and social damage they produce.

The Cumulative Arithmetic of Legal Disabilities

Figure 10.2, taken from a 2017 analysis by Sarah Shannon and associates, begins at the extreme end of the punishment spectrum with estimates of persons currently in prison or on parole, and those who ever were in prison.

Figure 10.2 combines current prison and parole status because parole is limited to conditional discharge from prison. The span of time reported by this study doesn't cover the entire imprisonment growth (that started after 1972) but covers more than 80% of the growth in current imprisonment that happened after 1972.

The rate of imprisonment and parole more than quadruples between 1980 and 2010, an increase of 334% in 30 years, but the rate of in-prison growth slows in the last decade of the three, with only a 12% increase, from 2.1 to 2.4 million. The aggregate growth over 30 years was still stunning by comparison with any other stable nation in recorded history.

But the growth in the population of Americans who were ever in prison grew even faster than those currently locked up—472% instead of 334% and, more ominously, did not slow down nearly as much as growth in the number of current prisoners. The "ever imprisoned" group grew nearly four times as fast as current prisoners after 2000 (41% versus 12%)—more than 2 million more persons ever imprisoned were added in the decade after 2000, an increase in ever-imprisoned in 10 years alone of 2.1 million persons, considerably more added in this "slowing down" period of growth than the 1.5 million aggregate national total of those ever in prison for 1980.

This demonstration of the more sustained growth for the "ever imprisoned" is important to the problem of legal and economic disabilities because

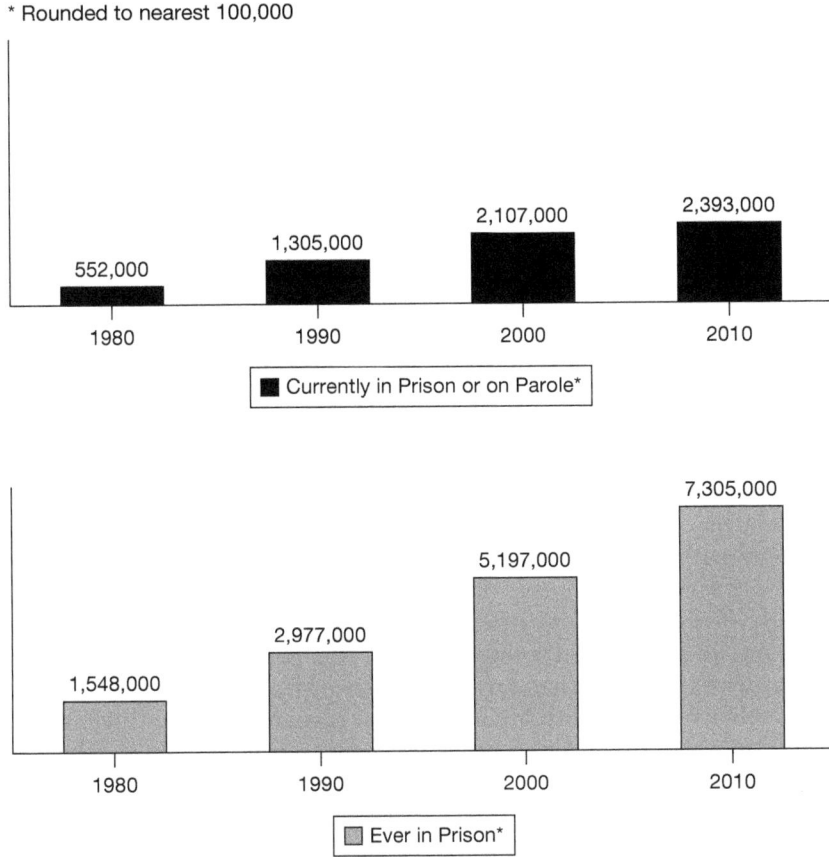

Figure 10.2 Volume of Persons in Prison or on Parole from Prison by Decade, 1980–2010. *Note*: Rounded to nearest 100,000. *Source*: Shannon et al. 2017.

disabilities of most kinds last for a long time, often forever. If the disability lasts a lifetime, the population of its subjects will keep expanding long after the population of currently imprisoned stabilizes. This is of critical importance in determining the size of the population of those primarily disabled by legal restrictions. The "ever imprisoned" are the still-expanding living legacy of the high growth rates of the decades when an aging population was much younger. Figure 10.2 showed us that about half a million persons were in prison in 1980. If they averaged age 30 in 1980, they will contribute close to that number of the average age 60 "ever imprisoned" in 2010. But in 2030, almost four times as many prisoners will be in the equivalent group above age 60 in the "ever imprisoned" cohort. The living legacy will not stop growing two decades after the currently-in-prison number has reached its peak.

This demonstrates the impact of policy choices on the length of imposed penal disabilities on the size of populations damaged by such restrictions, an issue that will be discussed after population trends have been further documented.

The large numbers of ever-imprisoned in Figure 10.2 are only part of the population covered by legal disabilities. Both the coverage of particular penal disabilities and the length of terms will vary from state to state and from specific disability to specific disability, but the usual category that is targeted for the most substantial general disabilities is all persons convicted of felonies. And this population is always at least twice as large as the group with a prison history. Figure 10.3 provides the estimated volume of living persons with current status of felons, the volume of what the authors estimate as living "former felons" and the estimated volume of living persons who have either status in the four census years profiled in the Shannon et al. study (2017).

The estimates of living current and former felons are only the total population at risk for legal disability because not all states impose disabilities and many states do not continue disabilities for the lifetime of the former felon. So the number of persons with a felony history is larger than those currently disabled in states when there are temporal limits on disability. Texas ends its disability on voting two years after parole supervision ends so that former felons more than two years removed from that landmark are no longer subject to that disability in that state (Brennan Center 2018b). Any national total for a population under currently active disabilities is impossible to estimate.

But the population at risk for such restrictions is the total number of persons with felony history in Figure 10.3, which shows one sharp difference with the prison estimates in Figure 10.2 and one important similarity with the pattern noted in that figure. The difference is the volume in the ever-convicted-of-felony population—over 19 million in 2010 instead of over 7 million for the "ever in prison" for the same year, a difference of over

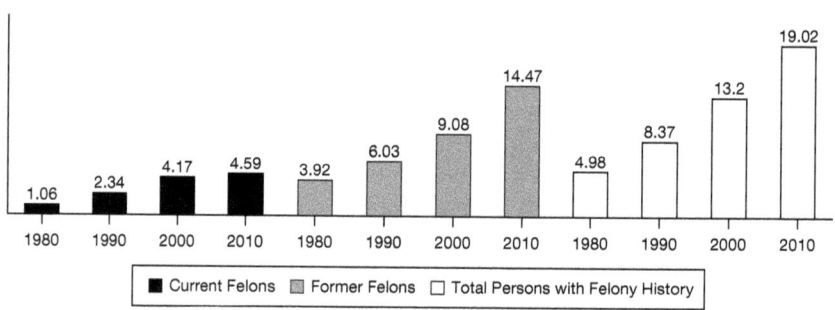

Figure 10.3 Current Felons, Former Felons, and Total Felons 1980–2010.
Source: Shannon et al. 2017.

2.5 to 1 by 2010 that will stay that high in 2020 and 2030. So the ever-convicted-of--a-felony population at risk will stay more than twice as large for the foreseeable future. We know this because of the similarity in the sustained pattern of increase for both "ever" populations. While the number of current felons only increased from 4.17 million to 4.59 million between 2000 and 2010, or 10.1% in 10 years, the growth of "ever convicted of a felony" grew from 13.2 million to 19 million, or 44%, the same growth in that decade of the ever-in-prison category: Only the numbers are much larger. Six million people were added to the population at risk for any permanent disabilities that government units choose to impose on those with felony criminal records.

In one generation, the felony record population grew from just under 5 million to just under 20 million. It is probably still growing and may reach its all-time high in the middle of the three-decade future that is the central concern of this book. The maximum impact of postconviction penal disabilities in the United States will reach a new all-time high between 2020 and 2040 unless laws and policies change.

Vicarious Victimization

This analysis has so far only considered the intended targets of penal disabilities instead of the partners, children, relatives, and close associates of persons convicted of felonies, who also face economic and social disadvantages. If a parent can't find or keep employment, the partner and child of a former felon also suffers substantially. I call these the "vicarious" victims of penal disabilities because, for the most part, those who designed the disabilities did not intend harm to nonoffenders, although in some cases, such as the ban on public housing, it requires willful blindness to ignore the harm to dependents and partners that a disability to a family member produces.

With 19 million former felons and an estimate of at least two vicarious victims for each punished offender, does this mean that we can estimate a total population at risk of at least 57 million distinct direct and vicarious victims? Not quite. Even though each offender's disability harms an average of two other people, if offenses are concentrated in particular socially disadvantaged populations, many persons will suffer not once when a parent or a partner or a child is convicted and punished but several times. Shannon et al. (2017) estimate that 23.4% of African American adults have felony criminal histories. But that doesn't translate into an estimate that 70% of all African Americans are direct or vicarious victims of penal disabilities (23.4% + 46.8% = 70.2%) because many vicarious victims may have two or more relations under penal disabilities.

In social groups with very high concentrations of arrest and punishment, some persons will have four or five or more vicarious links, so that others in the group may have lower rates. Instead of 70% of African Americans having criminal records or close relations who have serious criminal records, it might be "only" 40% or 45% of African American citizens with close links to a punished felon. But many of those with multiple prejudicial contacts may suffer more than vicarious victims with only single contacts. And the concentration of criminal record problems in low-income communities of color may put former offenders and vicarious victims at greater risk.

Whatever the aggregate social cost of penal disabilities in 1980, it is four or five times as large in 2020 as in 1980. And many new types of disability have also been added in the intervening years. How did this happen? How can this still expanding population at risk be protected from gratuitous further damage?

Mixed Motives and Problematic Assumptions

What are the reasons for imposing penal disabilities on convicted offenders, and why do they so often extend long beyond the time when confinement and probation have finished? A book could (and should) be written on this subject, but this is not that book!

There is an enormous range of disabilities imposed on convicted offenders, ranging from residential housing restrictions to ineligibility to vote to exclusion from food stamps to registration with police or state agencies, but all varieties of penal disability are motivated by a mix of punitive and regulatory motives, according to their architects. The disability is almost always intended as a further punishment of the offender no matter what its announced or regulatory function. Both sex offender "registration laws" and the ban on convicted drug offenders from public housing are justified as risk reduction and crime prevention measures. When sex offender registration provisions were first created in the United States, the idea was to give local police some indication of type of sex crime the offender had previously committed so that the offender might be contacted if that type of offense happened again in the community where the former offender lived. How often this happened and how useful such registrations might prove to be would depend, of course, on both how often prior offenders repeated similar crimes and how rarely other persons committed such crimes. When these registration obligations were combined with notifying the public that a convicted sex offender resided in a particular place, there was again a pretense that potential victims could consult the registry and protect themselves by residing where no previously convicted sex offenders also lived. And laws that prohibit convicted sex offenders from living close to schools or playgrounds could also be justified as child protective if there is any relationship between the distance between residence and schools or playgrounds and the rate of child victimization by repeat sex offenders. And if one factor that influenced the availability of drugs in public housing developments was the number of previously convicted drug offenders who lived in the same facility, then prohibiting convicted drug felons from living in such projects might reduce the rate of drug offending in public housing.

But the dominant motive for all of the special prohibitions and for every variety of public notice requirement like "Megan's Laws" is punishment and stigma. The enthusiasm of proponents of sex offender residence bans and public registries is in no way conditioned on belief in the preventive effectiveness of such laws but instead seems to reflect an assumption that anything that harms sex offenders should be considered a public benefit to be celebrated. The only sustained evaluations of "Megan's Laws" have been conducted by skeptical criminologists, and these studies provide little evidence of effectiveness (Bonnar-Kidd 2010; Ackerman, Sacks, and Greenberg 2012), but also little discomfort to those who created the laws. In part this enthusiasm for unlimited punishment seems linked to strong feelings that criminal justice processes should be regarded as status competitions between the victims of crime and criminal offenders. If an observer really believes that anything that hurts criminal offenders must also benefit crime victims, then any additional pain and suffering on offenders can be seen as a public benefit. Gordon Hawkins and I called such an assumption "the zero-sum fallacy" in our study of the politics of punishment in the United States in the 1990s (Zimring, Hawkins, and Kamin, 2001). And it was exactly this period that produced many of the drastic expansions in penal disabilities such as Megan's Laws.

There are two problems associated with the zero-sum fallacy. The first problem is imagining that crime victims benefit from any additional hardship imposed on offenders decades after the offense. The second problem, which was emphasized in the first two sections of this chapter, is that many, even most, of the people who suffer from the effects of penal disabilities are innocent persons who are dependent on or care about criminal offenders: the 1.3 children per prison inmate who have neither a parent or the economic benefit of a parent while a father or mother is locked up, or who cannot gain full support because of the economic damage that a felony criminal record imposes on a parent. It is impossible to restrict the harms associated with criminal punishment to those who committed the offenses.

One of the common penal disabilities in the United States is restrictions on eligibility to vote, which often covers all persons while imprisoned and in some states is extended to felons for sustained periods. Since the original distinction between felony and lesser crimes in English criminal law was eligibility for the death penalty, the rhetorical support for permanent deprivation of political capacity was that a felony conviction was itself a form of "civil death," although why this might be so in the United States where there was never any powerful overlap between felony conviction and execution is hard to imagine (Saunders 1970). There is in fact no justification for loss of voting rights as a penal disability other than punishment, and there are particular problems with imposing this disability on a permanent basis that illustrate the emptiness of the theoretical justifications for penal disabilities of many kinds.

Why should a person convicted of a felony crime never be permitted to vote? While there were historical periods when voting was restricted to privileged subsets of the citizenry, property owners, then men, such restrictions have long been considered inconsistent with democratic citizenship, which carries its branches to all adults. Does a person convicted of crime lose citizenship? *Trop v. Dulles*, one of the first announcements of Eighth Amendment restrictions by the US Supreme Court, held in 1958 that loss of citizenship as a criminal penalty would violate the offender's right to be free of cruel and unusual punishment (see 356 U.S. 93–104). Are there other citizens forbidden to vote? Minors suffer a delay in voting eligibility, but this is not permanent exclusion. In theory, there may be minimum standards of competence such as literacy that are linked to the capacity to make choices in the voting booth, but these are probably minimal and if methods exist to inform those not capable of reading short of denial of the franchise, the better policy given current understanding of the link between citizenship and voting eligibility is always to provide informational assistance.

Is there any sense in which the commission of a felony crime makes a person's continued ability to vote into an important threat to American democratic government? Not that has been discovered and announced. But if the punitive denial of the opportunity to vote is bad political philosophy, it is by equal measure also terrible empirical criminology. The denial of voting on a permanent basis makes conviction for a single act into a permanent status. Commit one crime and your permanent identity is as a criminal offender. Much if not most of American criminal justice policy depends on assumptions about the capacity of persons who have offended to change their behaviors, not just rehabilitation and juvenile justice but also special deterrent threats that depend on the capacity of potential offenders to respond to incentives.

Is there any evidence that restoration of voting privileges has ever created problems in any of the many nations and several American states that allow this? None. Why then are restrictions still in force in American states? This is a question of both political policy and of constitutional law. As a matter of politics, the practical wisdom holds that right-wing state politicians support voting restrictions because disproportionate numbers of persons who can't vote are minorities and other low-income groups who would probably favor their political opponents. What makes my protracted analysis frightening is that voting restrictions may be typical of a wide variety of senseless but obscure penal disabilities.

For the most part, penal disabilities are low-visibility issues without sustained importance in state political life. The exceptions to low visibility are campaigns to impose special restrictions such as registries and public notification on sex offenders and residential limits of various kinds of sex offenders and drug offenders. There are 44,000 separate statutes spread among 50 states and the federal government and an uncounted number of county and codes. How might a reform effort of modest proportions to address this ocean of disabilities best be organized?

Lessons from the Florida Miracle

The 2018 midterm elections in Florida produced one high-profile reform of a long-standing penal disability that had prohibited persons with records of felony conviction from eligibility to vote. Penal reformers had been trying to remove this barrier for almost a decade through legislative proposals and litigation. But the political stakes of expanding voter eligibility were quite high—more than a million potential new voters—and the tug of war over reform proposals was resisted by an incumbent Republican governor. His proposed system for restoring voting rights involved required clemency petitions and individual decisions by the governor, a process that a federal court struck down as unduly restrictive in early 2018.

The proreform groups collected more than 800,000 signatures to put reform on the ballot as Proposition 4 to amend the Jim Crow–era Florida constitution, which had imposed the ban.[1] Proposition 4 obtained the supermajority requirement with a 64.1% majority.[2]

The passage of a law that restores voting rights to all but a small number of convicted felons is obviously good news, but the protracted struggle that delayed and this final decisive effort is also an important indication of how difficult and costly individual reforms can be even when public opinion will support efforts to generate change. One reason that disenfranchisement was such a struggle was the vested interest of Republicans in the state to avoid a substantial expansion of voters from racial minorities. So restrictions on voting continue in a number of states. But the saga of Proposition 4 is also an illustration of the energy required to combat the inertial power of tens of thousands of obscure penal disabilities.

Florida is also a stunning case study in the long road ahead for the removal of penal disabilities. Without doubt, the denial of voting rights to former felons was one of the most offensive restrictions in Florida law, but it was one of more than a thousand barriers that state law maintains to inhibit the liberty of people with criminal convictions. Figure 10.4 provides a partial breakdown of the restrictions that were left on the books in the aftermath of the landslide victory for voting rights in November 2018.

---

[1] ABC News, November 7, 2018
[2] *New York Times* Tracker, November 7, 2018.

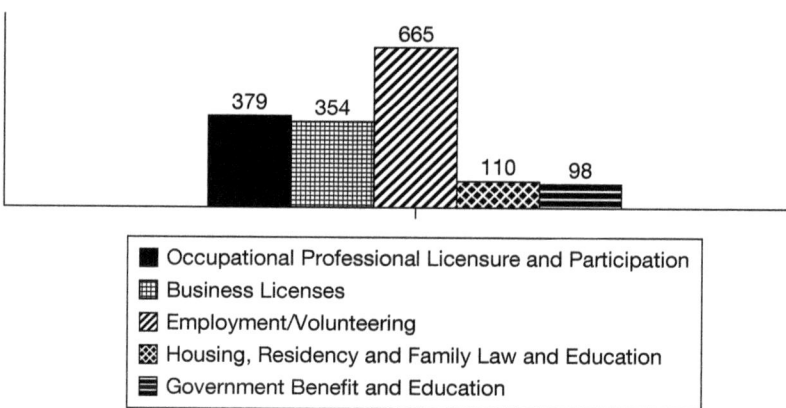

Figure 10.4 Current Restrictions on Florida Citizens with Felony Criminal Records. *Note*: Laws frequently impose restrictions in more than one activity. *Source*: Justice Center 2019.

There were 1,011 separate provisions in Florida law identified in the report prepared by James Stone for this study. How can observers find and categorize this vast and miscellaneous dictionary of civil disability? How can each of these provisions be evaluated and subjected to legislative assessment?

One Path to Progress

While the precise number of persons currently subject to penal disabilities cannot be calculated, the volume of those directly covered in 2020 is many times greater than in earlier periods because of the fivefold expansion of felony convictions in the penal expansion after 1970. The variety of disabilities also has expanded, particularly for sex and drug offenders. Tens of millions of those related to and dependent on persons with criminal records also suffer vicarious victimizations for conduct that was neither their fault nor within their control. So penal disabilities have innocent victims, and this population at risk has also expanded with the penal explosion documented in this volume.

For some of the newer variety of registration and public notification requirements, there is an overlap between punitive and preventive or regulatory justifications for practices, and this will frequently be impossible to unravel. For other penal disabilities such as restrictions on voting, it is difficult to imagine a rationale other than punishment. There are two reasons why the issue of penal disability as government policy belongs in a study of mass incarceration and the penal expansion that produced it. The fabulous explosion in the number of felony convictions that Chapter 2 documented and Chapters 3 and 4 attempted to explain made attaching collateral disabilities into a practice that damages much larger numbers of offenders and those whose destiny is linked to them. The ideological and moral assumptions that justify these collateral damages are twins of the assumptions that generated mass incarceration. Prohibitions of voting opportunities are secondary symptoms of the same assumption that the person who has committed a crime is a permanent social enemy of the citizenry.

Why do these disabilities persist? The public support for most penal disabilities is minimal, but so is the intensity and priority of those who wish to generate reforms in such practices. The thousands of penal disabilities are candidates for obscure but eternal existence.

How can these obscure irritants be dealt with without diverting time and resources from reducing imprisonment in the United States? I want to suggest both a mechanism and a methodology that could both improve our knowledge base about penal disability and its effects and also increase the prospects for immediate reform in federal and state legislation.

The mechanism that will add substantial value for this topic is a national commission of experts on criminal justice policy and offender rehabilitation programs. The commission's activities could be supported by the National Academy of Sciences Committee on Law and Justice or the National Institute of Corrections. Indeed, a joint effort by these two institutions might be an ideal launching strategy.

The methodology this topic needs is a scientific review and a policy analysis. What do we know about the justification for each subtype of penal disabilities, voting restrictions, ineligibility for professional license, registration requirements, public notification programs, residential restrictions, prohibition of presence in areas frequented by children, and so on? If there are documented preventive or crime solution effects from any disability strategies, what is their duration?

What are the effects of various restrictions on persons with qualifying conviction records, and what are the vicarious victim effects on children, partners, other family, and on persons economically dependent on convicted offenders subject to disqualifications? How many vicarious victims are at risk from each type of penal disability, and what are the major consequences for them? There is at present no rigorous and thorough inventory of the effects of penal disability policies. For once, this would be a national commission creating new knowledge and organizing a field of inquiry for the first time.

The second major task of a national assessment on penal disability would be a detailed analysis of whether specific disabilities should be permitted to continue and, if so, for how long after conviction and for what purposes?

A Zero-Based Budget?

Commissions of inquiry on criminal justice normally come late in the process of policy debate and empirical research. Many decades of research and debate preceded the activities of Britain's Royal Commission on Capital Punishment that reported results in 1953. Similar research and debate histories preceded the US President's Commissions on Crime (1967) on Pornography (1970), and on Violence (1969 and 1981).

But a Commission on Penal Disability and Policy would differ from those antecedents in three respects. There is little information or analysis in existing scholarship or debate on penal disability—some history, a few court cases, and very few studies of the number of persons affected or the nature of any behavioral effects. Rather than summarizing the knowledge on a topic with an extensive history, a commission of inquiry on this topic would have to create and organize a field of inquiry. The second difference between a commission on penal disabilities and prior commissions on penal issues is that the usual governmental commission report comes after governments have already been actively involved in making policy on the topics to be investigated. For penal disability, little attention has been paid to the definition, justification, and evaluation of these policies. Legislation is passed and all but forgotten. Most penal disability provisions in state law have low visibility and get little attention from policy actors. The third difference between penal disability and many other issues is the level of government where most of the legislation resides. State and local governments have few resources for research and evaluation, and for the most part the national government has not paid attention to the proliferation of disabilities throughout the federal system. The net effect of this legacy of inattention is that the value that a serious national commission could add to research and to policy analysis is much greater than for topics with more substantial levels of prior attention.

The greatest value from a serious examination of the costs and benefits of the existing and proposed penal disabilities would be specific policy recommendations for each type of disability. The rhetorical appeal of what is called a "zero-based budget" is that it gives no priority to the continuation of previous practices. Zero-based budgeting is a framework in which everything in previous policies should be reexamined with no prejudice toward continuity. There is no preference in this strategy for the status quo. Radical changes stand on equal footing with incremental changes if they are justified by a plausible calculus of cost and benefit.

A sustained analysis by an expert panel that presented detailed proposals for abolishing, limiting, or altering existing disabilities could become a blueprint for federal and state legislation and a new standard against which the rhetoric about the need for and value of penal disabilities could be measured.

With the probable exception of sex offender registration, the continuity of most penal disability owes much more to inattention than to public anger and hostility. The drug war public housing pattern shows a brief period of attention that either generates a new prohibition or doesn't. What happens next is usually that nothing happens. No abolitions but no new provisions. The new status quo, whatever it is, reigns in obscurity.

Strategies for Removing Unnecessary Penal Disabilities

There are three alternative ways that a comprehensive analysis of state, federal, and local penal disabilities could be used as a path to reforming state and federal laws governing those disabilities. The least aggressive strategy is to provide information but leave states, the federal government, and local governments free to make their own decisions about changing current laws. The obvious problem with this passive policy is that very few laws would be changed. At the other extreme would be using the findings of such a commission as the foundation for challenging state restrictions as violations of the Eighth Amendment. This is a high-cost and high-risk enterprise that risks outright rejection by an increasingly conservative Supreme Court and would also encounter skeptical federal court judges in many of the states (like Florida) with extensive punitive portfolios of penal disability.

A more modest use of federal law would be legislation providing that states must curtail a variety of penal restrictions to qualify for federal financial aid for criminal justice. This strategy has been used in federal legislation, including the Juvenile Justice and Delinquency Prevention Act of 1974 and, ironically, also to require punitive registration requirements in the federal Megan's Law and its 2006 amendments (Adam Walsh Child Protection and Safety Act 2006). This is less objectionable than massive Eighth Amendment litigation and might be sufficient motivation for substantial pruning back of obscure and unimportant penal restrictions.

Competition or Complementarity?

Many of the penal disabilities that put former offenders and their families at risk are unjustified and silly, but with millions of persons in prisons and jails, are these accessories to the penal state really worth priority as a reform objective in a million-cage nation? To imagine that sentencing reform and examining penal disabilities compete in the marketplace of public opinion is probably inaccurate. In most eras, public opinion is not often concerned with prisoners, or with the operation of the penal law or with the administration of justice. The real challenge that any penal reform needs to survive is to capture public attention from other topics, economic, political, or entertainment. Any appeal that makes people pay attention to the struggles and prospects of former offenders in or out of secure confinement is an important step toward continuing to pay attention to issues of justice and proportionate punishment. Paying serious attention to reforms of thousands of arbitrary penal disabilities will only help to focus attention on the other problems of penal justice that require reform.

References

Ackerman, A. R., M. Sacks, and D. F. Greenberg. 2012. "Legislation Targeting Sex Offenders: Are Recent Policies Effective in Reducing Rape?" 29 *Justice Quarterly* 858–887.
ACLU. 2014. *The Dangerous Overuse of Solitary Confinement in the United States*. https://www.aclu.org/report/dangerous-overuse-solitary-confinement-united-states.
Alexander, Michelle. 2011. *The New Jim Crow*. Rev. ed. New York: New Press.
American Law Institute. [1963] 2018. *Modern Penal Code: Sentencing*. Philadelphia, PA: American Law Institute.
Anderson, Rick. 2017. "California Prisons Struggle with Environmental Threats from Sewage Spills, Contaminated Water, Airborne Disease." *Prison Legal News*, December 5. https://www.prisonlegalnews.org/news/2017/dec/5/california-prisons-struggle-environmental-threats-sewage-spills-contaminated-water-airborne-disease/.
Arpaio, Joe. 1996. *America's Toughest Sheriff: How We Can Win the War against Crime*. Fort Worth, Texas: Summit Publishing Group.
Aussenberg, Randy Alison, David Carpenter, Gene Falk, and Maggie McCarty. 2016. "Drug Testing and Crime-Related Restrictions in TANF, SNAP, and Housing Assistance." Congressional Research Service, November 28.
Austin, J., and K. McGinnis. 2004. *Classification of High-Risk and Special Management Prisoners: A National Assessment of Current Practices*. US Department of Justice, Institute of Corrections. https://s3.amazonaws.com/static.nicic.gov/Library/019468.pdf.
Austin, James. 2010. "Reducing America's Correctional Population: A Strategic Plan." 12 *Justice Research and Policy*.

Barkow, Rachel. 2019. *Prisoners of Politics: Breaking the Cycle of Mass Incarceration.* Cambridge, MA: Harvard University Press.

Barnes, Harry Elmer, and Negley Teeters. 1946. *New Horizons in Criminology.* New York: Prentice Hall.

Bazelon, Emily. 2019. *Charged.* New York: Random House.

Beck, A. J., and A. Blumstein. 2012. *Trends in Incarceration Rates: 1980–2010.* For the National Research Council Committee on the Causes and Consequences of High Rates of Incarceration, Washington, DC.

Bird, Mia, and Joseph Hays. 2013. "Funding Public Safety Realignment in California." Public Policy Institute of California.

Blumstein, Alfred, and Allen Beck. 1999. "Population Growth in U.S. Prisons, 1980-1996." 26 *Crime and Justice* 17–61.

Blumstein, Alfred, and Jacqueline Cohen. 1973. "A Theory of the Stability of Punishment." 64 *Journal of Criminal Law and Criminology* 198.

Bonnar-Kidd, K. K. 2010. "Sexual Offender Laws and Prevention of Sexual Violence or Recidivism." 100 *American Journal of Public Health* 412–419.

Brennan Center for Justice. 2018a.

Brennan Center for Justice. 2018b. "Criminal Disenfranchisement Laws across the United States." April 18. www.brennancenter.org/criminal-disenfranchisement-laws-across-united-states.

Brown, Edmund G., Jr. 1975. "1975–76 Governor's Budget." June 10. https://archive.org/details/governorsbudget7576unse/page/n973.

Bureau of Justice Statistics. "Prisoners in 2010." https://www.bjs.gov/content/pub/pdf/p10.pdf

Bureau of Justice Statistics. 2005. *Special Report on Suicide and Homicide in State Prisons and Local Jails.*

Bureau of Justice Statistics. 2013. Prison Population Counts. https://www.bjs.gov/index.cfm?ty=tp&tid=131#data_collections.

Bureau of Justice Statistics. 2014. "Prisoners in 2014." https://www.bjs.gov/content/pub/pdf/p14.pdf.

Bureau of Justice Statistics. 2016. "Prisoners in 2015." https://www.bjs.gov/content/pub/pdf/p15.pdf.

Bureau of Justice Statistics. 2016. "Prisoners in 2016." https://www.bjs.gov/content/pub/pdf/p16.pdf.

Bureau of Justice Statistics. Various years. "Prisoners in the United States." Annual Reports 1970–2019.

Bureau of Justice Statistics. n.d. Federal Criminal Case Processing Statistics. In "Prisoners Entering Federal Prison." https://www.bjs.gov/fjsrc/var.cfm?ttype=one_variable&agency=BOP&db_type=Prisoners&saf=IN.

Bureau of Justice Statistics, Annual Probation Survey, Annual Parole Survey, Annual Survey of Jails, Census of Jail Inmates, and National Prisoner Statistics Program, 1980–2015.

Bureau of Labor Statistics. n.d. "CPI Inflation Calculator." https://data.bls.gov/cgi-bin/cpicalc.pl.

Bureau of the Census. 1970. "State Tax Collections in 1970." U.S. Department of Commerce. https://www2.census.gov/govs/pubs/state_govt_tax_collections/1970_state_govt_tax_collections.pdf.

Bureau of the Census. 2011. "State Tax Collections Summary Report: 2010." U.S. Department of Commerce. https://www2.census.gov/govs/statetax/2010stcreport.pdf.

Bureau of the Census. n.d.a. "Historical National Population Estimates: July 1, 1900–July 1 1999." https://www.census.gov/population/estimates/nation/popclockest.txt.

Bureau of the Census. n.d.b. "National Intercensal Tables, 2000–2010." https://www.census.gov/data/tables/time-series/demo/popest/intercensal-2000-2010-national.html.

Bureau of the Census. n.d.c. "U.S. and World Population Clock." https://www.census.gov/popclock/.

Cahalan, M. W. 1986. "Historical Correctional Statistics of the United States 1850–1985." Bureau of Justice Statistics, US Department of Justice.

California Department of Corrections. 2001. *California Prisoners and Parolees: Summary Statistics on Felon Prisoners and Parolees, Civil Narcotic Addicts and Outpatients and Other Populations.* https://sites.cdcr.ca.gov/research/wp-content/uploads/sites/9/2018/04/2000-archive.pdf.

California Department of Corrections and Rehabilitation (CDCR). 2007. *Successes and Challenges: The CDCR Story.* Sacramento, CA: Office of Public and Employee Communications.

California Department of Corrections and Rehabilitation (CDCR), Division of Juvenile Justice Research and Data Analytics. Population data available at https://www.cdcr.ca.gov/Juvenile_Justice/Research_and_Statistics/index.html.

Carson, E. Ann, and Elizabeth Anderson. 2016. "Prisoners in 2015." Bureau of Justice Statistics. https://www.bjs.gov/content/pub/pdf/p15.pdf.

Carson, E. Ann, and Daniela Golinelli. 2014. "Prisoners in 2012: Trends in Admissions and Releases, 1995–2012." Bureau of Justice Statistics, US Department of Justice, September 2.

Centers for Disease Control and Prevention (CDC). 2016. "Overdose Deaths Involving Opioids, Cocaine, and Psychostimulants—United States, 2015–2016." https://www.cdc.gov/mmwr/volumes/67/wr/mm6712a1.htm#T1_down.

Cronin, Thomas E., Tania Z. Cronin, and Michael E. Milakovich. 1981. *U.S. vs. Crime in the Streets.* Bloomington: Indiana University Press.

Davey, Monica. 2008. "Federal Report Finds Poor Conditions at Cook County Jail." *New York Times,* July 18. https://www.nytimes.com/2008/07/18/us/18cook.html?em&ex=1216526400&en=0fd5af153b22e24b&ei=5087%0A.

Drug Enforcement Administration Offices: www.leopulse.com/research/federal/dea/field-offices.

Diagard, L., S. Sullivan, and E. Vanko. 2018. "Rethinking Restrictive Housing: Lessons from Five U.S. Jail and Prison Systems." Vera Institute of Justice.

Drug Enforcement Administration. 2017. Budget request. https://www.justice.gov/jmd/file/822096/download.

Drug Enforcement Administration. n.d. "Staffing and Budget." https://www.dea.gov/staffing-and-budget.

Elmahrek, Adam. 2017. "Violence and Inhumane Conditions Plague Orange County Jails, ACLU Report Alleges." *Los Angeles Times,* June 27. http://www.latimes.com/local/lanow/la-me-ln-oc-jails-aclu-report-inhumane-20170627-story.html.

Federal Bureau of Investigation. 2014. Uniform Crime Report. https://ucr.fbi.gov/crime-in-the-u.s/2015/crime-in-the-u.s.-2015/tables/table-29.

Federal Bureau of Investigation. 2015. "Crime in the United States." https://ucr.fbi.gov/crime-in-the-u.s/2015/crime-in-the-u.s.-2015/tables/table-1.

Federal Bureau of Investigation. n.d. "Uniform Crime Reporting Statistics." https://www.ucrdatatool.gov/index.cfm.

Feeley, Malcolm M., and Austin D. Sarat. 1980. *The Policy Dilemma: Federal Crime Policy and the Law Enforcement Assistance Administration, 1968–1978*. Minneapolis: University of Minnesota Press.

Ferguson, Margaret. 2006. *The Executive Branch of State Government—People, Process and Policies*. Santa Barbara, CA: ABC-CLIO.

Finkelhor, David, and Lisa Jones. 2004. *Explanation for the Decline in Child Sexual Abuse Cases*. Washington, DC: US Department of Justice, Office of Juvenile Justice and Delinquency.

Forman, James. 2017. *Locking Up Our Own: Crime and Punishment in Black America*. New York: Farrar, Straus and Giroux.

Forst, Brian. 2000. "Prosecution's Coming of Age." *Justice Research and Policy* 2: 21.

Fryar, Cheryl, Margaret Carroll, and Cynthia Odgen. 2016. "Prevalence of Overweight and Obesity among Children and Adolescents Aged 2–19 Years: United States, 1963–1965 through 2013–2014." CDC: National Center for Health Statistics. July. https://www.cdc.gov/nchs/data/hestat/obesity_child_13_14/obesity_child_13_14.htm

Gallup. n.d. "Crime." http://news.gallup.com/poll/1603/crime.aspx.

Garland, David. 2001a. *The Culture of Control*. Chicago: University of Chicago Press.

Garland, David, ed. 2001b. *Mass Imprisonment: Social Causes and Consequences*. New York: Russell Sage.

Gartner, Rosemary, Anthony Doob, and Franklin E. Zimring. 2011. "The Past as Prologue? Decarceration in California Then and Now." 10 *Criminology and Public Policy* 291–325.

Gomez, Amanda Michelle. 2018. "States Waste Hundreds of Thousands on Drug Testing for Welfare, but Have Little to Show for It." ThinkProgress, May 7. thinkprogress.org/states-waste-hundreds-of-thousands-on-drug-testing-for-welfare-3d17c154cbe8/.

Gottschalk, Marie. 2006. *The Prison and the Gallows: The Politics of Mass Incarceration in America*. New York: Cambridge University Press.

Government of Canada. 1982. *Criminal Law in Canadian Society*. Ottawa: Government of Canada.

Governor of California. 2015. "Enacted Budget Detail." June 24. http://www.ebudget.ca.gov/2015-16/Enacted/agencies.html.

Guerino, Paul, Paige M. Harrison, and William J. Sabol. 2011. "Prisoners in 2010." Bureau of Justice Statistics, December. https://www.bjs.gov/content/pub/pdf/p10.pdf.

Harcourt, Bernard. 2006. "Should We Aggregate Mental Hospitalization in Empirical Research?" Public Law and Legal Theory Working Paper 114, University of Chicago Law School.

Harcourt, Bernard. 2011. "Reducing Mass Incarceration: Lessons from the Deinstitutionalization of Mental Hospitals in the 1960s." 9 *Ohio State Journal of Criminal Law* 53–88.

Heyman, Philip, and Carol Petrie, eds. 2001. *What's Changing in Prosecution? A Report of a Workshop*. Washington, DC: National Academy Press.

IIHS. 2019. "Fatality Facts 2018: Yearly Snapshot." December. http://www.iihs.org/iihs/topics/t/general-statistics/fatalityfacts/overview-of-fatality-facts.

Jacobs, James B. 2015. *The Eternal Criminal Record*. Cambridge, MA: Harvard University Press.
Jacobson, Michael. 2005. *Downsizing Prisons*. New York: New York University Press.
Johnson, David. 2002. *The Japanese Way of Justice*. New York: Oxford University Press.
Justice Center, Council of State Governments. 2019. https://niccc.csgjusticecenter.org/map/.
Kaiser Family Foundation. 2018. "Opioid Overdose Death Rates and All Drug Overdose Death Rates per 100,000 Population (Age-Adjusted)." https://www.kff.org/other/state-indicator/opioid-overdose-death-rates/?currentTimeframe=0&sortModel=%7B%22colId%22:%22Location%22,%22sort%22:%22asc%22%7D.
Kleiman, Mark. 2009. *When Brute Force Fails*. Princeton, NJ: Princeton University Press.
Kohler-Hausmann. 2017. *Getting Tough: Welfare and Imprisonment in 1970s America*. Princeton, NJ: Princeton University Press.
Krisberg, Barry, Linh Vuong, Christopher Hartney, and Susan Marchionna. 2010. *A New Era in California Juvenile Justice: Downsizing the State Youth Corrections System*. Oakland, CA: National Council on Crime and Delinquency.
Landau, Tammy. 1988. *Views of Sentencing: A Survey of Crown and Defense Counsel*. Toronto: University of Toronto.
Langer, Máximo, and David Sklansky, eds. 2017. *Prosecutors and Democracy: A Cross-National Study*. New York: Cambridge University Press.
Lehrman, Paul. 1975. *Community Treatment and Social Control*. Chicago: University of Chicago Press.
Loftstrom, Magnus, and Steven Raphael. 2015. "Realignment, Incarceration and Crime Trends in California." Public Policy Institute of California.
Love, Margaret Colgate, Jenny Roberts, and Cecilia Klingele. 2016. *Collateral Consequences of Criminal Conviction: Law, Policy and Practice*. Toronto, Ontario: Thomson Reuters.
Management Division, US Department of Justice. 2002.
Mears, Daniel and Joshua C. Cochran. 2015. *Prisoner Reentry in the Era of Mass Incarceration*. Thousand Oaks, CA: Russell Sage.
McPhersson, William. 1984. "A Better Class of Prisoner." *Washington Post*, October 30. https://www.washingtonpost.com/archive/politics/1984/10/30/a-better-class-of-prisoner/fa0d32d0-5aea-45ee-82e9-a08f59bb1190/?utm_term=.e05362e9f8a3.
Meriden Journal. 1967. "Board under Fire on Rights Issue." April. https://news.google.com/newspapers?id=YbNIAAAAIBAJ&sjid=bwENAAAAIBAJ&dq=frank%20rizzo%20appointed%20commissioner&pg=828%2C5233926.
Messinger, Sheldon, and Philip Johnson. 1978. *California's Determinate Sentencing Statute, History and Issues in Determinate Sentencing: Reform or Regression?* US Department of Justice, National Institute of Justice. Washington, DC: Government Printing Office.
Miller, Justin. 2010. "New Jersey's Riverfront Prison Demolished." *Prison Legal News*, August 15. https://www.prisonlegalnews.org/news/2010/aug/15/new-jerseys-riverfront-prison-demolished/.
Morris, Norval, and Gordon Hawkins. 1970. *The Honest Politician's Guide to Crime Control*. Chicago: University of Chicago Press.

Morris, Norval, and Gordon Hawkins. 1977. *Letter to the President on Crime Control.* Chicago: University of Chicago Press.

Morris, Norval, and David J. Rothman, eds. 1995. *The Oxford History of the Prison: The Practice of Punishment in Western Society.* New York: Oxford University Press.

Murray, J., D. P. Farrington, I. Sekol, and R. F. Olsen. 2009. *Effects of Parental Imprisonment on Child Antisocial Behavior and Mental Health: A Systematic Review.* Oslo: Campbell Corporation.

National Academy of Sciences (NAS). 2014. *The Growth of Incarceration in the United States.* Jeremy Travis, Bruce Western, and Steve Redburn, eds. National Research Council of the National Academies. Washington, DC: National Academies Press.

National Academy of Sciences (NAS). 2017. *Pain Management and the Opioid Epidemic: Balancing Societal and Individual Benefits and Risks of Prescription Opioid Use.*

National Corrections Reporting Program. 2000. "Most Serious Offense of State Prisoners, by Offense, Admission Type, Age, Sex, Race, and Hispanic Origin." https://www.bjs.gov/content/data/ncrpm00.zip.

Nitcher, E. 2018. "Federal Form Gives Incorrect Info on Federal Voting Rights in Nebraska." *Omaha World Herald.* http://www.omaha.com/news/nebraska/federal-form-gives-incorrect-info-on-felon-voting-rights-in/article_cb80be7b-270b-5d9d-a340-87cd3e6250c9.html.

Obama, Barack. 2017. "The President's Role in Advancing Criminal Justice Reform." 130 *Harvard Law Review* 811.

Office of National Drug Control Policy. 1989. *The National Drug Control Strategy.* Washington, DC.

Office of Juvenile Justice and Delinquency Prevention, US Department of Justice. 2017. "The Number of Juveniles in Residential Placement Reached a New Low in 2015." https://www.ojjdp.gov/ojstatbb/snapshots/DataSnapshot_CJRP2015.pdf.

Ohio Department of Corrections. 2000. Annual Commitment Report. http://drc.ohio.gov/LinkClick.aspx?fileticket=UaQdCkbiOxA%3d&portalid=0.

Ohio Department of Corrections. 2016. Annual Commitment Report. http://drc.ohio.gov/Portals/0/Reentry/Reports/Commitment%20Reports/CY2016%20COMMITMENT%20REPORT.pdf?ver=2017-03-10-103733-650.

Page, Joshua. 2011. *The Toughest Beat: Politics, Punishment and the Prison Officers Union in California.* New York: Oxford University Press.

Parent, Dale. 1988. "Structuring Criminal Sentences: The Evolution of Minnesota's Sentencing Guidelines." Lexis.

Pattillo, Mary, Bruce Western, and David Weiman, eds. 2004. *Imprisoning America: The Social Effects of Mass Incarceration.* New York: Russell Sage.

Pfaff, John. 2017. *Locked In: The True Causes of Mass Incarceration and How to Achieve Real Reform.* New York: Basic Books.

Pontell, Henry. 1984. *A Capacity to Punish.* Bloomington: Indiana University Press.

Raphael, Steven, and Michael Stoll. 2013. *Why Are So Many Americans in Prison?* Thousand Oaks, CA: Russell Sage.

Reaves, Brian A., and Lynn M. Bauer. 2003. *Federal Law Enforcement Officers 2002.* Washington, DC: Bureau of Justice Statistics, NCJ 199995.

Reiter, Keramet. 2016. *23/7: Pelican Bay Prison and the Rise of Long-Term Solitary Confinement.* New Haven: Yale University Press.

Reiter, Keramet. 2017. *Mass Incarceration*. New York: Oxford University Press.
Rhoden, William C., Michael Wright, and Caroline Rand Herron. 1982. "The Nation in Summary: Houston Gets a New Police Chief." *New York Times*, March 28. https://www.nytimes.com/1982/03/28/weekinreview/the-nation-in-summary-houston-police-get-a-new-chief.html.
Royston, P. 1983. "A Simple Method for Evaluating the Shapiro-Francia W Test of Non-normality." 32 *Statistician* 297–300.
Royston, P. 1991. "Estimating Departure from Normality." 10 *Statistics in Medicine* 1283–93.
Saunders, Harry David. 1970. "Civil Death: A New Look at an Ancient Doctrine." 11 *William and Mary Law Review* 988–1003.
Schwirtz, Michael. 2017. "Brutal Force at Rikers Island Continues at an 'Alarming Rate,' Report Says." *New York Times*, April 3. https://www.nytimes.com/2017/04/03/nyregion/brutal-force-at-rikers-island-continues-at-an-alarming-rate-report-says.html.
Sentencing Project. 2017. "Trends in US Corrections." https://justnet.org/pdf/Sentencing-Project-Trends-in-US-Corrections.pdf.
Shannon, Sarah K. S., Christopher Uggen, Jason Schnittker, Melissa Thompson, Sara Wakefield, and Michael Massoglia. 2017. "The Growth, Scope, and Spatial Distribution of People with Felony Records in the United States, 1948–2010." 54 *Demography* 1795–1818.
Shapiro, S. S., and R. S. Francia. 1972. "An Approximate Analysis of Variance Test for Normality (Complete Samples)." 67 *Journal of the American Statistical Association* 215–16.
Shapiro, S. S., and M. B. Wilk. 1965. "An Analysis of Variance Test for Normality (Complete Samples)." 52 *Biometrika* 591–611.
Sherman, Michael, and Gordon Hawkins. 1983. *Imprisonment in America: Choosing the Future*. Chicago: University of Chicago Press.
Shinar, Shlomo, and Reuel Shinar. 1975. "The Effects of the Criminal Justice System on the Control of Crime: A Quantitative Approach." *Law and Society Review* 9: 581–611.
Simon, Jonathan. 2014. *Mass Incarceration on Trial: A Remarkable Decision and the Future of Prisons in America*. New York: New Press.
Smith, Peter Scharff. 2014. *When the Innocent Are Punished: The Children of Imprisoned Parents*. New York: Palgrave Macmillan.
"State Prison Capacity, Overcrowded Prisons Data." 2013. *Governing*. http://www.governing.com/gov-data/safety-justice/state-prison-capacity-overcrowding-data.html.
"State Prison Capacity, Overcrowded Prisons Data." 2018. *Governing*. http://www.governing.com/gov-data/safety-justice/state-prison-capacity-overcrowding-data.html.
Steele, Allison. March 16, 2017. "Once a Prison, Soon to Be Waterfront Park in South Jersey." *Philadelphia Inquirer*. http://www.philly.com/philly/news/new_jersey/Camden-prison-waterfront-park-development.html.
Steiker, Carol. 2011. "Mass Incarceration: Causes, Consequences, and Exit Strategies." 9 *Ohio State Journal of Criminal Law* 1.
Stuntz, William. 2011. *The Collapse of American Criminal Justice*. Cambridge, MA: Belknap Press of Harvard University Press.

Su, Kai-Ping. 2016. "Revisiting the Concept and the Merits of Empirical Legal Studies: Lessons from Taiwan's Commutation Policy." 45 *National Taiwan University Law Journal*, 979–1043.

Sutherland, Edwin, and C. C. Van Vechten Jr. 1934. "Reliability of Criminal Statistics." 25 *Journal of Criminal Law and Criminology* 10.

Tran-Leung, Marie Claire. 2015. "When Discretion Means Denial: A National Perspective on Criminal Records Barriers to Federally Subsidized Housing." Sargent Shriver National Center on Poverty Law.

Twentieth Century Fund Task Force. 1976. *Fair and Certain Punishment*. New York: McGraw Hill.

US Department of Health and Human Services, Administration for Children and Families, Administration on Children, Youth and Families, Children's Bureau. 2018. *Child Maltreatment 2016*. Available from https://www.acf.hhs.gov/cb/research-data-technology/statistics-research/child-maltreatment.

Vera Institute of Justice. 2015. The Price of Jails: Measuring the Taxpayer Cost of Local Incarceration. Center on Sentencing and Corrections.

Vera Institute of Justice. 2018. "People in Prison in 2017." Vera Evidence Brief.

Von Hirsch, Andrew, et al. 1975. *Doing Justice: The Choice of Punishments*. New York: Hill and Wang.

Western, Bruce. 2007. Punishment and Inequality in America. New York: Russell Sage.

West Virginia Department of Military Affairs and Public Safety. 2017. "Drug Offenders Incarcerated in West Virginia: Characteristics and Population Trends, 1998–2015."

Wilson, James Q. 1975. *Thinking about Crime*. New York: Basic Books.

Windlesham, David James George Hennessy. 1998. *Politics, Punishment and Populism*. New York: Oxford University Press.

Wong, Julia Carrie, and Lauren Gambino. 2017. "Donald Trump Pardons Joe Arpaio, Former Sheriff Convicted in Racial Profiling Case." *The Guardian*, August 26. https://www.theguardian.com/us-news/2017/aug/25/donald-trump-joe-arpaio-pardon-arizona-sheriff.

World Prison Brief. n.d. "World Prison Brief Data." https://www.prisonstudies.org/world-prison-brief-data.

Zimring, Franklin E. 1983. "Sentencing Reform in the States: Lessons from the 1970s," 101–121. In Michael Tonry and Franklin E. Zimring, eds., *Reform and Punishment: Essays on Criminal Sentencing*. Chicago: University of Chicago Press.

Zimring, Franklin E. 2005. "Penal Policy and Penal Legislation in Recent American Experience." 58 *Stanford Law Review* 323–334.

Zimring, Franklin E. 2007. *The Great American Crime Decline*. New York: Oxford University Press.

Zimring, Franklin E. 2008. "Criminology and Its Discontents: The American Society of Criminology 2007 Sutherland Address." *Criminology* 46: 255.

Zimring, Franklin E. 2010. "The Scale of Imprisonment in the United States: Twentieth Century Patterns and Twenty-First Century Prospects." 100 *Journal of Criminal Law and Criminology* 3.

Zimring, Franklin E. 2014. "The Power Politics of Juvenile Court Transfer." In Franklin E. Zimring and David S. Tanenhaus, eds., *Choosing the Future for American Juvenile Justice*. New York: New York University Press.

Zimring, Franklin E. 2017. *When Police Kill*. Cambridge, MA: Harvard University Press.
Zimring, Franklin E., and Bernard Harcourt. 2007. *Criminal Law and the Regulation of Vice*. St. Paul, MN: Thomson West.
Zimring, Franklin E., and Bernard Harcourt. 2014. *Criminal Law and the Regulation of Vice*. 2nd ed. St. Paul, MN: Thompson West.
Zimring, Franklin E., and Gordon Hawkins. 1973. *Deterrence: The Legal Threat in Crime Control*. Chicago: University of Chicago Press.
Zimring, Franklin E., and Gordon Hawkins, eds. 1984. *The Pursuit of Criminal Justice: Essays from the Chicago Center*. Chicago: University of Chicago Press.
Zimring, Franklin E., and Gordon Hawkins. 1991. *The Scale of Imprisonment*. Chicago: University of Chicago Press.
Zimring, Franklin E., and Gordon Hawkins. 1992. *The Search for Rational Drug Control*. New York: Cambridge University Press.
Zimring, Franklin E., and Gordon Hawkins. 1995. *Incapacitation: Penal Confinement and the Restraint of Crime*. New York: Oxford University Press.
Zimring, Franklin E., and Gordon Hawkins. 1997. *Crime Is Not the Problem: Lethal Violence in America*. New York: Oxford University Press.
Zimring, Franklin E., Gordon Hawkins, and Sam Kamin. 2001. *Punishment and Democracy: Three Strikes and You're Out in California*. New York: Oxford University Press.
Zimring, Franklin E., and David T. Johnson. 2012. "The Dark at the Top of the Stairs: Four Destructive Influences of Capital Punishment on American Criminal Justice." In Joan Petersilia and Kevin R. Reitz, eds., *The Oxford Handbook of Sentencing and Corrections*. New York: Oxford University Press.
Zoukis, Christopher. 2017. *Prison Legal News*, February 8.

Index

Tables and figures are indicated by *t* and *f* following the page number
For the benefit of digital users, indexed terms that span two pages (e.g., 52–53) may, on occasion, appear on only one of those pages.

Adam Walsh Child Protection and Safety Act, 197
adversarial systems of criminal justice
 budgetary considerations among local governments and, 54, 77–78
 constitutional restrictions on police investigations and, 53
 defense attorneys and, 53, 54, 55
 election of prosecutors and judges and, 53, 69, 77
 imprisonment rates viewed as indicator of success in, 54–57, 58–59
 income disparities among defendants and, 53
 localized nature of prosecution and, 68–70, 77, 124, 148–49
 negotiated guilty pleas and, 54–55, 125, 142, 180–81
 prosecutors' incentives in, 53, 58, 79–80, 139, 142–44, 148, 150–52
 reform proposals regarding, 77, 79–80, 83
 sentencing considerations complicated by, 122–23, 127, 139, 142
 Warren Court reform cases and, 53–54, 55
African Americans
 drug crime imprisonment and, 107*f*, 107, 109, 111, 113
 family members of offenders among, 189–90
 race-based attitudes of fear regarding, 72
Alaska, 89
alternatives to imprisonment. *See also* decarceration
 drug decriminalization and, 103
 drug treatment and, 71, 103, 129–30, 138, 141–42, 178
 education programs and, 103
 electronic monitoring and, 44–45, 114, 175
 fear of violent crime as an obstacle to, 72
 financial penalties and, 70
 halfway houses and, 119, 169, 174, 175, 176
 probation and, 70, 130, 141–42
 public opinion regarding, 70
 restorative justice initiatives and, 44–45, 132, 133
 retributive inadequacy questions regarding, 70–71
 work release programs and, 174–75
American exceptionalism, 6
Argentina, 143
Arizona, 23–24
Arpaio, Joe, 23–24

assault
  aggravated *versus* other forms of, 26, 31*f*, 33
  arrest rates for, 25*t*, 30–31, 31*f*, 33, 130–31
  imprisonment rates for individuals convicted of, 26
  nonprison sanctions for, 132
  percent of all inmates imprisoned for, 25*t*, 26
  prison admission rates and, 46*t*, 47*f*, 130–31, 131*f*, 132
  prison impact metric regarding, 25*f*, 27
  time served to release policies and, 37*f*, 37
Austin, James, 84
Australia, 4–5*f*, 5, 53, 71–72, 143
auto theft, 25*f*, 25*t*, 27, 30–31, 31*f*

bail reform, 175–77, 178, 179
Barnes, Harry, 113–14
Beck, Allen, 36–37, 38*f*, 41
Bennett, William, 104, 112
Blumstein, Alfred, 8*f*, 8–10, 36–37, 38*f*, 41
Brown, Lee, 23–24
Brown v. Plata, 91–93, 98–99, 116, 152, 161
Bulgaria, 96*t*
Bureau of Prisons, 176
burglary
  arrest rates for, 25*t*, 30–31, 31*f*, 130–31
  comparative international data on, 71–72
  percent of all inmates imprisoned for, 25*t*
  prison admission rates and, 46–47, 46*t*, 47*f*, 130–31, 131*f*, 132
  prison impact metric regarding, 25*f*, 27
  time served to release policies and, 37*f*, 37
Bush, George W., 37–38

California
  Correctional Peace Officers Union in, 152, 176
  Department of Corrections and Rehabilitation in, 161–62
  imprisonment reduction (2007-17) in, 86–87, 89–90, 90*f*, 91–92, 94, 97–98, 99, 162–63, 164, 167, 171
  juvenile confinement system in, 95, 96*f*, 116, 117, 125, 135–36
  overcrowding of prisons in, 76, 91–92, 97, 116, 125–26, 136, 152, 161–62
  prison admission rates in, 94
  Proposition 36 regarding drug treatment in, 71, 138
  Proposition 47 on changing some crimes to misdemeanors in, 117, 119
  Proposition 57 on parole release for life-term prisoners in, 119
  prosecutors in, 94
  sentencing system in, 11, 30, 122, 135
  shifts in custodial jurisdiction for parole violators in, 91–92, 93*f*, 93–94, 97, 103–4, 115–17, 118–19, 135–36, 138, 152, 154–55, 161
  state prison system in, 13–14, 14*f*, 76–77
  state university system in, 13–14, 14*f*

Youth Authority (CYA) and, 95, 96*f*, 117, 125, 135–36
Canada
  adversarial nature of criminal justice system in, 53, 144–45
  crime rates in, 145–46
  federalist system of government in, 145
  homicide rates in, 145*f*, 145
  imprisonment rate in, 4–5*f*, 5, 145–46
  probation systems in, 70
  prosecutors (Crown attorneys) in, 143, 144–49, 145*f*, 147*f*, 151–52
  violent crime rates in, 71–72
CareCivic corporation, 175–76
child molestation, 20, 132–33
child pornography, 64–65, 132, 133
Cohen, Jacqueline, 8*f*, 8–9
Colorado, 97–98, 184
Connecticut, 89, 97–98, 171
correctional forecasting methodology, 160–62
crack cocaine, 20, 39–40, 105–6
Crime Control Act of 1994, 27
crime rates
  belief in mass imprisonment's ability to reduce, 72–74
  crime classification changes and, 33
  declines since 1990 in, xii, 16, 28*f*, 28–29, 72
  general trends (1970-2015) in, 27–38, 28*f*, 39, 145–46, 146*f*
  imprisonment rates and, 23, 34, 40, 71, 73–74, 123, 146*f*, 146
  juvenile crime rates and, 98
  prison admission rates and, 35
Czech Republic, 96*t*

death penalty, 64, 191–92
decarceration. *See also* alternatives to imprisonment
  Drug Enforcement Agency's institutional interest as potential obstacle to, 80
  families of prisoners as potential beneficiaries of, 83, 155
  federalist system of government as obstacle to, 75–77, 155
  local government budget incentives and, 79–80, 83, 138–39, 141–42
  low-risk offenders and, 172–73
  nonviolent criminal offenses and, 131–32
  parole reform and, 79–80, 134–35
  public fear of violent crime as potential obstacle to, 78
  redundant jurisdictions as a potential obstacle to, 75–76, 80
  state budgets as potential factor promoting, 76–77
  "thinning out" of populations *versus* closure of facilities in, 159–60, 171–72
Delaware, 89
Democracy in America (Tocqueville), 6, 61–62
deterrence purpose for incarceration, 11, 13, 49–50, 121–22, 192

District of Columbia, 184f, 184
driving while intoxicated and alcohol-related offenses, 46t
drug crimes
  arrest rates for, 25t, 32f, 32–33
  decriminalization reforms and, 103
  families of people incarcerated for, 48
  federal prisons and, 37–38, 65t, 75–76, 113
  history of drug dependency among people incarcerated for, 111
  increasing imprisonment after 1985 for, 19–20, 32, 37–38, 105
  overcrowding of prisons and, 48
  percent of all inmates imprisoned for, 25t, 48
  prison admission rates and, 46–48, 46t, 47f, 51, 76, 108–9, 109t, 112–13, 129–30, 131
  prison impact metric regarding, 25f
  public health *versus* legalist approaches to, 104–6, 112–13
  public housing sanctions against felons convicted for, 181–83, 189, 190–91, 192–93, 197
  racial demography of people imprisoned for, 107f
  redundant jurisdictions and enforcement resources for, 64–66, 65t, 76, 80
  salience in public opinion of, 39–40
  sentencing conventions regarding, 48–49, 104
  time served to release policies and, 37f, 37
  varying severity of, 32
  war on drugs policies and, ix–x, 19, 47–48, 63, 71, 76, 104, 112, 131
Drug Enforcement Administration (DEA), 66f, 66, 76, 80, 107–8, 108t, 110
drug use. *See also* drug crimes; *specific drugs*
  overdose deaths and, 105–7, 106–8f
  treatment for addiction and, 44–45, 71, 103, 110–11, 129–30, 138, 141–42, 178

Eighth Amendment (US Constitution), 183, 192, 197
electronic monitoring release programs, 44–45, 114, 175
England. *See also* United Kingdom
  family members of offenders in, 182
  imprisonment rates in, 3–4, 4–5f, 5, 62
  jail system during medieval era in, 113–14
  prison population declines during 1930s in, 7
  "ever imprisoned" population, 186–89, 187–88f

fear of crime, 29–30, 39, 40, 71–72, 78
federal prisons
  child pornography crimes and, 133
  drug crimes and, 37–38, 65t, 75–76, 113
  imprisonment rates in, 37–38, 75
  robbery and, 37–38
federal sentencing commission, 37–38, 136–37
fentanyl, 106–7, 111
Florida
  federal court judges in, 197
  Republican Party in, 193
  voting rights for offenders in, 193–94
forgery and fraud crimes, 46t, 47f, 131f, 132
Forst, Brian, 56
France, 3–4, 4–5f, 143
Frankel, Marvin, 136–37

Garland, David, 3–4
GEO (private prison corporation), 175–76
Georgia, 149
Germany, 3–5, 4–5f
Gideon v. Wainwright, 53

halfway houses, 119, 169, 174, 175, 176
Harcourt, Bernard, 80–81
Henderson, Thelton, 91–93, 152
Henry II (king of England), 113–14
heroin, 105, 111
Hispanics, 107f, 107, 111, 112–13
Holder, Eric, 75
home confinement programs, 44–45
homicide
  annual rates of, 132, 145
  arrest rates for, 25t, 30–31, 31f, 33, 130–31
  comparative international data on, 72, 145f, 145
  families of offenders and, 48
  percent of all inmates imprisoned for, 25t, 48
  prison admission rates and, 46–48, 46t, 47f, 130–31, 131f
  prison impact metric regarding, 25f, 27
  in prisons and jails, 173
  time served to release policies and, 37f, 37
Hungary, 96t

Illinois
  overcrowding of prisons in, 165
  sentencing system in, 11
  Tamms Supermax Prison in, 165, 168, 170, 173
imprisonment rates. *See also* projections regarding imprisonment rates in 2050
  adversarial systems of criminal justice's emphasis on, 54–57, 58–59
  arrest rates and, 30, 32f, 32, 34–35, 40
  assault and, 26
  in comparative international context, 3–6, 4–5f, 61, 62, 66–67, 95–97, 96t, 145–46
  crime rates and, 23, 34, 40, 71, 73–74, 123, 146f, 146
  decline (2007-17) in, 42, 87f, 87–92, 89t, 98–99, 155, 171
  economic conditions' correlation with, 73–74
  era of relative stability (1930-70) in, 8–9f, 8–10, 18–19
  era of vast expansion (1972-2007) in, xi, 4–20, 9f, 24, 32–34f, 33, 39, 40, 44–45, 46t, 47f, 48, 52–53, 145–46, 160–63, 186, 187f
  federalist system of US government and, 7–8, 12–13, 15–18, 20–21, 23–24, 63, 140

imprisonment rates (*cont.*)
  federal *versus* state prison systems and, 37–38, 38*f*
  financial costs associated with, 13–15, 59, 76–77, 91
  government wealth levels and, 66–67
  governors' offices and, 152–53
  local government budget incentives and, 51–53, 58–59, 77–78, 79–80, 116–18, 135, 138–39, 150, 177–78
  mental health facility reductions in the 1960s and, 80–81
  negotiated guilty pleas and, 40
  parole factors and, 36, 42
  peak (2007) of, x, 87
  police efficiency levels and, 34
  potential impact of demographic change on, 73–74
  prison admission rates and, 40, 42–43, 45, 48, 76, 128–29
  prison capacity as potential factor limiting increase in, 91, 97, 98
  prison impact metric regarding, 25*f*, 25–26
  prosecutors and, 40, 41–42, 59, 77, 141–42, 143, 144–45, 151–53
  public perceptions of fear and, 29*f*, 29–30, 39, 40
  redundant jurisdiction and enforcement resources as factor influencing, 64–66, 75–76
  salience of crime in public opinion and, 39–40, 55, 59–60, 143, 144
  sentencing's impact on, 48–49, 127, 177
  state-level variations in, 17*f*, 17–18, 18*t*, 24, 88–99, 89*t*
  time served to release policies and, 36–37, 178–79
  variation by type of crime in, 25*t*, 30–31
incapacitation purpose for imprisonment
  claims regarding effectiveness of, 51, 72–74
  decarceration reforms and, 78
  drug crimes and, 51
  increased interest starting in 1970 in strategy of, 50, 51
  prosecutors' belief in, 143
  rationale behind, 50
  recidivism and, 121–22
  retribution purpose for imprisonment and, 50
inquisitorial judicial systems, 53, 144
Italy, 3–4, 4–5*f*, 62, 70

Jackson Prison (Michigan), 168
jail confinement
  community programs and, 119–20
  conditions in, 81, 115, 119, 136, 159, 168, 173–74
  continuity of service relationships offered by, 114, 168
  flexibility of, 115, 116, 118–19
  geographic proximity to offenders' communities and, 114, 136, 164–65, 168
  as less serious alternative to prison confinement, 45, 70, 71, 103–4, 113–17, 130, 141–42
  local government budgets and, 52, 114, 116, 117–18, 119, 169
  medieval English origins of, 113–14
  parole violators and, 91–92, 93*f*, 93, 116–17
  pretrial detention and, 45, 70, 168, 175–77, 178–79
  reform efforts designed to diversify facilities involved in, 173–77
  shorter duration of sentences and, 114–15, 119, 130, 168–69, 179
  time served to release policies and, 116
  treatment for drug addiction and, 115, 169
Japan, 3–4, 4–5*f*, 143
Joliet Prison (Illinois), 168
Journal of Criminal Law and Criminology, 6–7
judges
  elections and, 68–69, 77
  imprisonment rates impacted by, 77, 141, 151–52
  localized nature of the work of, 68–69, 77
  police conduct evaluations by, 68
  reforms designed to offer more sentencing discretion to, 127, 144
  sentencing recommendations from prosecutors and, 142
  sentencing restrictions placed on, 41, 122, 126, 127, 139
  vested institutional interests of, 140
juvenile confinement
  budget considerations and, 125, 135–36
  in California, 95, 96*f*, 116, 117, 125, 135–36
  declines starting in 1990s in, 98
  Juvenile Justice and Delinquency Prevention Act of 1974 and, 197
  state *versus* local administration of, 95, 98–99, 125

Kentucky, 107

larceny
  arrest rates for, 25–26, 25*t*, 130–31
  percent of all inmates imprisoned for, 25–26, 25*t*
  prison admission rates and, 46*t*, 47*f*, 130–31, 131*f*
  prison impact metric regarding, 25*f*, 27
Law Enforcement Assistance Administration, 56, 160
local governments
  adversarial systems of criminal justice and, 54, 77–78
  decarceration initiatives and, 79–80, 83, 138–39, 141–42

imprisonment in state institutions and
  budgetary considerations of, 51–53, 58–
  59, 77–78, 79–80, 116–18, 135, 138–39,
  150, 177–78
 parole management and, 91–97, 93f, 135–36,
  138, 152, 161
Louisiana, 24

Maddox, Lester, 149–50
Maine, 24
mandatory minimum sentences, 41, 135
Mapp v. Ohio, 53
marijuana, 103, 112–13
Mattick, Hans W., 115
maximum-security prisons, 165, 169, 170–71
Megan's Laws, 191, 197
mental health institutions, 80–81,
  94–95, 176–77
Minnesota, 136–37
Miranda v. Arizona, 53
Model Penal Code, 121–22
Montana, 89
Morris, Norval, 71, 135, 153
murder. *See* homicide
Murphy, Patrick, 23–24

National Academy of Sciences Committee on
  Law, 195
National Institute of Corrections, 195
New Hampshire
  Drug Enforcement Agency in, 108, 108t
  drug overdose deaths in, 107–8, 109, 110f
  imprisonment rates in, 24
  prison admission rates in, 108–9, 109t
New Jersey
  closure of penal institutions in, 172
  imprisonment reduction (2007-17) in, 89,
    97–98, 171
  Riverfront Prison in, 172, 173
New York State
  closure of penal institutions by, 172
  drug overdose deaths in, 107
  fixed costs in prison system of, 76–77
  imprisonment reduction (2007-17) in, 89,
    97–98, 171
North Carolina, 24

Obama, Barack, 75
Ohio
  Drug Enforcement Agency in, 108, 108t
  drug overdose deaths in, 107–8, 109, 110f
  prison admission rates in, 108–9, 109t
opioids
  age demographics of population addicted to,
    107, 108f
  decriminalization reform proposals
    regarding, 110–11, 112
  Drug Enforcement Agency and, 80
  heroin and, 111
  medical prescriptions and, 80, 106–7, 110
  National Academy of Sciences report (2015)
    on, 111, 112
  overdose deaths from, 105–7,
    106–10f, 109–10
  public health approach to addiction
    and, 112
  racial demographics of population addicted
    to, 107f, 107, 111, 113
  treatment for addiction to, 110–11
overcrowding of prisons
  aggregate rates in US state prisons of,
    163, 164f
  Brown v. Plata and, 91–93, 98–99, 116,
    152, 161
  in California, 76, 91–92, 97, 116, 125–26, 136,
    152, 161–62
  drug crimes and, 48
  financial costs and, 14, 76
  medical care and, 14, 76, 91–92, 116, 152
  parole and, 125–26, 137
  prison construction and, 163–64, 164f,
    166, 167
  security problems associated with, 14
  society's lack of urgency regarding, 140,
    152, 162–63
OxyContin, 106–7

parole
  budget considerations
    and, 125–26, 135–36
  expansion during 1980s of, 20
  health of individual prisoners as potential
    factor in, 137
  imprisonment for violations of, 38f, 41
  individual *versus* systemic perspectives
    regarding, 125–26
  in-prison behavior as factor in, 122, 137
  limited jurisdiction of boards
    granting, 125–26, 127, 134
  new criminal convictions for
    people on, 40
  overall imprisonment rates affected
    by, 36, 42
  overcrowding of prisons as potential factor in
    decisions regarding, 125–26, 137
  prisoners' changed circumstances as factors
    in, 134
  reform proposals regarding, 77, 79–80,
    127–28, 134–35
  sentences without the
    possibility of, 135
  shifts to local custodial jurisdiction for
    violators of, 91–97, 93f, 135–36, 138,
    152, 161
  size of population on, 186, 187f
  state governments' role in
    administering, 41
Pelican Bay Prison (California), 170–71

penal disabilities for offenders
  cumulative duration of the impact of, 183, 186–89
  education restrictions and, 185t, 194f
  employment barriers and, 181–82, 189, 194f
  enduring stigma of imprisonment and, 180, 191
  "ever imprisoned" population and, 186–89, 187–88f
  family and domestic rights and, 185t, 194f
  family members as vicarious victims of, 180, 182–83, 185–90, 191, 194, 195
  felony offenders as primary population affected by, 185
  firearms restrictions and, 185t
  in Florida, 193–94, 194f
  formal restrictions on jobs and, 183–84, 185t, 194f
  government benefit restrictions and, 183, 184, 185t, 190–91, 194f
  housing restrictions and, 181–83, 185t, 189, 190–91, 192–93, 197
  motor vehicle restrictions and, 185t
  prosecutors' role in, 180–81
  publicly available criminal records and, 181–82
  public opinion regarding, 195, 197–98
  rationale for imposing, 190–94
  reform proposals regarding, 185, 195, 196–97
  residency restrictions and, 185t
  size of population affected by, 185–86, 187–88f, 194–95
  state-by-state variations and, 184, 188, 192–93
  state laws *versus* federal laws and, 181–82, 184f, 184, 185t, 197
  voting rights suspensions and, 181–82, 183, 185t, 188, 190–92
  zero-sum fallacy regarding, 191
Petersilia, Joan, 183–84
Poland, 96t
Pontell, Henry, 13
pretrial detention, 45, 70, 168, 175–77, 178–79
prison admission rates
  arrest rates and, 35
  assault and, 46t, 47f, 130–31, 131f, 132
  crime rates and, 35
  data-driven methods of reform regarding, 130–31
  decline (2005-2017) in, 42–43, 87f, 87–88, 128–29
  drug crimes and, 46–48, 46t, 47f, 51, 76, 108–9, 109t, 112–13, 129–30, 131
  homicide and, 46–48, 46t, 47f, 130–31, 131f
  larceny and, 46t, 47f, 130–31, 131f
  mass increase (1970-2015) in, 34–36f, 34–35, 45–48, 46t, 47f, 79, 128–29, 129–31f, 131
  in opioid epidemic states, 108–9, 109t
  overall imprisonment rates and, 40, 42–43, 45, 48, 76, 128–29

  projections toward 2050 and, 128–29, 129f
  rape and, 46–48, 46t, 47f, 130–31, 131f
  robbery and, 46–48, 46t, 47f, 130–31, 131f
  sex crimes and, 46–48, 47f, 132–33
  US population increase rates compared to, 47
prison and jail construction
  costs associated with, 13, 168–69
  drug abuse treatment facilities and, 167
  era of mass imprisonment expansion (1970-2015) and, 163, 166
  federal funding for, 169
  location-oriented needs and, 164–65, 167–68
  moratorium proposals regarding, 167–69
  overcrowding of current facilities and, 163–64, 164f, 166, 167
  projections regarding future of, 163–66, 167–69
  security-oriented needs and, 165, 167–68
  state budgets and, 168–69
  variation in conditions across states and, 166
Prison Litigation and Reform Act, 91–92
private for-profit prison companies, 175–77
probation, 70, 130, 141–42
Project Hope, 119, 169
projections regarding imprisonment rates in 2050
  agenda setting and, 83
  bail reform and, 178, 179
  correctional forecasting methodology and, 160–62
  disadvantaged minority populations and, 81
  drug treatment programs and, 178
  imprisonment decline (2007-17) and implications for, 87–88, 155
  "law of penal gravity" concept and, 84–88
  obstacles regarding decarceration initiatives and, 79, 154–55
  parole reform and, 92
  population reductions in analogous forms of institutional confinement and, 94–97
  prison admission rates and, 128–29, 129f
  remote megaprisons and, 170
  sentencing reform and, 177
  state variations and, 88–99, 177–78
  time served to release policies and, 178–79
  unprecedented nature of imprisonment boom of 1970-2015 and implications for, 85–87
Proposition 4 (Florida), 193
Proposition 36 (California), 71, 138
Proposition 47 (California), 117, 119
Proposition 57 (California), 119
prosecutors
  accountability measures for, 58
  adversarial nature of US criminal justice system and incentives of, 53, 58, 79–80, 139, 142–44, 148, 150–52
  in Canada, 143, 144–49, 145f, 147f, 151–52
  charging restrictions placed on, 122, 126, 127
  data management systems for cases and, 56, 57–58

elections of, 53, 69, 77, 146, 148–49
imprisonment rates and, 40, 41–42, 59, 77, 141–42, 143, 144–45, 151–53
"Lester Maddox Theory of Reform" and, 149–51
local government budget considerations and, 51, 52, 59, 150
localized nature of the work of, 68–69, 77
negotiated guilty pleas and, 40, 41, 51, 54–55, 139, 142, 180–81
opioid-related crimes and, 110
penal disabilities for former felons and, 180–81
police conduct evaluations by, 68
power to influence punishment choices among, 142, 143
prioritization of punishment over other objectives among, 142, 143–45
provincial *versus* local selection of, 146, 148–49
punishment preferences among, 142–43, 144, 146–49, 147f, 150, 151–52
reforms designed to offer more discretion to, 127
retribution purpose for imprisonment and, 51
salience of public concern about crime and, 55, 59, 143, 144
vested institutional interests of, 140
Prosecutor's Management Information System (PROMIS), 56
provincial dominance of criminal law and punishment, 63–64, 75
public housing sanctions for drug offenders, 181–83, 189, 190–91, 192–93, 197
public order charges, 46t
Puerto Rico, 184f, 184

rape
 arrest rates for, 25t, 30–31, 31f, 130–31
 imprisonment rates for, 132–33
 percent of all inmates imprisoned for, 25t, 48
 prison admission rates and, 46–48, 46t, 47f, 130–31, 131f
 prison impact metric regarding, 25f, 27
 time served to release policies and, 37f, 37
Raphael, Stephen, 79–81
Reiter, Keramet, 170–71
remote megaprisons, 170–71
restorative justice initiatives, 44–45, 132, 133
retribution purposes for imprisonment, 49, 50–51, 78
Rhode Island, 107
Riverfront Prison (New Jersey), 172, 173
Rizzo, Frank, 23–24
robbery
 arrest rates for, 25t, 30–31, 31f, 130–31
 comparative international data on, 72
 families of prisoners and, 48
 federal prisons and, 37–38
 percent of all inmates imprisoned for, 25t, 48

prison admission rates and, 46–48, 46t, 47f, 130–31, 131f
prison impact metric regarding, 25f, 27
sentencing conventions and, 48–49
time served to release policies and, 37f, 37
Romania, 96t
Royal Commission on Capital Punishment (United Kingdom), 196

sabermetrics, 57–58
San Quentin Prison (California), 171
Scale of Imprisonment analysis, 6–7, 12
Schwarzenegger, Arnold, 161, 162
securities fraud, 181–82
sentencing
 adversarial systems of criminal justice as a complicating factor in, 122–23, 127, 139, 142
 budget concerns and, 122, 123–24, 124f, 126, 127, 135–36
 courts of appeals and, 139
 determinate systems of, 11, 122–23
 deterrence purpose of imprisonment and, 49–50
 disparities between similar cases and, 134
 drug crimes and, 48–49, 104
 electoral incentives for judges and, 68–69
 federalist system of US government and, 123–27, 124f, 140
 federal sentencing commission and, 37–38, 136–37
 firearm enhancements and, 135
 imprisonment rates and, 48–49, 127, 177
 indeterminate systems of, 11
 individual offender release provisions for sentencing commissions and, 137
 individual *versus* systemic perspectives in, 124f, 125, 126, 127–28
 localized nature of, 68–70, 77, 79–80
 mandatory minimum sentences and, 41, 135
 Minnesota's system of, 136–37
 overcrowding of prisons as potential factor in, 126
 prison admission reduction goals and, 127–30, 129f
 public opinion regarding, 30, 39
 reform proposals regarding, 77, 79–80, 127–28, 130, 131–32, 139–40
 retributive purposes of, 122
 robbery and, 48–49
 sentencing commissions and, 126–28, 130, 134, 136–39, 144, 149, 177
 state legislatures' role in establishing, 41, 122, 135–36, 138, 143, 161
 status competition between prosecutors and defense attorneys and, 69
 truth in sentencing laws and, 11, 79–80, 123, 135
 victim status recognition and, 69–70

sex crimes. *See also* rape
  Adam Walsh Child Protection and Safety Act and, 197
  child molestation and, 132–33
  child pornography and, 64–65, 132, 133
  imprisonment rate increase after 1985 for, 19–20
  Megan's Laws and, 191, 197
  prison admission rates and, 46–48, 47*f*, 132–33
  public notification requirements regarding persons convicted of, 183, 190–91, 192–93, 197
  recidivism and, 133, 190–91
  reporting rate increases for, 132–33
  residential restrictions for persons convicted of, 181–82, 190–91, 192–93, 197
  restorative justice interventions and, 133
Shannon, Sarah, 186, 187*f*, 188, 189
Slovakia, 96*t*
Social Security, 94–95
South Korea, 143
Soviet Union, 95–96
state governments. *See also specific states*
  attorneys general and, 138
  budgets of, 13–14, 14*f*, 52, 67, 76–77, 80–81
  corrections departments and, 138
  criminal codes established by, 7, 41
  death penalty and, 64
  dominance of criminal law and punishment system by, 63–64, 75
  education and, 13–14, 14*f*, 63–64
  governors' offices and, 138, 152–53
  law enforcement background of members of, 64
  legislatures' role in determining sentencing regimes and, 41, 122, 135–36, 138, 143, 161
  mental health institutions and, 80–81, 94–95
  parole systems and, 41
  penal systems of, 13–14, 14*f*, 67
  prison capacity decisions and, 128
  roads and, 63–64
  susceptibility to one-party dominance and, 63, 64
  taxes collected by, 67
Stateville Prison (Illinois), 168
Stoll, Michael, 79–81
Stone, James, 194
Stuntz, William, 53–54, 55
Sutherland, Edwin, 7–8

Tamms Supermax Prison (Illinois), 165, 168, 170, 173
Teeters, Negley, 113–14
Texas, 188
Tocqueville, Alexis de, 6, 61–62
Trop v. Dulles, 192
truth in sentencing laws, 11, 79–80, 123, 135

United Kingdom, 53, 68, 70, 143, 196. *See also* England
US President's Commission on Crime (1967), 196
Utah, 107–8

Van Vechten Jr., C. C., 7
Vermont, 89
victims
  child pornography and, 133
  family members of offenders as, 182–83, 185–90, 191, 194, 195
  retribution purpose for imprisonment and the status of, 50–51, 69–70, 121–22, 191
Virgin Islands, 184*f*, 184
voting rights
  "civil death" philosophy and, 191–92, 194–95
  in Florida, 193–94
  minimal standards of competence and, 192
  right-wing state politicians support for restrictions on, 192

Wales, 3–4, 4–5*f*, 5, 62. *See also* United Kingdom
war on drugs policies. *See also* drug crimes
  crack cocaine and, 105–6
  drug treatment and decarceration policies as alternative to, 71, 131
  federal penalties and, 76
  increasing imprisonment rates and, 19–20
  public health *versus* legalist approach to drug use and, 104–6, 112
Warren Court, 53–54, 55
weapons charges, 46*t*, 64–65
West Virginia
  Drug Enforcement Agency in, 108, 108*t*
  drug overdose deaths in, 107–8, 109, 110*f*
  prison admission rates in, 108–9, 109*t*
Wilson, James Q., 50
work release programs, 174–75

zero-based budgeting, 196
Zimring, Franklin (previous research citations)
  on drug crimes and imprisonment rates by, 32–33
  on federalism and mass expansion in imprisonment rates, 16–17
  on the history of correctional forecasting, 160–61
  on incapacitation purposes of imprisonment, 50
  on increasing salience of crime in public opinion, 39
  on public health approach to drug use, 104
  "scale of imprisonment" research and, 6–7
  on victims' status and the retribution purpose for imprisonment, 50–51
  on the "zero-sum fallacy" in the politics of punishment, 191

www.ingramcontent.com/pod-product-compliance
Ingram Content Group UK Ltd.
Pitfield, Milton Keynes, MK11 3LW, UK
UKHW022153230426
12049UKWH00003BA/78